CW01645487

AAT LEVEL 4

Business Tax

FA2024

Tax Year FY2024

April 2024 to March 2025

For Q2022 assessments from 27 Jan 2025

AAT Level 4
Business Tax FA2024
(Q22 1.1)

Published by Accountext

The content of this pack is frequently updated but on occasion, changes to legislation or accounting standards may not be reflected until sometime after implementation.

The content of this publication is intended to prepare students for AAT examinations and should not be used as professional advice. Accountext Publishing Ltd does not accept any liability for any losses or damage suffered, directly or indirectly, as a result of the information within this text. Professional advice should always be sought.

Accountext Publishing Ltd
First Floor Unit B
Meltex House
65-67 Kepler
Tamworth
B79 7XE

www.accountext.co.uk

Introduction

The manual is split into chapters from 1 to 10 and contains many exercises. You should start at the beginning and work through each chapter in order. Should you become stuck at any point, ensure you review the content again – a second or third reading often helps.

The manual contains a number of icons to provide assistance along the way:

The Activity icon indicates that you have an activity to complete at that stage of the manual. Activities aid learning – have a go and then check where the answer came from.

When you see this icon, an answer to the activity you have carried out, will be displayed. Take time to appreciate how the answer was arrived at.

Where you see this icon, an example is provided. This may be an illustration of a document that is used in business or an illustration of how a calculation or activity is to be completed.

Take note. This is information that is important or information that you may need for examination purposes.

This is one of the most important icons – it represents a requirement for you to complete an online assessment.

This page is left intentionally blank.

Contents

This page is left intentionally blank.

Introduction to L4 Business Tax

This course introduces students to UK taxation that is relevant to businesses. Students will understand how to compute business taxes for sole traders, partnerships, and limited companies. They will also be able to identify tax planning opportunities while understanding the importance of maintaining ethical standards.

In learning how to prepare tax computations, students will gain the skills required to apply the tax treatment of capital expenditure and the adjustment of accounting profits for tax purposes.

Students will allocate profits to tax years for ongoing businesses as well as in opening and closing years. In addition, students will allocate profits between partners in a partnership and will calculate National Insurance contributions (NIC) for the self-employed, advising clients on the tax implications of making losses.

Students will understand the administrative requirements of UK tax law, including the implications of errors in tax returns, late filing of returns, late payment of tax and not retaining records for the required period. Students will compute tax on the sale of capital assets by companies and will understand the capital gains implications of the sale of a business and the tax reliefs available to businesses.

Tax advice is an important part of many accountancy roles in recognising tax planning opportunities for businesses. Students will discuss the ethical issues facing business owners and managers in reporting their business tax and the responsibilities that an agent has in advising on tax issues to business clients.

This page is left intentionally blank.

Chapter 1: Underpinning knowledge of the tax framework

By the end of this chapter, you should:

- Understand the structures of different types of businesses and what taxes would be applicable to each.
- Understand the duties and obligations of a Tax Practitioner.
- Understand the definitions of:
    - Tax planning
    - Tax avoidance
    - Tax evasion.
- Understand the need to adhere to ethical requirements.
- Understand the tax legislative rules and the role of HMRC.
- Appreciate the components of the types of income.
- Have knowledge of the different tax rates that apply to individuals trading as sole traders and partners.
- Understand what an accounting period is for Corporation Tax for limited companies.
- Have knowledge of the tax rates that apply to limited companies.

Different types of trading businesses

To accurately consider and calculate business tax implications, it is necessary to understand the different types of businesses that may be liable to taxes.

Unincorporated

This will cover sole traders (a self-employed individual) and partnerships (self-employed individuals working together). They will pay income tax, Class 4 National Insurance contributions and capital gains tax. A sole trader is not a separate legal entity and as well as income from trading (business tax) they may also have other personal income (personal tax). A partnership is not a separate legal entity and each individual partner is responsible for paying their own income tax and capital gains tax on their share of the partnership's profits and gains.

Incorporated

This covers companies with limited responsibility who pay a business tax that is referred to as Corporation Tax, which is paid on all business profits. Incorporated businesses also pay tax on gains on the disposal of assets.

According to the business entity concept, the financial statements for limited companies are prepared purely from the perspective of the business – they do not include any valuations of personal assets or liabilities of the owners and are therefore a legal entity, separate from any owners and managers/directors.

This type of business can be recognised as its trading name will end with a Ltd (Limited) or Plc (Public limited) company.

Private expenses **do not apply** to incorporated businesses.

Example 1.1

The following types of businesses will pay corporation tax as they are incorporated companies:

Nirvana Garages Ltd

Garage Habitats Plc

The following types of businesses will pay income tax as they are either sole traders or partnerships:

Holmes & Watson (private investigators)

Petula Heave trading as Pet Heaven (pet shop)

Duties and responsibilities of a Tax Practitioner

Tax is a very specialised area of accounting and being a Tax Practitioner means keeping up to date with current tax legislation and following a strict regime of CPD (Continuing Professional Development).

On this basis, an AAT member must **not** accept any work which:

a) they lack sufficient expertise or competence to complete
b) would involve them or any other person in the commission of any criminal act
c) they do not have adequate time or opportunity to complete promptly

Becoming a Tax Practitioner involves a very high level of responsibility and at all times an AAT member must follow the AAT's fundamental ethical principles.

These fundamental principles were covered in AAT Level 2 and Level 3 but a brief overview is given below as a reminder of the level of standard required to be able to operate as a Tax Practitioner.

Objectivity means all AAT members must not compromise their professional or business judgement because of bias, conflict of interest or the undue influence of others. This means being able to take a balanced view of any given situation and to make decisions based on an unbiased viewpoint.

Integrity means all AAT members must be straightforward and honest in professional and business relationships. Integrity also implies fair dealing and truthfulness. Clients - and the public in general - expect accountants to work in ways which are **honest, transparent** and **fair.** Tax Practitioners must ensure that all tax returns submitted on behalf of clients are completed fairly and honestly, with no attempt to under-declare the amount of taxes owing by the taxpayer.

- **Honest**: Honesty means that the accountant has acted at all times in a way which is truthful.
- **Transparent**: Transparency means that the accountant would not mind others knowing how or why a decision was made.
- **Fair:** Fairness means that the accountant is confident that people affected by his/her decision would consider it fair, rather than biased or based on personal preferences or for personal gain.

Confidentiality means that AAT members must refrain from disclosing confidential information acquired as a result of professional and business relationships without proper and specific authority, or unless there is a legal or professional right or duty to disclose. It also means that members must refrain from using confidential information acquired as a result of professional and business relationships to their personal advantage or the advantage of third parties.

Professional Competence and Due Care means that members must maintain professional knowledge and skill at the level required to ensure that clients or employers receive competent professional service *and* also act diligently in accordance with applicable technical and professional standards when providing professional services.

Clients expect their accountants to be **competent** to complete the work they say they can do and to approach any work with due care and professionalism to ensure that the work is completed accurately and on time.

Professional Behaviour means that members must comply with relevant laws and regulations and avoid any action that may bring disrepute to the profession.

Registering as a Tax Practitioner

HMRC has its own relevant standard that is applicable to individuals and businesses involved in professionally representing or advising taxpayers.
This standard sets out the expectations of HMRC from Tax Practitioners to maintain high standards to promote tax compliance.

Again, the HMRC standard covers the fundamental principles required by the AAT. Full details of the requirements of the HMRC standard can be found at:

https://www.gov.uk/government/publications/hmrc-the-standard-for-agents/hmrc-the-standard-for-agents

To act as a Tax Practitioner, you will need official authorisation from HMRC.

You will be required to register as an agent in HMRC online services. To do this you will need a Government Gateway user ID and password – if you have not already got these you can create them when you register.

Here is a screenshot of the sign-in to HMRC online services page:

https://www.gov.uk/log-in-register-hmrc-online-services

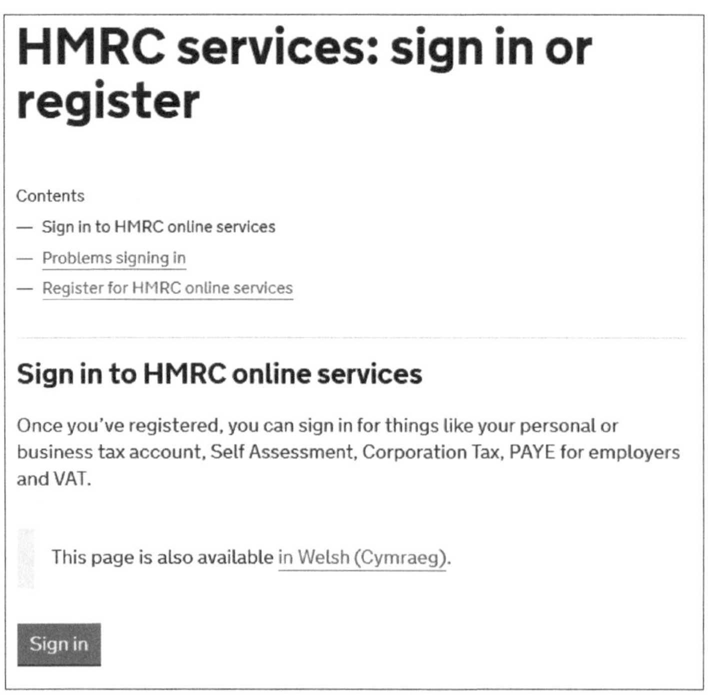

By clicking 'Sign In' you will be guided to the Government Gateway sign-in page.

You can then enrol for each of the individual services you require, i.e. Corporation Tax or Self-Assessment.

As a Tax Practitioner, you must have an agent code before you can set up agent authorisation for Tax to be able to deal with your client's tax details. This code is required for both online and paper filing and is obtained in writing from HMRC, Central Agent Maintainer Team, National Insurance contributions and Employer Office. BX91AN.

You will need the following to complete your written application:

- full name and/or trading name if different to the full name
- trading address
- telephone contact number
- email contact address
- HMRC Anti Money-Laundering (AML) Supervision registration number (obtained through an official practice licence)
- UTR (Unique Taxpayer Reference) Number
- Detail of which tax you want to deal with.

It can take up to 28 days for HMRC to make their decision.

Once the agent has registered with HMRC the client must then give HMRC formal authorisation by completing form 64-8 for the Tax Agent to be able to deal with their Corporation Tax. A company is able to have more than one agent, each one dealing with a different area of their business, for example, one for PAYE and one for Corporation Tax.

This will not transfer any of your client's legal obligations to yourself. It is the taxpayer's responsibility to ensure the calculated return is correct and the tax is paid on time. The taxpayer is also referred to as the 'Principal'.

Form 64-8 allows the client to give you authorisation to act on their behalf for:

- Individual, partnership and trust tax affairs
- Corporation tax for limited companies

- Tax Credits
- PAYE for employers
- CIS for contractors
- VAT

If you already have an online services account, you will just need to add the relevant Tax for Agents to your list of services and this is done by logging in to your online account and going to 'Your HMRC services' and adding for instance 'Corporation Tax for Agents', etc, to your portfolio from the 'Services you can add' section.

To be able to achieve agent authorisation you will then need to follow the instructions under 'Request an authorisation'. You will need (for Corporation Tax):

- the client's Corporation Tax UTR
- postcode of the client's registered office or Companies House registration number
- authorisation code HMRC will send to your client's registered office address by post (begins with CT).

Once set up you will be able to file your clients' Company Tax Returns and any relevant tax payments electronically. HMRC and Companies House collect data from electronic filing as the old paper and PDF formats are obsolete apart from a few companies who have special exemptions for not filing online.

The online service allows you to use internet filing-enabled software and forms which are available from recommended suppliers. A list of these can be found on the HMRC website. These commercial software suppliers can also assist with the reporting of annual accounts which require iXBRL tagging.

iXBRL tagging (Inline Extensible Business Reporting Language) came into force through legislation on 1 January 2010 and means it is compulsory for companies to send their Company Tax Returns online using iXBRL for accounts and computations.

Financial Statements and returns which have been converted into iXBRL may appear unchanged to the human eye but they contain tags which can be computer read. iXBRL can provide an identifying tag for each individual item of business data. For example, 'operating profit' has its own unique tag, as does 'current assets'.

It is up to the Company to make sure that it adequately covers the requirements for filing in iXBRL and ensure that its accounts software and tax software are adequate to do the job.

There is a free Corporation Tax online service from HMRC that can be used by small companies with simple accounts that do not use accounting software but involve templates. HMRC and Companies House also provide an optional joint filing service that enables small companies to enter their accounts data once. The service can be used to submit full or micro entity accounts over the Internet to HMRC as part of the Company Tax Return and also to send these, or an abridged version, to Companies House.

The following link gives a good overview of iXBRL and the terminology involved.
https://assets.publishing.service.gov.uk/government/uploads/system/uploads/attachment_data/file/366116/online-xbrltag.pdf

Activity 1.1

a) An agent code is only required for authorisation for self-assessment. Is this statement true or false?

b) Which of the following statements regarding a tax agent for a business is/are incorrect?

i) A business must only appoint one tax agent for their tax affairs.

ii) A business can appoint more than one agent to deal with their tax affairs.

iii) A tax agent is entirely responsible for the payment of the business tax on time.

iv) A tax agent can file the business tax returns on behalf of the business.

c) Match the correct word/s to the relevant description in the table below:

- HMRC standard for Agents
- Form 64-8
- Government Gateway User ID and password

Description	Word/s
Allows the client to give you authorisation to act on their behalf.	
Sets out the expectations from HMRC by Agents.	
Required to register as an Agent online.	

Tax planning, tax avoidance and tax evasion

At all times a tax practitioner needs to consider the following when dealing with their own or their clients' tax calculations and be aware of any warning signs that may highlight that one of the following is going on:

- **Tax evasion –** this is always illegal and can incur fines and imprisonment if anyone is involved in deliberately trying to conceal taxes that are due and payable to HMRC by reducing the tax bill by illegal means such as under-declaring income or overstating expenses. It is a requirement that any suspected tax evasion is reported and this can be done by phone or online to HMRC by using the HMRC fraud hotline report form.
- **Tax avoidance –** trying to bend the rules of the tax system to gain a tax advantage that Parliament never intended. According to HMRC, "it involves operating within the letter, but not the spirit, of the law". HMRC are able to challenge any potential tax avoidance 'artificial' transactions which may result in the company paying more tax than the amount

they saved by trying to avoid tax in the first place. Tax avoidance uses loopholes in the tax system and although not illegal – HMRC will be able to open an enquiry, seek payment where necessary and charge penalties where appropriate if found to be "avoiding tax".

- **Tax planning** – legally being able to reduce tax liability by using available legal exemptions and deductions. However, by being excessive and aggressive and going beyond the intention of the Acts of Parliament to pay less tax, may infer tax avoidance, even when under the umbrella of "planning". HMRC states that where this is the case, it is right to take action because it is important the tax system is fair and perceived to be so.

HMRC (His Majesty's Revenue and Customs)

Tax is collected by the Government to finance expenditure on items such as education, the welfare system, the NHS, local government, defence and so on. The main forms of taxation which are currently charged in the UK include:

- **Income Tax** – levied on the earnings of individuals, including profits from self-employment as a sole trader or partner.
- **Corporation Tax** – levied on the profits of limited companies.
- **Capital Gains Tax** – levied on individuals on gains made by selling assets.
- **Chargeable Gains and Allowances** – levied on limited companies on gains made by selling assets.
- **Value Added Tax** – A tax on expenditure on many goods and services.
- **Inheritance Tax** – levied on the estates left by people when they die.

The legislative rules around tax are **statute law** brought into effect from Acts of Parliament which are amended annually by the Finance Act in operation in that year. **Statutory instruments** are further rules instigated by the government where they have the ability to amend an act rather than have to pass a new act completely.

This course currently covers Finance Act 2024 and the fiscal tax year from 1 April 2024 to 31 March 2025. This means that calculations will be based on **2024/2025** rates dependent on the dates of accounting periods.

His Majesty's Revenue and Customs (HMRC) is the government organisation responsible for administering the UK's many varied and complex tax laws put into effect by the Acts of Parliament, ensuring that the correct amount of tax is collected from each individual taxpayer and company each year.

'Case law' is where the courts are required to give guidance to interpret the law in making decisions on taxation cases.

In addition, HMRC provides support to taxpayers and tax agents in making sure they submit their tax returns correctly and on time. This guidance has no force of law, whereas the legislation of Statute law is enforceable by law. There is a lot of support on the HMRC website, including the following:

- **Statements of Practice** – these are HMRC's interpretation of the law and how they intend to apply it in given situations.

- **Extra-Statutory Concessions –** in some situations HMRC may elect **not** to apply the strict letter of the law – for example, where it would be unfair. However, these situations are becoming rarer and so the number of Extra Statutory Concessions (ESCs) is expected to fall in coming years.
- **Explanatory Leaflets –** providing basic guidance to a wide range of tax issues.
- **Revenue & Customs Briefs –** these give the HMRC view on specific points of tax legislation.

Activity 1.2

a) You work as a Tax Practitioner for Cottone Ltd and have prepared the Company Tax Return for review by Cottone Ltd. The Managing Director has asked if it could be amended which would incur using a loophole in current tax legislation to reduce the tax due. Is this legal and should you comply with the request?

Give a brief description with details of any items that may be relevant to the question.

b) Which of the fundamental principles could be breached if you agreed to the amendment in question 1 above?

Fundamental principle	Breached Yes/No?
Integrity	
Professional competence and due care	
Professional behaviour	
Confidentiality	
Objectivity	

c) A Limited Company would be liable to pay Income Tax on its annual profits.

Is this statement, True or False and why?

d) Which of the following types of businesses would not pay corporation tax?

i) Whillans & Son (window cleaners)
ii) Fox Fixtures Ltd (Furniture makers)
iii) Motor Emporium Plc (Nationwide car sales)
iv) CF Counts & Co (partnership of accountants)

Sources of income for an individual

For the purpose of calculating income tax, an individual (sole trader or partnership) may obtain income from a variety of sources. For many taxpayers, they will earn income solely from a single employed job and will have tax taken at source by their employer through the PAYE (Pay As You Earn) system.

However, there are many other sources of income which could mean the taxpayer will need to consider the tax implications of receiving that other income.

The first stage of a tax computation is to identify and calculate all the taxpayer's income for the year. There are many different possible sources of income for a taxpayer, including:

1. **Non-Savings Income**
   From employment, self-employment, pensions, certain state benefits and property.

2. **Savings Income**
   From bank and building society accounts, ISAs and other investments.

3. **Dividend Income**
   From dividends received in respect of shares held in limited companies.

These sources of income are always taxed in the order of the list above.

Any of these sources of income will be added together to form **'total income'.**

From this total income, any items like loss relief would be deducted to form **'net income'.**

From this net income there may then be a deduction of a '**personal allowance'.** The personal allowance rate for 24/25 is **£12,570**. This means that an individual is allowed to earn £12,570 tax-free before being taxed on the balance.

Net income less the personal allowance is then referred to as **'taxable income'.** This is the income that the applicable tax rates would be applied against.

The personal allowance is always deducted from non-savings income first. If there is insufficient non-savings income then any remaining balance of the personal allowance is transferred to be used against savings income, and then (if there is still a remainder) against dividend income.

Once the correct personal allowance has been deducted from the income, you will have calculated the **taxable income** – i.e. how much of the taxpayer's income for the year must be chargeable to tax.

Example 1.2

Types of income

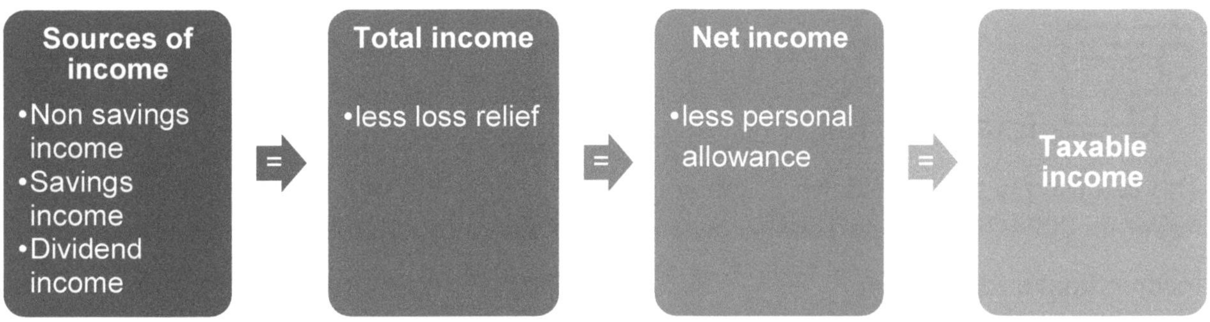

Rates of tax for individuals

There are also exemptions applied to certain types of income – some savings and dividend income, for example, is not taxed (depending on the taxpayer's situation). Income from an Individual Savings account (ISA), for example, is tax-free.

Not everybody pays tax at the same rate, individuals residing in England, Wales and Northern Ireland who are **basic rate taxpayers** are taxed at 20% on the majority of their income, whilst **higher rate taxpayers** (who have taxable income above £37,700) will pay some tax at 20% and some at 40%, and **additional rate taxpayers** (with taxable income above £125,140) will pay some tax at 45%. These rates apply to both employed income and trading income.

Individuals residing in Scotland will pay tax at 5 different rates on their income.

Income from dividends is taxed at different rates, these being:

- **8.75%** for basic rate taxpayers
- **33.75%** for higher rate taxpayers
- **39.35%** for additional rate taxpayers

Example 1.3

Income taxation for 2024/25 for England, Ireland and Wales

Band	Taxable Income	Tax Rate
Personal Allowance	Up to £12,570	0%
Basic Rate	£12,571 to £50,270	20%
Higher Rate	£50,271 to £125,140	40%
Additional Rate	Over £125,140	45%

This means an individual can earn up to £50,270 (£12,570 + £37,700) before paying tax at 40% and any income above £125,140 will then be taxed at 45%.

Example 1.4

The following is the breakdown of the sources of income for an individual trading as a sole trader for 2024/25. Their personal allowance is the standard £12,570.

Income from trading	£30,000
Building society interest	£2,500
Dividends	£4,250

Their taxable income would be:

£30,000 + £2,500 + £4,250 = £36,750 less personal allowance of £12,570 = **£24,180.**

Activity 1.3

Benjamin has non-savings income before the deduction of any personal allowances in 2024/25 of £15,800 and he has no other forms of income in the tax year. He has the standard personal allowance rate for this tax year. What is the taxable income for Benjamin?

Example 1.5

Paris has non-savings income (before the deduction of any personal allowances) in 2024-25 of £39,000. She has no other forms of income in the tax year.

What is Paris's tax liability for 2024-25?

Non-savings income	= £39,000
Less Personal allowance	= £12,570
Taxable income	= £26,430
All taxed at 20%	= £5,286 (basic rate)
Tax liability	**= £5,286**

Activity 1.4

Ralph has non-savings income (before deduction of the standard personal allowance) in 2024-25 of £37,700. He has no other forms of income in the tax year. What will Ralph's tax liability be for the year?

Example 1.6

Amanda has taxable income (after the deduction of the personal allowance) of £42,000 which is all non-savings income.

What would be Amanda's tax liability for 2024/25?

The first £37,700 would be at the basic rate of tax of 20% = £7,540.

The difference between £42,000 and £37,700 would be at the higher rate of 40% = £1,720. Total tax liability would be £9,260.

Activity 1.5

Sylvester has a total taxable income of £172,000 being all non-savings income.

What would be Sylvester's tax liability for 2024/25?

£ ________ @ 20% = __________

£ ________ @ 40% = __________

£ ________ @ 45% = __________

Total tax liability = £__________

£1,000 personal trading allowance for individuals

A £1,000 allowance is eligible for taxpayers with very low levels of income from trading. Essentially the allowance means that individuals who have low earnings from trading or casual income can earn up to the £1,000 allowance and not pay tax on those earnings.

The allowance is also available to those people who earn more than £1,000 in each category (before the deduction of expenses), in which case those people will be able to earn the first £1,000 tax-free **instead** of claiming any expenses.

The allowance is aimed at people who may make relatively small profits from selling goods on eBay, selling at car boot sales, making and selling cakes or having odd jobs doing gardening or similar work – but who would not necessarily class it as a “business”.

Anyone whose earnings are less than £1,000 a year will not need to fill in a tax return to declare any of this income but people earning over £1,000 will need to declare those earnings and deduct the £1,000 allowance from the income, any income above the allowance would then be taxable.

Understand what an accounting period is for corporation tax purposes

The relevant laws applicable to Corporation Tax are the Corporation Tax Act 2009, the Corporation Tax Act 2010 and the Taxation of Chargeable Gains Act 1992, all of which can be amended by the Finance Acts. The Finance Acts are normally changed annually for tax and duty changes which have been outlined in principle by the Chancellor of the Exchequer in his Budget Day speech being March 2024 for the Finance (No.2) Act 2024. The Finance Bill then has a passage through the House of Commons, and the House of Lords and then receives Royal Assent when it becomes law, which happened on 24 May 2024 for Finance Act 2024.

A “**chargeable accounting period**” or CAP for Corporation Tax (CT) normally coincides with a company’s period of account for its annual accounts. However, this may not always be the case as an accounting period for CT **cannot be longer than 12 months**.

If a period of account exceeds 12 months, due to when the business started trading, it would be required to be split into two chargeable accounting periods. For example, if annual accounts have been produced from 1 April 2024 to 30 June 2025 (15 months) then this would be split as:

- first 12 months being 1 April 2024 to 31 March 2025
- remainder of 3 months balance – being 1 April 2025 to 30 June 2025.

The date of your first tax return depends on whether your company started trading on the same day it was set up or didn’t start trading until after it was set up. The first chargeable accounting period can also commence when a company acquires a source of taxable income like opening an interest-bearing bank account before the actual commencement of trading. This will then give a short CAP before the commencement of trading.

Example 1.7

Tweade Ltd was first incorporated on 1 January 2024 and opened up an interest-bearing bank account on 1 March 2024. The business started trading on 1 June 2024 and its first set of accounts are due to be drawn up to 30 June 2025 (an 18-month period from 1 Jan 2024 to 30 June 2025).

The first chargeable accounting period for tax will commence on 1 March 2024 when the interest-bearing bank account was opened and end on 31 May 2024 (prior to the commencement of trading).

Limited companies are classed as dormant until they start to trade for the first time and are regarded as being active if:

- they carry on a business activity such as a trade or professional activity
- buying and selling goods with a view to making a profit or surplus
- providing services
- earning interest
- managing investments
- receiving any other income.

For example, incorporated on 1 March 2024 and started trading on 1 May 2024.

The accounts would be prepared for 1 March 2024 to 28 February 2025 and the CT return would cover the period 1 May 2024 to 28 February 2025. After this, the dates for accounts and tax returns will match the company's financial year from 1 March 2025 to 28 February 2026.

Other points to keep in mind for accounting periods are:

- An accounting period begins immediately after the end of the last accounting period or when a company is chargeable to corporation tax.
- An accounting period also commences when a company enters liquidation or commences a winding up or goes into administration. The final CAP for CT purposes would be *the date the business goes into administration*, *when the administrator is appointed*, and ends when it ceases to trade.
- An accounting period will also come to an end when a company ceases trading, ceases to be within the charge to UK corporation tax or ceases to be in administration.
- After a company ceases trading a further accounting period may apply to a final set of accounts until the company is no longer receiving any transactions (like interest on a bank account) and is "dormant". A dormant company is dormant for corporation tax purposes if it is not trading and does not receive any other income.
- With accounts prepared for longer than a 12-month period, gains and profits should be apportioned between the relevant accounting periods using a time basis. However, in

some circumstances a different apportionment is possible, for example, chargeable gains could be allocated to the accounting period that the disposal takes place. This is covered in detail in Chapter 5.

Example 1.8

Swade Ltd was incorporated on 7 February 2024 and started trading on the same day. Its period of account end date will therefore be 28 February 2025 the end of the month in the next financial year.

The company's first accounts and financial statements must cover 12 months and 3 weeks from 7 February 2024 to 28 February 2025.

The company tax return can only be for 12 months and no longer. Therefore, you may have to file 2 tax returns covering the first period of account. This will also incur 2 payment deadlines.

The first accounting period for Corporation Tax ends on 6 February 2025, this being a 12-month period from 7 February 2024.

The second accounting period for Corporation Tax ends on 28 February 2025. This will then cover the 3-week period.

After this initial period of account, Swade Ltd will have a period of account end date of 28 February 2026 and an accounting period for CT ending 28 February 2026.

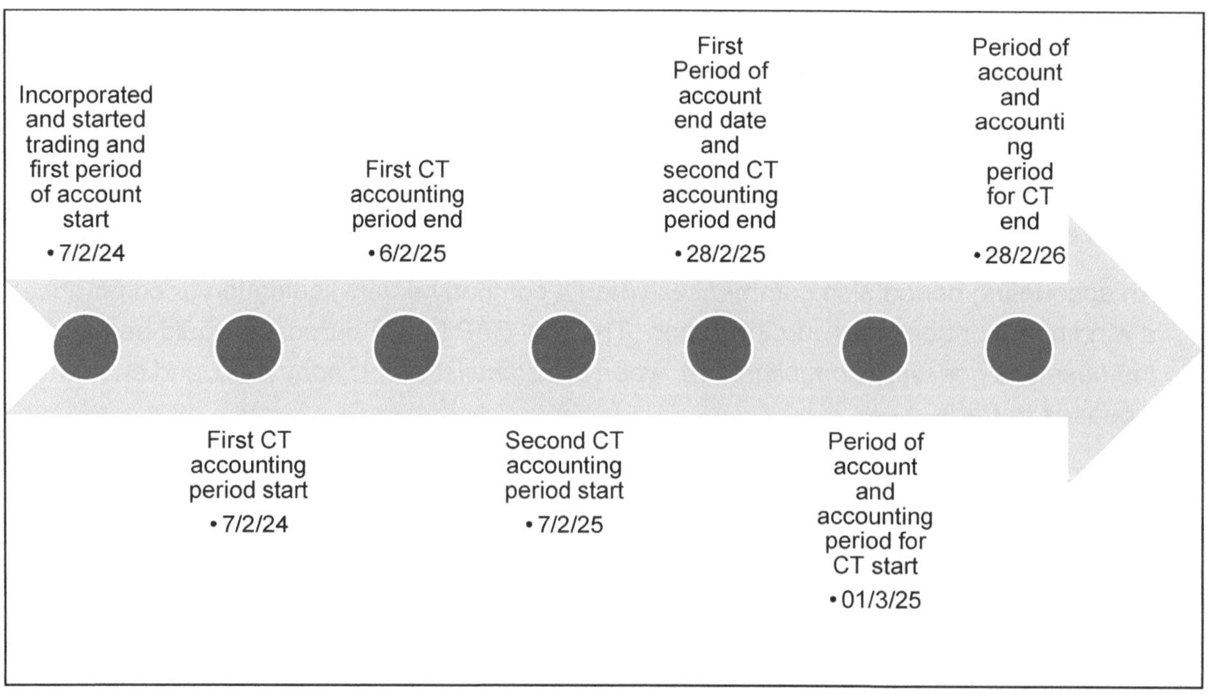

Activity 1.6

a) Whull Limited was incorporated and started trading on 5 March 2024 and its period of account end date is 31 March 2025.

1) What will be the first accounting period for Corporation Tax?

2) What will be the second accounting period for Corporation Tax?

b) Thredd Limited was incorporated on 1 August 2023 and commenced trading on 1 October 2023.

The first set of financial accounts was prepared to the end of March 2024. An administrator was appointed on 1 February 2025, as the business was financially struggling, but they were unable to save the business and the company ceased trading on 31 August 2025.

Choose from the following to give the final chargeable accounting period for CT.

a) 1 September 2024 to 31 August 2025

b) 1 February 2025 to 31 August 2025

Rates of tax for Limited companies

Taxable profits for Corporation Tax include the money your company or business makes from:

- doing business (trading income profits)
- investments
- selling assets for a profit (gains on disposal of assets)

If your company is based in the UK, it pays Corporation Tax on all its profits from the UK and abroad.

If your company isn't based in the UK but has an office or branch here, it only pays Corporation Tax on profits from its UK activities.

Corporation Tax rates are fixed for financial years beginning 1 April to the following 31 March. So, for the year ending 31 March 2025, this would be the Financial Year 2024 as it began 1 April 2024.

The following are the rates of Corporation Tax taken from the Government website. The main rate for Financial Years 2017 through to 2022 has remained consistent at 19%.

Rates for Corporation Tax years starting 1 April

There are different rates for ring fence companies.

Rate	2024	2023	2022	2021	2020	2019	2018	2017
Small profits rate (companies with profits under £50,000)	19 %	19%	—	—	—	—	—	—
Main rate (companies with profits over £250,000)	25%	25%	—	—	—	—	—	—
Main rate (all profits except ring fence profits)	—	—	19%	19%	19%	19%	19%	19%
Marginal Relief lower limit	£50,000	£50,000	—	—	—	—	—	—
Marginal Relief upper limit	£250,000	£250,000	—	—	—	—	—	—
Standard fraction	3/200	3/200	—	—	—	—	—	—
Special rate for unit trusts and open-ended, investment companies	20%	20%	20%	20%	20%	20%	20%	20%

From 1 April 2023, there is no longer a single Corporation Tax rate for non-ring fence profits.

At the Spring Budget 2021, the government announced that the Corporation Tax main rate for non-ring fence profits would increase to 25% for profits above £250,000.

A small profits rate of 19% was also announced for companies with profits of £50,000 or less.

Companies with profits between £50,000 and £250,000 will pay tax at the main rate, reduced by a marginal relief. This provides a gradual increase in the effective Corporation Tax rate.

For profits from 1 April 2023, use the Marginal Relief calculator to work out how much Marginal Relief you can claim on your Corporation Tax.

Apportionment of corporation tax rates

Because the taxation is calculated on the accounting periods for Corporation Tax it may be necessary to apportion different percentages of corporation tax based on the rate for the financial (fiscal) year which is always 1 April to 31 March. The rate for FY2024 - 1 April 2024 to 31 March 2025 is **25% (main rate for companies with profits over £250,000)**. Any companies with profits of £50,000 or less will incur a 'small profits rate' **of 19% from 1 April 2024.** Any companies with profits between £50,000 and £250,000 will pay tax at 25% being reduced by a marginal relief.

The financial year will therefore not always be the same as the accounting period for CT and where this happens, apportionment will be required to calculate the correct amount of tax payable.

Apportionment is generally based on the time within the financial years that are applicable for the accounting periods for CT. The rate of CT is then applied to the apportioned periods.

Example 1.9

Sateen Ltd has the following information relevant to the year ending 30 June 2023.

	£
Trading Income	1,300,000
Property income	125,000
Total profits	1,425,000

Total profits would be apportioned as follows:

1/7/22 to 31/3/23 (financial year 2022) 9/12 x £1,425,000 = £1,068,750

1/4/23 to 30/6/23 (financial year 2023) 3/12 x £1,425,000 = £356,250

The Corporation Tax rate for 2022 was **19%** and for 2023 was **25%**.

Tax chargeable based on the above apportionment would therefore be:

£1,068,750 x 19%	= £203,062.50
£356,250 x 25%	= £ 89,062.50
Total tax chargeable	= **£292,125.00**

This only happens when an accounting year covers two different rates of Corporation Tax as in the years 2022 and 2023 and does not apply to 2023 to 2024 as this has been 25% for these two years. The above example is for information only on split rates.

When you have 2 chargeable accounting periods that cover two different financial years for Corporation Tax then there will be a further step.

Example 1.10

Organsa Limited was incorporated and started trading on 7 February 2023 and the period of account end date for the financial statements is 29 February 2024.

The first accounting period for Corporation Tax would be 7 February 2023 to 6 February 2024 – 12 months. This covers part of the FY2023 and part of the FY2024 split as follows:

07/02/23 to 31/03/23 (FY2022 which is 01/04/2022 to 31/03/2023)

01/04/23 to 06/02/24 (FY2023 which is 01/04/2023 to 31/03/2024)

The second accounting period for Corporation Tax would be 7 February 2024 to 29 February 2024 and this would also apply to FY2023.

This example would also cover two different rates of CT 19% for FY2022 and 25% for FY2023.

Activity 1.7

Taffeeta Ltd was incorporated on 1 July 2023 and started trading on 1 November 2023. The first set of accounts was drawn up to 31 March 2024. Unfortunately, they entered into administration on 1 January 2025 and the administrator was called in but was unable to save the business and the company ceased trading at the end of July 2025.

a) What is the start date of the final chargeable accounting period for corporation tax purposes?

b) What is the end date of the final chargeable accounting period for corporation tax purposes?

Summary of Chapter 1

- An unincorporated business covers sole traders and partnerships whereas an incorporated business covers a limited company.
- Individuals trading as a sole trader or a partner pay income tax, capital gains tax and NICs.
- Companies and individuals must complete and submit regular tax returns.
- A tax practitioner or agent has an obligation to maintain client confidentiality and a high ethical standard at all times.
- A tax practitioner needs to keep up to date with current tax legislation and update CPD on a continuing regular basis.
- Consideration should be paid to tax evasion which is illegal, and tax avoidance and planning which is legal.
- The legislative tax rules are brought into effect from Acts of Parliament which are amended annually by the Finance Act in operation in that year.
- A company should register for Corporation Tax within 3 months of the start of trading.
- A period of account refers to the Financial Statements.
- An accounting period refers to Corporation Tax and cannot be longer than 12 months.
- A CT Return must be filed within 12 months of the end of the CT accounting period.
- Accounts prepared for longer than a 12-month period, gains and profits should be apportioned between the relevant accounting periods.
- An individual's sources of income are taxed in the order of non-savings income, savings income and dividend income to arrive at total income.
- Trading losses are deducted from total income to achieve net income.
- The personal allowance is deducted from net income to achieve taxable income.
- AAT's fundamental ethics must be adhered to.

Assessment 1

You are now required to log in to your ROGO account to complete your first online assessment before progressing to the next chapter.

This page is left intentionally blank.

Chapter 2: Adjustment of trading profits

By the end of this chapter, you should:

- Understand how to identify if unincorporated businesses are trading through the application of the badges of trade.
- Understand that the cash basis is the new default basis but an election can be made for the accruals basis.
- Understand the differences between the cash basis and the accruals basis.
- Be able to identify deductible and non-deductible expenditure when adjusting trading profits.
- Apply any rules relating to allowable and non-allowable expenditure.
- Understand how expenditure is classified as being either revenue or capital.
- Be able to adjust accounting profit and losses for tax purposes.

Introduction

Each year a sole trader, partnership or limited company will record their income and expenses within their financial accounts with the intention of making a profit.

Any profits made by a business are chargeable to tax. However, there are always a number of adjustments which must be made to the **'accounting profit'** (i.e. the net profit from the **business's** statement of profit or loss account) before we can determine the **'taxable profit'.** (The profits that tax will be liable and required to be paid on).

Badges of trade

In the process of being able to tax the profits of the trade of an **individual**, there are some attributes to trading that have been summarised into the following nine badges of trade by HMRC. This is to understand if an actual 'trade' is being carried out and the tests (since the 1950's) are used by the courts to determine trading or capital transactions in case law.

A distinction needs to be made, as this will determine how profits will be treated and how individuals may pay for any taxation.

Badges of trade	Description
Is there a ***profit seeking motive?***	For an activity to be referred to as a trade, then it must be carried out with a view to making a profit.
The frequency and ***number of transactions.***	Very few transactions may indicate non-trading activity but there may be other factors that may indicate trading if other badges are also apparent.
Has the underlying ***asset been modified?***	If an asset is enhanced to make it more saleable there is likely to be a trade.
The ***nature of how the asset*** is acquired.	If acquired through a gift or inheritance, this is unlikely to constitute trading on sale.
Is the taxpayer involved in a ***similar trade*** or subject matter?	If the individual is involved in transactions that are very similar to existing trades, then it indicates trading.
What ***type of finance*** has been used?	If funded by a short-term loan which is paid off on disposal, this is an indication of trading.
Length of ***ownership*** of the asset?	When a sale follows a purchase within a short period of time, this will indicate trading. Items held for a long time indicate non-trading.
The way the ***transaction is carried out.***	If the sale of the asset is carried out in a manner that would apply to a trading organisation, then this could indicate trading.
The ***reason*** for the sale.	If sold to alleviate a cash flow problem, then this is more likely to indicate non-trading.

When trying to determine trading or non-trading, all the badges described above must be taken into consideration to achieve the result.

Example 2.1

In the case *Rutledge v CIR – CS1929, 14 TC 490*, the taxpayer was on a business trip to Germany where the taxpayer purchased one million toilet rolls. On returning to the UK, the sole consignment of toilet rolls was sold to one individual for a profit. The profit made on this large quantity, single purchase and resale item was 'an adventure in the nature of trade'. The case was decided on the fact that the purchase was not made for own use or investment purposes, so must therefore be for trade and a profit seeking motive.

Example 2.2

In the case of *Taylor c Good – CA 1974, 49 TC 277; (1974) STC 148; (1974) 1 WLR 556; (1974) 1 All ER1137*, a taxpayer purchased a house with the sole intention of using it as a family home. However, the taxpayer's partner refused to move in as they did not like it. The taxpayer was forced to sell the house immediately although the taxpayer genuinely did not have the intention of buying the property for a profit. Even though the sale was a short period of time after purchase, it was **not** deemed to be a trade.

Activity 2.1

Andrew Hodges purchases pieces of art, some of which he displays in his family home, some of which he keeps in a safe storage facility.

This was a hobby while he was employed, but after retiring from employment he has started purchasing works of art on a more frequent basis, setting up a stall in the local market bi-monthly where he sells pieces for a profit that he doesn't want to keep as an investment for himself.

Would Andrew be classed as an art collector or an art dealer? What badge of trade, if any, would determine that trading is happening?

A written summary explaining your answer should be given:

Establishing the net profit figure

There is a difference between **accounting profit** and **taxable profit** and this will apply irrespective of the type of business.

- **Accounting profit or loss** for a period is before the deduction of applicable taxation. This is the profit or loss shown in the financial statements by deducting trading expenditure from trading income. Profits before tax from the financial statements need adjusting according to tax legislation.
- **Taxable profit or loss** for a period is the profit or loss determined by the taxation authorities' regulations and rules that are relevant for taxation.

The starting point will always be to identify the **net profit** figure in the profit or loss account for the period; however, this will need to be adjusted for the following:

- **Disallowed Expenses** – these are the most common adjustments. Not all items of expenditure which are perfectly acceptable to be included in a profit or loss account are permitted for tax purposes – remember that expenses will reduce the profit made by the business, resulting in a lower tax liability. There are therefore a number of expenses which HMRC has said are not allowable in calculating the taxable profit – these items must be **added back to the net profit.** This would include drawings taken as wages for a sole trader.
- **Income taxed elsewhere or not taxable** – sometimes a business will include sources of income in its profit or loss account which are taxed differently. These could include grants or subsidies received by the business which are not taxable or income from property or savings which are taxed elsewhere under self-assessment. Any income which is either taxed elsewhere or is not taxable must be **deducted from the net profit.**

Taxable trading profits for an individual are very similar to a company as they start with the net profit, then the adjustments for adjusted trading profit, and then less any capital allowances. Any differences for individuals will be highlighted later in this chapter under **unincorporated** business private expense, salary and drawings, income included/not included in the accounts but is taxable as trading income.

The following gives the process on how you achieve the adjusted taxable profit figure from the accounting profit figure and this is shown in a step-by-step process for ease of understanding:

1. The first step in adjusting profits is to take the net profit before taxation. This is the starting point for any adjustments to achieve the taxable profit.

Steps	Adjustment of Profits	£
1	Net profit before tax as per accounts	X

2. **Disallowed expenses** are the most common adjustments.

Allowable expenses would include expenses that are:

- Revenue and 'not capital'
- 'Wholly and exclusively' for the purpose of the trade

If the expenses fully adhere to the above rules, then they should normally be **allowable.**

However, not all items of expenditure which are perfectly acceptable to be included in the statement of profit or loss are permitted for tax purposes. Expenses in the accounts reduce the gross profit made by the business. If expenses have been included that are not allowable for tax, this would reduce the tax liability to the business.

There are a number of types of expenses which HMRC state are ***not allowed*** in calculating taxable profit – these items must therefore be **added back to the net accounting profit.** A comprehensive list of disallowed and allowable expenses is shown later in the chapter.

Steps	Adjustment of Profits	£
1	Net profit before tax as per accounts	**X**
	Add	
2	Disallowable expenses e.g. depreciation which has been entered as an expense in the accounts	X

3. After the additions of disallowable expenses have been adjusted there is a requirement to add income that has not been included in the accounts but **taxable as trading income**. (Individual trader only). An example of this would be goods taken by the owner for own or private use.

Steps	Adjustment of Profits	£
1	Net profit before tax as per accounts	**X**
	Add	
2	Disallowable expenses e.g. depreciation which has been entered as an expense in the accounts	X
3	Income not included in the accounts but taxable as trading income	X

4. The next steps are the deductions for items in the accounts that are **not taxable as trading profits**. An example of this would be rental or property income received. In the accounts, this would have increased the profit figure as it is a source of income. However, for tax purposes, this is not trading income and will be **deducted from the net profit** which will then decrease the tax liability at this point. These items, however, will be treated separately under self-assessment or corporation tax rules later on in the course.

Steps	Adjustment of Profits	£
1	Net profit before tax as per accounts	**X**
	Add	
2	Disallowable expenses e.g. depreciation which has been entered as an expense in the accounts	X
3	Income not included in the accounts but taxable as trading income	X
		X
	Deduct	
4	Items in the accounts not taxable as trading, e.g. property rental income	**(X)**

5. The last step in the calculation of adjustment of profits is to deduct expenditure that has not been charged in the accounts for profit valuation but is **allowable for tax purposes.** Capital expenditure should not be included in the profit or loss account in any event – however, it is not always easy to determine what is revenue expenditure (e.g. repairs and renewals) and what is capital expenditure (e.g. enhancement of new purchases). Capital allowances are available to be deducted from profit and these will be looked at in detail later in the course.

Steps	Adjustment of Profits	£
1	Net profit before tax as per accounts	**X**
	Add	
2	Disallowable expenses e.g. depreciation which has been entered as an expense in the accounts	X
3	Income not included in the accounts but taxable as trading income	X
		X
	Deduct	
4	Income in the accounts not taxable as trading income, e.g. property rental income	(X)
	Adjusted trading profit before deduction of capital expenses	**X**
5	Expenditure deductible from trading profits, e.g. capital allowances	**(X)**

6. You are then left with the adjusted trading profit figure. The following template can then be used for calculating the adjustment of profits.

Example 2.3

Template for adjustment of profits.

Steps	Adjustment of Profits	£
1	Net profit before tax as per accounts	X
	Add	
2	Disallowable expenses	X
3	Income not included in the accounts but taxable as trading income	X
		X
	Deduct	
4	Income in the accounts not taxable as trading income, e.g. property rental income	(X)
	Adjusted trading profit before deduction of capital expenses	X
5	Expenditure deductible from trading profits, e.g. capital allowances	(X)
6	**Adjusted trading profit**	X

Example 2.4

Kingsley Field is a sole trader working as an electrician. His latest accounts show a net profit of £26,000 (Step 1). Within this figure in the accounts, he has deducted entertaining expenses of £1,750 and depreciation expenses of £5,000 (Step 2). These amounts are not allowable for tax purposes. Capital allowances of £5,000 are available for tax purposes. (Step 5).

The adjustment of profits template can be completed as:

Steps	Adjustment of Profits	£
1	Net profit before tax as per accounts	**26,000**
	Add	
2	Disallowable expenses (1,750 + 5,000)	6,750
3	Income not included in the accounts but taxable as trading income	0
		32,750
	Deduct	
4	Income in the accounts not taxable as trading income	(0)
	Adjusted trading profit before deduction of capital expenses	**32,750**
5	Expenditure deductible from trading profits, e.g. capital allowances	(5,000)
6	**Adjusted trading profit**	**27,750**

Deductions are shown with brackets but it may be that a minus sign will be required in an assessment.

Because the entertaining and depreciation expenses have been added back to profit but a deduction has been made for capital allowances, Kingsley will now have to pay tax on the £27,750 adjusted trading profit rather than the original £26,000 net accounting profit.

Activity 2.2

Kirstie Robin is a landscape gardener and her net profit for the year is £15,000. She has arrived at this figure in her accounts by deducting £1,500 for depreciation expense and £800 for entertaining suppliers. Capital allowances are £2,400.

What would be the adjusted trading profit for Kirstie?

Identify deductible and non-deductible expenditure and income

The following table gives examples of adjustments to net accounting profit and if they are to be added back, deducted or no action to be taken from the net profit figure. It is a useful table to refer to but you need to ensure you are aware of and understand the reasoning behind the adjustments to the accounting profit and the effect on the net profit figure.

Remember allowable expenses must be:

- **Revenue and 'not capital'**
- **'Wholly and exclusively' for the purpose of the trade**

Apply this principle to any examples given. Note that there may be some small differences that apply to limited companies that do not apply to sole traders and partnerships and vice versa, and this will be pointed out as we progress through the chapter and the course.

Example 2.5

The treatment of expenses/income for taxation

Adjusted Trading Profit changes	Disallowed (Add back)	Disallowed (Deduct)	Allowed. No action if it is in P&L
Assets should not be in P & L – capital expenditure	Add		
Asset improvement or making second-hand assets useable	Add		
Asset depreciation/amortisation – capital allowances granted instead	Add		
Asset purchase legal fees and installation costs	Add		
Asset loss on disposal	Add		
Asset profit on disposal		Deduct	
Asset repairs to keep in good condition			✓
Bad/Irrecoverable debt write-offs – non-trade (such as an employee loan)	Add		
Bad/Irrecoverable debt write-offs - trade			✓
Bad/Irrecoverable debt recovered - trade			✓
Bad/Irrecoverable debt provision – increase in specific bad debt provision (ltd company)			✓
Bad/Irrecoverable debt provision – decrease in specific bad debt provision (ltd company)			✓
Bad/Irrecoverable debt provision – increase in general bad debt provision	Add		

Bad/Irrecoverable debt provision – decrease in general bad debt provision		Deduct	
Capital allowances for assets			✓
Corporation tax itself is not deductible			✓
Debenture interest (trading loan)			✓
Depreciation of assets	Add		
Dividends payable included in P & L before tax	Add		
Dividends received included in P & L before tax		Deduct	
Donations - to local charities (wholly and exclusively for trading and promotion)			✓
Donations – Qualifying charitable donations under gift aid – disallowed for adjusted trading profit	Add		
Donations to political parties	Add		
Entertaining Customers and Suppliers	Add		
Entertaining Employees at Social Events			✓
Expenses – normal business trading expenses • distribution • administration • salaries and wages • employers NI • rent and rates • insurance • repairs • advertising • business travel and subsistence • accountancy services • research and development			✓
Fee for chasing a bad debt			✓
Fines for law breaking and late payment of taxes	Add		
Fines for employee (while working at job)			✓
Fines for Director (or owner) (like motoring)- never deductible	Add		
Fraud – Bribes and payments from threats	Add		
Fraud – Petty theft by employee (non-director or non-senior management)			✓
Gifts to customers and clients (exceptions below)	Add		
Gifts to customers that contain: a conspicuous advert, under £50 value per recipient per year and not including food, drink, tobacco or gift voucher			✓
Gifts to employees			✓

Income – rental income received		Deduct	
Income – gain or profit on sale of shares		Deduct	
Income – non-trading interest received		Deduct	
Income – normal trade sales			✓
Income tax and NI (sole trader/partners)	Add		
Interest paid on trading loans			✓
Interest received on trading loans			
Interest paid on non-trading loans	Add		
Interest received on non-trading loans		Deduct	
Lease – car on operating lease with emissions more than 50g/km CO^2 for over 45 days	15% add		✓ 85%
Lease – car lease with emissions less than 50g/km CO^2			✓
Legal expenses – incorporation or acquiring new leases	Add		
Legal fees – successful tax appeal	Add		
Legal fees – breach of regulations	Add		
Legal fees and costs – registration of patents and trademarks			✓
Legal fees – renewing long lease (over 60 years)	Add		
Legal fees – renewing short lease or defending title to asset			✓
Legal fees – connected to issue of share capital	Add		
Loans to Directors or Employees written off (and subject to BIK)	Add		
Loan finance – *incidental costs to obtain* Applies to individuals and not companies			✓
Patent and copyright royalties – for trade only		Deduct	
Private use adjustments – not calculated for a Limited Company, ***see notes for individuals***			✓
Salary or interest paid to a sole trader or partner	Add		
Share disposal – profits on disposal		Deduct	
Subscriptions to a trade or professional association required for trading			✓
Trade samples – not for resale			✓

Capital expenditure

For expenses to be allowable they must be **revenue and not capital** in nature which means that capital expenditure should not be included in the profit or loss in any event. This follows the principle that allowable expenses should be 'wholly revenue and not capital'.

An understanding of what is capital and what is revenue is required especially where additions, fees, repairs, etc. to assets are concerned.

Asset purchases including any legal fees and any installation costs are all capital expenditure and if they have been included in the P & L incorrectly, they must be **added back** to net profit in the adjusting profit calculation. This also applies to legal fees on the purchase of a **new** short lease or the **renewal** of a lease over 65 years.

Improvements to existing assets or making purchased second-hand assets useable are classified as capital expenditure and are disallowed expenses and must be **added back** to net profit if they have been incorrectly included in net profit in the accounts.

The profit on the disposal of an asset would have been entered as income in the profit or loss thereby increasing profit. Asset disposal is covered for taxation purposes under capital allowances so the amount would be disallowed and **deducted from** net profit at the adjusting profit stage.

Loss on disposal of an asset would be disallowed and **added back**.

Repairs to existing assets **just to keep in good condition** are running expenses and allowable expenses so no action would be required.

Example 2.6

Ismaeel Schroeder runs a sweet shop on the High Street and when a window was broken on the facia of the building, he decided to change the whole appearance of the front of the shop and not just the window. The cost of replacing one window would have been £600. Ismaeel spent £9,400 changing the shop front.

Ismaeel put the £9,400 expense into his accounts as a repair. This should have been treated as an improvement and therefore a capital item and should be **added back** to profit.

There are occasions when the use of new technology as part of the repair does not then mean that the repair becomes an improvement. An example of this is double glazing. At one stage replacing single-glazed windows with double glazed would have been an improvement. As time has gone on, double glazing is now normal within the industry and ceased to be an improvement and became allowable for tax.

Activity 2.3

Identify which of the following are revenue or capital by ticking the correct box:

	Revenue ✓	Capital ✓
Buying a vehicle		
Repainting an existing office		
Purchasing new premises		
Extending existing premises		
Paying rent on shop outlet		
Paying for repairs to machinery		

There are some disallowable expenses that appear on a regular basis and these are explained in more detail below:

Depreciation

Depreciation is an annual reduction in the value of the assets owned by the business. There is considerable freedom in the way in which a business may choose to depreciate its assets (e.g. using the straight line or diminishing balance methods). The expense is shown in the statement of profit or loss which reduces the net profit.

This flexibility with depreciation expense can lead to different businesses having different profits – even though they have had similar results. This would then cause differences between businesses with regard to taxation. The depreciation expense is required to be **added back** for the purposes of adjusted profits. To replace depreciation, capital allowances are available for assets, which is covered in detail in Chapter 3. Capital allowances are allowances that are the same **for every company** that can be used to reduce adjusted profits to make the results fairer for companies as they will all be subjected to the same rules.

Example 2.7

Barry and Larry are both plumbers, operating as sole traders. In 2024-25, each made identical profits of £30,000, before deducting depreciation charges for the year. Both have assets valued at £10,000.

Barry depreciates his assets on a straight-line basis over ten years, whilst Larry depreciates his assets on a reducing balance basis at a rate of 40% per annum.

The following shows how this will affect the net profit for each business.

Barry:	Profit	£30,000	
	Less Depreciation	£ 1,000	*£10,000 x 1/10*
	Net Profit	**£29,000**	
Larry:	Profit	£30,000	
	Less Depreciation	£ 4,000	*£10,000 x 40%*
	Net Profit	**£26,000**	

We can see in this example that if depreciation were to be classed as an allowable expense, businesses could reduce the amount of tax they pay (at least in the short term) by changing their depreciation policy.

HMRC therefore have 'disallowed' depreciation as an expense when calculating taxable profit, and any depreciation expenses in the profit or loss account must be added back.

Instead of allowing depreciation, there is an alternative system called **Capital Allowances** which apply at the same rate to all businesses. Capital allowances are a very involved calculation and Chapter 3 is dedicated to them.

Depreciation is recorded in **Step 2** of the template for adjusted profits.

Entertaining

Businesses will entertain customers and suppliers as part of their promotion of their business and feel it is a valid cost which would legitimately be seen as an expense in their statement of profit or loss which would therefore reduce profits.

However, HMRC does not allow the entertaining of customers or suppliers for tax purposes, so any expense incurred on this is **added back** via the adjustment of profits.

Entertaining staff or employees of the business is allowable if the cost is £150 per person or less. However, the employees may incur an income tax liability if the amount exceeds this limit. A staff party is allowable as long as all members of staff have been invited.

Entertaining customers and suppliers are recorded as part of **Step 2** of the template for adjusted profits.

Fines

A business is required to operate within the law so if a business incurs fines or penalties due to infringement of the law they are **not** regarded as allowable for tax purposes and should be **added back**. Examples of this are late payment of taxes or breaches of Health and Safety legislation.

Motoring fines by Directors in a company are **never allowable** and must be **added back**. The same applies to owners of a business like a sole trader. However, fines incurred by an employee while working at their job are **allowable** and will not cause a change.

Fines are recorded in **Step 2** of the template for adjusted profits.

Charitable and political donations

Any small local charity donations are treated as a form of advertising as these donations improve the image of the business within the local community. The **local charity donation is allowable** as an expense for tax purposes for both incorporated and unincorporated businesses. (These will only be examined for unincorporated businesses.)

An unincorporated business may make donations via the gift aid scheme. These are **not allowed** and must be **added back**. However, the individual may be able to reclaim tax relief through self-assessment.

All other national charitable donations are **not allowed** as trading expenses and will be added back to net profit.

A limited company may obtain relief under qualifying charitable donations (QCDs). This is not given through the adjusting profits but under corporation tax rules and will be covered in a later chapter.

No political donations are allowable.

Charitable donations are recorded in **Step 2** of the template for adjusted profits.

Gifts

Gifts to employees are **allowable**, although the **employee** may be **taxed** on them as a benefit. Gifts to third parties are generally **not allowable** unless they fulfil the following three conditions:

- They must clearly state the business's name
- Each gift cannot cost more than £50
- They cannot be food, drink, or tobacco (or anything that can be readily exchanged for it.)

The usual gifts that are allowable are things like diaries, pens and calendars which state the business' name.

Disallowable expenses for gifts are recorded in **Step 2** of the adjusted profits template.

Activity 2.4

The following expenses have been incurred by a limited company. You are required to determine whether any or all of the expenses are allowable for tax purposes:

Expense	Amount £	Allowable Yes or No?
Staff outing to the races for 30 employees.	3,600.00	
A gift to a customer of a bottle of aged port with company emblem on bottle.	49.99	
A floral gift to an employee who has just given birth.	25.00	
Company embossed diaries of £15 each to customers at Christmas.	450.00	
Donation to the local conservative party.	200.00	
Speeding fine incurred by a director.	75.00	
Donation to the local hospice.	100.00	

Irrecoverable debts and allowances for specific and general doubtful receivables

When an irrecoverable (bad) debt has been written off for a customer this is classified as an **allowable** expense. Any recovered irrecoverable debts that have been written off (when the customer has eventually paid) are also allowable and **no adjustment** would be required to net profit.

When you have an **allowance for specific doubtful receivables** or any increase or decrease in the specific doubtful receivables allowance then this usually applies to a particular customer. This customer may not yet be a bad debt but the company may be experiencing difficulty in paying and you are uncertain that the debt will ever be paid. An allowance for specific doubtful receivables is made in the accounts for the value of the debt of this one customer. Again, this is an **allowable** expense because the debt passes the principle that it has been incurred "wholly and exclusively" for the purposes of the trade.

A specific allowance for doubtful receivables usually applies to one particular customer and not to the whole receivables ledger and is normally calculated for limited companies only. This is because companies need to follow the rules of the Companies Act requirements when producing their accounts, whereas unincorporated businesses are not bound by this act and may contain general allowances.

However, where a **general** allowance for doubtful receivables has been calculated (usually by a percentage of the total balance of the receivables ledger), any increase in the general allowance will be disallowed by being **added back** and any decrease in the general allowance for doubtful receivables will be **disallowed and deducted.**

This is because it is not an actual expense or deduction, it is just an accounting adjustment.

Any non-trade debts like a loan to an employee written off are not an allowable expense and should be **added back** to net profit.

Irrecoverable debts are recorded in **Step 2 and Step 3** of the template for adjusted profits.

Example 2.8

Phillett Limited has a receivables ledger balance of £120,000 at the end of their financial year. They are required to write off an irrecoverable debt for £4,750 plus VAT for Surloyn Limited, which is now over 6 months old and the customer is no longer trading.

The irrecoverable debt write-off for Surloyn Limited creates an expense of £4,750 in the accounts in the statement of profit or loss and is **allowable** for tax purposes.

Phillett Ltd also has a customer Rhump Ltd, who has not yet paid their balance on the receivables ledger of £10,000 plus VAT. The debt is now 5 months old and Phillett Ltd has heard through the trade that Rhump Ltd **may** go out of business. They are required to make an allowance for specific doubtful receivables within the year-end accounts to ensure the accounts give a "true and fair view".

The specific doubtful receivables allowance for Rhump Ltd creates an expense of £10,000 in the accounts on the statement of profit or loss and is **allowable** for tax purposes. This is then shown on the Statement of Financial Position as a liability on the allowance for doubtful receivables ledger account.

After the irrecoverable debt for Surloyn Limited has been written off, the receivables ledger balance is £114,300 being £120,000 - £5,700 = £114,300.

Phillett Ltd also feels they should make a general allowance for doubtful receivables of 2% of the receivables ledger balance.

This general provision is classified as a "guess" at future debts that may not get paid.

The general allowance for doubtful receivables is £2,286 (£114,300 x 2%) and this is **disallowed** for tax purposes and needs to be **added back** in the adjusting profit calculation.

Legal and professional expenses

Legal expenses are allowable if they relate to the day-to-day running of the business and have been incurred wholly and exclusively for the purposes of the trade – if they relate to the purchase of a capital item, for example, then they are **disallowed** and must be **added back**.

So, for example, legal expenses relating to defending the business against a claim for unfair dismissal by a former employee **would** be allowable; however legal fees relating to the purchase of a new factory **would not** be.

Disallowable legal and professional expenses are recorded in **Step 2** of the adjusted profits template.

Pre-trading expenditure

This is allowable as long as it satisfies the wholly and exclusively test and is incurred in the seven years before the business commenced trading and they are business expenses that would be allowed after the commencement of trade.

Any expenditure from more than seven years before the start of trade is **disallowed** and must be **added back** in **step 2** of the adjusted profits template.

Unincorporated business – private expenses

Any expenses that are **private** and belong specifically to an owner of a business should be **disallowed** and **added back,** this will include any personal income tax or national insurance amounts.

If there is a business/personal split on the expense, such as in the case of a telephone bill then it will be just the private element that is disallowed.

Private expenses do not apply to incorporated businesses.

Private expenses are recorded in **Step 2** of the adjustments to profits.

Unincorporated business – salary and drawings

Any salaries or drawings withdrawn by an owner of a business are **disallowed** and must be **added back** to profit. However, reasonable salaries of family members for work done within the business are allowable.

Salary and drawings do not apply to incorporated businesses.

Salaries and drawings are recorded in **Step 2** of the adjustments to profits.

Example 2.9

Show whether the following should be allowed, disallowed and added back or disallowed and deducted.

	Allow	Disallow and add back	Disallow and deduct
Increase in general bad debt provision		✓	
£1,250 expense for patent registration	✓		
Repair to office roof	✓		
£700 donation to a political party		✓	
Drawings by owner		✓	
Profit on disposal of an asset			✓

Activity 2.5

Show whether the following should be allowed, disallowed and added back or disallowed and deducted.

	Allow	Disallow and add back	Disallow and deduct
Owner's parking fine			
Decrease in general bad debt provision			
Depreciation charge			
Donation to a local charity			
Patent registration legal fees			
Rental income received			
£7 stolen from petty cash by employee			
Employees salaries			
Fee for chasing an irrecoverable debt			
Entertaining suppliers			

Example 2.10

Ajay Gunn runs an art shop business. The following are his accounts for year the ended 31 December.

	£	£
Gross Profit		90,000
Less - Expenses		
Salaries	35,000	
Motor expenses	4,500	
Allowable expenses	26,000	
Total expenses		65,500
Net Profit for the year per the accounts		**24,500**

Ajay has included £1,600 in the accounts for running his own car but he uses it 50% for personal use and 50% for business. Also included is his salary of £25,000.

Ajay's adjusted trading profit would be:

Adjustment of Profits	£
Net profit before tax as per accounts	24,500
Add	
Drawings for salary Private motor expense usage (50% of £1,600)	25,000 800
Adjusted trading profit before deduction of capital expenses	50,300

Activity 2.6

Kristen Vasquez is a sole trader who runs a beauty treatment clinic from her home.

Her home heating bill for the 12 month period of her accounts is £3,000. This amount has been deducted as an expense in full to achieve the accounting profit for the year.

40% of the utility bills are for use in her business.

How much, if any should be added back in the calculation of adjusting trading profit?

Activity 2.7

Amy runs her own convenience store selling products from her store as well as online. Her accounts show the following information:

	£	£
Gross Profit		120,000
Less - Expenses		
Depreciation charges	12,300	
Advertising	2,450	
Motor expenses	1,500	
Entertainment	3,000	
General allowance for doubtful receivables	1,800	
General expenses	17,000	
Total expenses		38,050
Net Profit for the Year		**81,950**

Capital allowances have been calculated at £8,200 for the year.

Calculate the taxable profit by making relevant adjustments to the accounting net profit.

Adjustment of Profits	£
Net profit before tax as per accounts	
Add	
Adjusted trading profit before deduction of capital expenses	
Capital allowances	
Adjusted trading profit	

Unincorporated business – Income not included in the accounts but taxable as trading income

This category at **Step 3** of the adjustment for trading profits does not apply to a limited company and will only apply to sole traders or partners within a partnership.

This normally applies in the instances where an owner takes goods for their own use. This should be **added back** to the accounting profit. The owner should be taxed at market value on the profit that would have been achieved if sold to retail or wholesale.

If the owner has reduced the cost of sales in the statement of profit or loss for the goods taken, the amount to be **added back** will be the **profit**.

However, if the owner has not reduced the cost of sales for the goods taken for their own use, the amount to be **added back** to arrive at the adjusted profit would be the **selling price.**

Example 2.11

Lyle Lister runs an independent stationery business as a sole trader. He has taken goods for his own use within the last financial year that originally cost £1,500. The cost of the goods has been adjusted in the accounts to account for the recording of the taking of the goods.

Lyle operates on a gross profit margin of 40%.

If the gross profit is 40% of sales, the cost of sales is 60%.

Profit is therefore £1,500 x 40 / 60 = **£1,000 to be added back in adjusting profit**.

Income included in the accounts but not taxable as trading income

Income received that is not referred to as "trading income" will need to be deducted from net profit in the adjustment of profits for all businesses and will include the following:

- Gains on the disposal of assets
- Non-trading interest received
- Rental income received
- Dividends received

Chargeable gains on fixed assets are usually the gain when disposing of an asset, the difference between what you paid for it and how much it has been sold for. Chargeable gains are dealt with in detail later in the course. These chargeable gains are taxed separately and therefore will initially be deducted from profit under the adjusted trading profit calculation.

If you make an allowable loss from the disposal of an asset you can reduce your total **chargeable gains** by deducting any allowable losses. You can only deduct allowable losses from your chargeable gains **– not from trading income** or other profits.
These gains/losses are calculated separately and therefore will initially be **added back** to profit under the adjusted trading profit calculation in Step 4.

Non-trading interest received covers interest received on things like business bank deposit accounts or building society accounts. If this income has been shown in the statement of profit or loss it should be deducted from the profit figure in adjusting trading profits at Step 4, but will be dealt with when calculating taxable trading profits later in the course.

Non-trading interest payable covers interest on loans taken out for example on a property purchase, and is disallowed in adjusting trading profits at Step 4 and again will be dealt with later in the course.

Trading interest is allowable and if it is showing in the statement of profit or loss, there will not be any adjustment. This covers loans that are specifically for the trade of the business like the purchase of an asset by a loan.

Rent receivable or property business income will have the expenses applicable to the property deducted to achieve a separate profit or loss figure. Property business income is then taxed on an accrual basis. Therefore, it is deducted from profit for adjustment of profits and is dealt with separately which is covered in detail later in the course.

Dividends received by UK companies are usually exempt from tax irrespective of where they are received from, although there are some exceptions to this (not covered by this syllabus). Dividends received should be deducted from profit if they have been included in the net profit before tax.

Treatment of dividends payable

Dividends are what companies pay to their shareholders out of the profits of the company.

Dividends payable cannot count as a business expense when working out Corporation Tax for companies.

However, the shareholder or receiver of the dividend may have to pay Income Tax on any dividends received depending on their value, the status of the recipient and what dividend allowances are available.

If dividends payable have been included in the statement of profit or loss before taxation, then they must be disallowed. Dividends are always paid from **profits after tax.** So, if net profit in the accounts is given after dividends are paid then the amount should be adjusted and disallowed.

If a limited company has profits before corporation tax of £50,000 and a dividend is required to be paid from these profits, the corporation tax must be paid on the profits before a dividend is paid.

£50,000 x 19% (small profits) corporation tax = £9,500 tax due. This is deducted from the profits of £50,000 and the maximum dividend that can be received from the shareholder/s is £40,500.

Lease charges for cars

By finance leasing, you may **never own** the asset depending on the arrangements of the lease. A finance lease is where the finance company (lessor) purchases the asset and owns the asset, and then "leases" it back to the lessee (who leases the asset).
For short finance leases (up to 7 years) the ownership always remains with the lessor (who is able to claim capital allowances as the owner) and are similar to an operating rental lease where the rental expense is recorded as an expense in the statement of profit or loss as and when invoiced by the lessor to the lessee.

This type of lease is sometimes chosen when ownership is not required. When the short lease is for a car with CO^2 emissions **exceeding 50 g/km (for leases beginning on or after 1 April 2021)** there is a flat rate disallowance of **15%** on the amount of lease payments allowed for tax purposes. This means that **only 85% is allowable** for tax purposes.

Any lease costs for cars with CO^2 emissions **below 50 g/km are allowable.**

Example 2.12

Minee Ltd is planning to lease a new car for their Sales Director in April 2024. The list price of the car is £27,000 and the CO^2 emissions are 170g/km.

The annual cost of the lease is £3,800 and it will run for a period of 3 years after which time the car will be returned to the dealer for a newer model. 25% of the Sales Director's mileage is for private use.

The tax treatment of the lease of the vehicle would be:

The lease is similar to an operating lease as it is less than 7 years. £570 of the annual cost of the lease must be added back in calculating the taxable trading profit for Minee Ltd because the car's CO^2 emissions are more than the limit of 50g/km.

85% is allowable and 15% is added back. Therefore, £3,800 x 15% = £570.

The private mileage for private use would be treated separately as a benefit to the Sales Director.

Where a sole trader leases a vehicle for business and private usage, and the vehicle is a high emissions car, the amount to be disallowed will initially be the 15% rental charges. The private element will then be calculated on the balance of the 85% as well depending on the percentage of private use. These two figures will then be added together.

Activity 2.8

Feehat Ltd leases the following two cars on 1 March 2024.

1) Cost price £22,000 with CO^2 emissions of 45 g/km. Lease charges for 10 months to the end of the financial year 31 December 2024 are £6,500.

2) Cost price £17,500 with CO^2 emissions of 130 g/km. Lease charges for 10 months to the end of 31 December 2024 are £4,500.

What would be the total disallowed expenditure for the financial year ending 31 December 2024?

Computing adjusted trading profit before capital allowances

The following is a full working example to assist with the different changes that may be required to net accounting profit:

Example 2.13

The statement of profit or loss for Bewghatti Limited for the year ending 31 March 2025 shows a net profit of **£50,000** after accounting for and including the following items:

- Depreciation £16,000
- Entertaining customers £600
- Gifts of wine to customers £600
- Increase in general allowance for doubtful receivables £450
- Profit on sale of production machine £3,400
- Penalty for late payment of VAT £300
- Bank interest received on deposit account £50
- Rental income £2,000
- Donation to a national charity £500
- Car leasing costs for a director with Car CO^2 emissions exceeding 50 g/km £1,500
- Employee parking fine £250
- Director fine for parking £250

The first step is to enter the net profit figure of £50,000 into the template.

Steps	Adjustment of Profits	£
1	Profit before tax as per accounts	**50,000**

The next step is to determine if there are any disallowable expenses in the list to **be added back.**

Go through the list and analyse the entries to determine their status in the computation of adjusted profit. Always apply the principles of 'revenue and not capital' and 'used wholly and exclusively for the purpose of the trade'.

- Depreciation is disallowed expenditure along with any **loss** on the sale or disposal of a fixed asset and must be added back to profit as the original posting entry would be as an expense which originally reduced the profit.
- Entertaining customers is a disallowed expenditure. Any entertaining costs associated with staff are allowable.
- Gifts of wine to customers are disallowed expenditure. Any food or drink items are not allowable for tax. Gifts for employees are allowable.
- The increase in the general allowance for doubtful receivables is a disallowed expenditure. This is because there is no evidence that the general allowance is actually going to be

written off as an irrecoverable debt. This is required to be added back to profit as the original general bad debt provision increase would have been entered as an expense and this would have reduced profit. If the general allowance for doubtful receivables had decreased then this would have increased profit.

However, if an increase in the specific allowance has been entered then this is allowable and there would be no change to the net profit. A specific allowance for doubtful receivables is one where a reliable amount of certainty is placed that the provision will become an irrecoverable debt in the future. Again, if a decrease in a specific allowance has been entered in the statement of profit or loss then this is reliable that it has already been written off or is not going to happen and no change to profit is required.

- The penalty for a late payment of VAT is disallowed as the company should be trading within the law. As this was originally entered as an expense it has reduced profit so would be required to be added back.
- Donation to a national charity is a disallowable expense as it does not qualify as "wholly and exclusively" for the purpose of the trade. Any small donations to local charities can be classified as being local advertising and can be allowed for tax purposes.
- Car leasing costs for a Director with CO^2 emissions exceeding 50 g/km. 15% of the leasing costs are disallowed and 85% allowable with no change to profit. Therefore, on a leasing cost of £1,500, £225 would be disallowed.
- In general expenses, there are two parking fines, one for the employee on company business which is an allowable expense and one for a director, which is a disallowable expense and would need adding back to profit as it was originally an expense in the statement of profit or loss.

These adjustments can now be added to the template for adjusting profits and then added to the profit figure to give a new adjusted profit figure. This then increases the profit from £50,000 to £68,925.

Steps	Adjustment of Profits	£
1	Profit before tax as per accounts	**50,000**
	Add	
2	Depreciation	16,000
	Entertaining customers	600
	Gifts of wine	600
	Increase in general allowance for doubtful receivables	450
	Penalty for late payment of VAT	300
	Donation to a national charity	500
	Car leasing costs for Director with CO^2 exceeding 50 g/km	225
	Director parking fine	250
		68,925

Step 3 involves deciding which items in the list are **not taxable** as trading profits.

Profit on the sale of a production machine is disallowed as this is treated under chargeable gains in the Corporation Tax computation. As the gain would have been entered as income this would have increased the profit so this would be required to be deducted from profit.

Interest received by companies on bank deposit accounts is non-trading interest income and this is deducted from profit in the adjustment of profits, as it is taxed in a different way (shown later).

Rental or property income will have the relevant expenses relating to any income deducted from it to achieve an individual profit or loss for this section. Net property income is dealt with in detail later in the course. Property income is deducted from trading profits at this point as this is non-trading profit.

These deductions can now be entered at step 3 and deducted from **£68,925**.

This will then give the figure for the adjusted trading profit before the deduction of capital allowances.

Steps	Adjustment of Profits	£
		68,925
	Less	
3	Profit on sale of production machine	(3,400)
	Bank interest received	(50)
	Rental Income	(2,000)
	Adjusted trading profit before deduction of capital allowances	**63,475**

Activity 2.9

IKA Limited prepare their accounts to 31 March annually. The information from their statement of profit or loss for the year ending 31 March 2025 is as follows:

	£	£
Gross Profit		60,000
Add – Other Income		
Bank deposit interest received		1,920
Dividends Received		4,800
Less - Expenses		
Allowable expenditure	21,600	
Irrecoverable debts w/off recovered	(1,200)	
Making second hand asset useable	1,800	
Re-plastering damaged wall	840	
Motor expenses	8,400	
Depreciation	4,200	
Loss on sale of asset	480	
Accountancy fees	2,400	
Legal fees breach of official regulations	4,500	
Director's fine	3,000	
Legal fees for debt collection	1,440	
Trade subscriptions	240	
Entertaining customers	3,600	
Customer gifts with logo (£12 ea.)	540	
Sundry allowable expenses	3,444	
Total expenses		55,284
Net Profit for the Year		**11,436**

Calculate IKA Ltd.'s tax adjusted trading profit for the year ending 31 March 2025 using the following template.

Add back disallowed items and subtract the items that are not taxable as trading income, placing brackets () around them to show that they are to be subtracted.

Steps	IKA Ltd Adjustment of Profits	£
1	Profit before tax as per accounts	
2	**Add**	
3	**Less**	
	Adjusted trading profit before deduction of capital allowances	

Cash basis vs accruals basis

Starting from the tax year 2024-25, the default method for calculating income and expenses for self-assessment tax returns is the cash basis. If you are unable to use the cash basis or prefer the traditional accounting method (accruals), you must opt-out by ticking the appropriate box on your self-assessment tax return. Certain specific businesses are not eligible for the cash basis, but these exclusions generally do not apply to most self-employed individuals. Limited companies and limited liability partnerships are also excluded from using the cash basis.

The cash basis records income and expenses only when they are actually received and paid within the tax year.

Example 2.14

Your business invoices a customer on 20 March 2024 but the money is not received until 20 April 2024. Under the cash basis, this income should be recorded in the tax year 2024 to 2025 and not in the tax year 2023 to 2024.

In contrast, traditional accruals accounting records transactions when they are incurred or earned, regardless of when payment is made or received. For instance, income is recorded when an invoice is issued, not when the payment is actually received.

Example 2.15

Your business invoices a customer on 20 March 2024 but the money is not received until 20 April 2024. Under the accrual basis, this income should be recorded in the tax year 2023 to 2024 and not in the tax year 2024 to 2025.

The cash basis is a more simplistic method compared to accruals accounting, making it suitable for small business owners with straightforward accounting needs. However, it might not be the best option for your business, especially if you need your accounts to provide a more accurate reflection of your financial performance and position.

Summary of Chapter 2

Accounting profit/(loss) for a period, is before the deduction of applicable taxation. Profits before tax from the financial statements need adjusting according to tax legislation.

Taxable profit/(loss) for a period is the profit or loss determined by the taxation authorities' regulations and rules that are relevant for taxation.

The main types of **allowable** expenditure are:

> **"wholly and exclusively for the purpose of the trade"**
> **"revenue and not capital"**

Disallowed expenses can include:

- Fines incurred by Directors
- Depreciation expense
- Customer and supplier entertaining
- Fines for law breaking
- Qualifying charitable donations

Car rental expenses are normally allowable as an expense when adjusting profits. However, there is a percentage restriction on vehicles over **50g**/km if purchased after April 2021. **15% is disallowed** on these vehicles and **85% is an allowable** rental cost.

Income that is not taxable as trading profit:

- Gains on disposal of assets
- Non-trading interest received
- Rental Income receivable
- Dividends received

Dividends payable cannot count as a business expense when working out Corporation Tax.

Individuals adjust their accounting profits in the same way as limited companies apart from:

- Disallowance of drawings and salaries
- Adjusting goods taken for personal use
- Private expenses

- Restriction of owner's own use of assets for capital allowances
- Trading allowance of £1,000 available for sole traders and partners

Cash basis is the default basis for calculating self-assessment from 2024-25.

Assessment 2

You are now required to log in to your ROGO account to complete your online assessment before progressing to the next chapter.

Chapter 3: The nature and purpose of capital allowances

By the end of this chapter, you should:

- Understand why and when capital allowances are given instead of depreciation.
- Understand what applies as qualifying expenditure.
- Understand which capital allowances are available and at what rates:
  - Full expensing (FE)
  - First year allowances (FYA)
  - Annual investment allowance (AIA)
  - Writing down allowances (WDA)
  - Treatment of cars
  - Small pool allowance
- Understand which capital allowances apply to different assets:
  - Plant and machinery
  - Structures and buildings
- Prepare capital allowance computations for accounting periods:
  - Longer than 12 months
  - Shorter than 12 months
  - Equal to 12 months

Depreciation expense and capital allowances

As mentioned in the previous chapter, depreciation is a **disallowable** expense for tax purposes.

This is to minimise the discrepancies which can arise when businesses are allowed to choose their own depreciation policies, i.e. straight line or diminishing balance at varying percentage rates.

Capital allowances are given instead, as a type of depreciation, to businesses to replace depreciation in their tax calculations. This ensures that all businesses write off the value of their assets against tax at the same rate and under the same rules. HMRC produce the capital allowances rates for incorporated businesses currently from January - December to give what is available by way of allowances on each type of asset.

A business can only claim capital allowances on assets that qualify as **plant and machinery**. Therefore, fixed assets such as buildings **will not qualify** for normal capital allowances, see the section on *structures and buildings allowances* later in the chapter.

The amount of capital allowances claimed is then deducted from the business's profits in the calculation of the adjusted taxable profit or trading income.

Example 3.1

GCM Ltd and Hondha Ltd are both small businesses making parts for the car industry. They are identical businesses and both use a production machine for making parts that originally cost the same value of £100,000 for each company.

GCM uses straight-line depreciation over 5 years and Hondha Ltd uses the diminishing balance method @ 15%.

Both companies made profits before depreciation of £160,000 and can claim capital allowances of £80,000 (*for example only, not calculated*).

The example below shows that although the accounting profits before depreciation are the same, when the different rates of depreciation have been applied the accounting profits are then different and Hondha Ltd have made £5,000 more profit than GCM Ltd. However, after adding back depreciation and adjusting for the same capital allowances the adjusted trading profit remains the same. This would then have the application of tax applied at the same rate.

	GCM Ltd £	Hondha Ltd £
Profit before depreciation	160,000	160,000
Less depreciation expense	(20,000)	(15,000)
Accounting profits	**140,000**	**145,000**

Adjustment of profits		
	GCM Ltd £	Hondha Ltd £
Accounting profits	**140,000**	**145,000**
Add back depreciation	20,000	15,000
Adjusted profit before capital	160,000	160,000
Less capital allowances	(80,000)	(80,000)
Adjusted trading profit	**80,000**	**80,000**

Qualifying expenditure

A distinction always needs to be made between what is capital and what is revenue expenditure.

Capital expenditure is usually large expenditure on fixed or non-current assets that will be used for a long period of time within the business.

Revenue expenditure are expenses that are "wholly and exclusively" for the purpose of the trade and are not capital expenses.

A business can only claim capital allowances on assets that qualify as **plant and machinery**.

Therefore, fixed assets such as buildings will not qualify along with land and goodwill. Buildings include walls, floors, ceilings, doors, gates, shutters, windows and stairs and these are now (since 29 October 2018) provided for under Structures and Buildings (S & B) Allowance as a form of tax relief. The S & B allowance is described in detail later in the chapter.

Non-current assets such as buildings do not qualify but alterations to a building to enable the installation of machinery **would qualify** as part of the cost of the asset.

Main types of capital expenditure

There is no specific definition of plant and machinery that all assets can be tested against. Machinery is not too hard to define and it is reasonably obvious if something is a machine or not. Plant, however, can be more difficult to define.

There are two main characteristics of plant which give some indication:

- Plant should have some degree of permanence and longevity, i.e. it will be used over a number of years.
- It should be something that has an active **function** in the business – therefore, it should be something that is used in the trade or business, as opposed to being where the business is carried out (referred to as its **setting**).

There have been many cases brought before the courts to try to establish what does and does not constitute 'plant' – examples include:

1) Moveable partitions, atmospheric lighting, advertising hoardings; signs, displays and similar assets, a dry dock to repair ships, a swimming pool at a holiday camp and specialist window lighting have all been held to be plant as they **have an active function**.

2) General lighting, false ceilings, a canopy at a petrol station and a football stand have all been held not to be plant as they have been classified as **the setting** in which the business is carried on.

The main assets for capital allowances that will be referred to in this course are:

- Plant and machinery including moveable partitions
- Fixtures and fittings
- Motor Vehicles, being cars, vans and lorries
- Computer equipment

Some examples of plant and machinery according to HMRC's capital allowances manual include:

- Kitchen and bathroom fittings
- Computer, telecommunication and surveillance systems
- Business machines like printing presses, lathes and tooling machines
- Tractors, combine harvesters and other agricultural machinery
- Gaming machines, amusement park rides
- Robotic machines
- Wind turbines and fibre-optic cabling
- Refrigeration or cooling equipment

Capital allowances are available on expenses for the following, but are considered separately because they follow different rules under the **special rate pool** (covered later):

- Thermal insulation of buildings
- Items with a long life
- Integral features of a building or structure (not the building itself) like lifts, water heating systems, air conditioning/cooling systems
- Personal security
- Software and rights to software

Example 3.2

A ship used as a floating restaurant that is owned by the proprietor is not plant as the ship is the **setting** for the trade of the restaurant.

However, a ship used by its owner in a trade of shipping is plant as it is used in the active **function** of the business.

Activity 3.1

Identify which of the following would be defined as plant and machinery for capital allowances calculations:

Description	Plant and Machinery, Yes or No
An item of land purchased for £200,000	
Printing press for a business selling magazines	
Heating and ventilation system in new offices	
An additional wall to an existing building	
Drainage ditch around premises	
False ceiling to hide pipework	
Shower unit in bathroom facilities	
Advertising hoarding signage on building front	

Capital allowances available

Capital allowances are a way in which businesses can claim tax relief and reduce their tax liability and the government hopes that this will assist companies to invest in new plant and machinery.

When calculating capital allowances for Limited (incorporated) companies there will **never be any private use** in the computation as there would be for an unincorporated business like a sole trader. With a Limited Company, the director or employee will be required to have any private use deducted as a taxable benefit through their own self-assessment, and the business can then deduct the capital allowance in full.

The allowances are calculated in relation to the CAP (chargeable accounting period) for a Limited Company and they are then deducted from the taxable profits for that period.

The main types of capital allowances available are:

- Full expensing (FE) is **only available to incorporated businesses**
- Annual Investment Allowance (AIA) is available to both incorporated and incorporated
- First Year Allowances (FYA)
- Writing Down Allowances (WDA)
- Special Rate Allowances (SRA).

Full Expensing (FE)

In the Spring Budget 2023, the Chancellor brought in a new type of capital allowance that would be available **only to incorporated businesses that pay Corporation Tax**. Initially, the period announced was from 1 April 2023 until the end of March 2026. However, in the Autumn Statement 2023, the government announced that full expensing would be **made permanent**. This means that qualifying companies can claim **100%** capital allowances on qualifying new main rate **plant and machinery** investments. The plant and machinery must be new and unused and cannot be a car, given to the company as a gift, or purchased to lease to someone else. Used or second-hand assets can still qualify for the Annual Investment Allowance. The purpose of this new capital allowance is to encourage investment in the economy and stimulate growth in productivity.

Annual investment allowance (AIA)

The Annual Investment Allowance (AIA) allows all businesses, both incorporated and unincorporated, to write off **100%** of the cost of **new** qualifying assets in the business against its profits **up to the specified annual limit**. The maximum amount of AIA a company can claim each 12-month accounting period is as follows.

From January 2019, the AIA has been - 100% on £1m (applicable to Finance Act 2024).

Where a business has an accounting period of less than twelve months, the AIA must be pro-rated accordingly.

For example, if a business has a chargeable accounting period of 6 months within the calendar year 2024 (1 April 2024 to 31 March 2025), it would only be able to claim AIA of £500,000 (£1,000,000/2) for that period.

When the AIA rate changes within the accounting period you would need to divide your accounting period into sections and apply the relevant rate to the split period.

Example 3.3

As an example, if your accounting period runs from 1 July 2024 to 30 June 2025, but the AIA from 1 April 2025 is reduced to £200,000 (example only). You would calculate the AIA for the first nine months of July 2024 – March 2025 as £1,000,000 / 12 x 9 = **£750,000.**

The remaining three months of April – June 2025 would be calculated as £200,000 / 12 x 3 months = **£50,000.** Add the two amounts together to get the AIA maximum entitlement you can claim for the full accounting period 1 July 2024 to 30 June 2025 being £750,000 + £50,000 = £800,000.

However, with regard to the second part period falling on or after 1 April 2025, no more than £50,000 of the business's actual expenditure in that part period would be covered by its transitional AIA entitlement.

For example, if a business purchased £250,000 worth of computer equipment in the last part period (May 2025), they would only be able to claim £50,000 against the AIA and the balance would need to be put against other allowances like the Writing Down Allowance (covered later).

The Annual Investment Allowance (AIA) cannot be used against the purchase of cars.
It is, however, available on other vehicles.

Activity 3.2

Jeap & Sons starts trading as a partnership business on 1 April 2024. In the nine months chargeable accounting period to the end of December 2024, they incur the following capital expenditure:

Date	Asset Purchased	Amount
30 April 2024	Computer equipment	£180,000
15 May 2024	Delivery van	£30,000
12 July 2024	Office furniture	£50,000
28 November 2024	Car	£20,000
	Total	**£280,000**

a) What is the total of the eligible assets for AIA for the period?

b) What is the maximum entitlement for AIA for the period?

c) How much can Jeap & Sons claim against AIA for the CAP?

AIA can only be claimed in the period the item was purchased. The date of purchase can be identified as:

- The date the contract was signed, if payment is due within less than 4 months
- When payment is due, if it is more than 4 months later

For example, if a new machine was ordered in June 2024 for delivery and invoice in August 2024, the date of purchase would be June 2024 (payment is less than 4 months from contract signing in June 2024.)

However, if a new machine was ordered, the contract was signed in June 2024 and the machine was expected to be delivered and invoiced in December 2024 with immediate payment on delivery, then the date of purchase would be December 2024 as payment due is more than 4 months later from contract signing in June 2024.

An asset that is part-paid with a balance being paid at a later date would have the claim for capital allowance split over the relevant accounting periods according to purchase payment.

Example 3.4

Rhowver & Balance ordered a new machine in May 2024 for delivery and invoice in January 2025. The total cost of the machine is £52,000 with £40,000 payable on delivery and the balance of £12,000 to be paid on 1 June 2025. The machine has a useful life of 25 years.

As the purchase date is when payment is due, (more than 4 months later than the order) capital allowances can be claimed on the cost of £40,000 in tax year 24/25 year ending March 2025. The balance of £12,000 would be applicable to tax year 25/26 ending March 2026 relevant to the June 2025 payment date.

If the business has purchased more qualifying assets than it has available AIAs, any excess is placed in the general pool and will be calculated separately under Writing Down Allowances. However, if the expenditure is less than the AIA available, any unused AIA **will be lost**.

First year allowances (FYA)

Some expenditure on new assets like energy efficient cars qualify for enhanced capital allowances, referred to as a **First-Year Allowance (FYA)** and these are available on both incorporated and unincorporated businesses. This is to encourage businesses to invest in some cars with 0g/km CO^2 emissions or electric cars.

HMRC allows a higher writing down allowance of **100%** than the standard WDA in the **first year of ownership** for this type of asset

Currently, for the financial tax year FY2024 being 1 April 2024 to 31 March 2025, the following are available at the **100%** rate for FYA expenditure incurred:

- On zero-emission goods vehicles
- On cars with zero CO^2 emissions or the car is electric
- On new plant and machinery installed at a gas refuelling station to refuel vehicles with natural gas, biogas or hydrogen fuel, such as storage tanks and pumps
- On plant or machinery for an electric vehicle charging point
- Plant and machinery for use in a freeport tax site, if you're a company.

Example 3.5

The adjusted profit (before deduction of capital allowances) for Jag'U'are Ltd for the year ending 31 December 2024 was £240,000. Within their financial year, they invested and purchased £125,000 in new qualifying plant and machinery under FE. In February 2024, they also invested a further £30,000 on a zero-emissions goods vehicle under FYA.

To calculate the taxable profit for Jag'U'are Ltd:

Adjusted trading profit before deduction of capital allowances	**240,000**
Less capital allowances	
FE claimed	(125,000)
FYA claimed	(30,000)
Taxable profit	**85,000**

By claiming tax relief on the capital allowances available Jag'U'are Ltd is able to reduce its taxable profit from £240,000 to £85,000. This has greatly reduced the liability to corporation tax for the period.

FYAs will never be apportioned for short or long accounting periods and will always be 100%.

Activity 3.3

WV Ltd.'s year-end is 30 November 2024 and the adjusted profit before deduction of capital allowances is £257,000. Within the period they purchased a new car with CO^2 emissions of 0g/km at a cost of £22,000. Other assets included computer equipment worth £75,000 and some office furniture valued at £30,000.

Calculate the taxable profit for WV Ltd for the year ending 30 November 2024.

Adjusted trading profit before deduction of capital allowances	
Less FE claimed FYA claimed	
Taxable profit	

Writing down allowances (WDA)

Capital allowances are not normally calculated on individual assets within the business but instead, any expenditure over the new asset AIA eligibility, would be pooled together and the capital allowance calculated on the value of the "pool" and not on any individual assets within the pool.

Previously owned assets or assets that have been transferred from a different business or even privately owned and introduced to the business at a later date will not be eligible for FE or AIA as they are **not new** assets. A business may be able to get the assets valued which could then allow them to qualify for Written Down Allowance (WDA).

The 3 types of pools a business would use are:

- General pool (main pool)
- Special rate pool
- Short-life asset pool (not tested in this syllabus)

Most expenditure over the AIA is placed into the general pool and written down using the Writing Down Allowance (WDA). The current rate of **18%** on a reducing balance is attributable to WDA for general pool allowances based on a 12-month period.

However, there are some assets which **will not** be pooled in the general pool:

- Cars with CO^2 emissions exceeding 50 g/km
- Long-life assets – with an expected life of 25 years or more
- Integral features of a building or structure
- Thermal insulation of buildings

These particular assets will be grouped under the **special rate pool**. The special rate for the tax year 2024/2025 from April 2024 is **6%** on a reducing balance.

Example 3.6

John Crème trading as Coconut Crème started trading on 1 January 2024, with accounts being prepared for the financial year ending 31 December 2024. On 1 March 2024, they purchased £1,110,000 worth of machinery and a car with CO^2 emissions of 50 g/km costing £25,000 on 1 May 2024. Capital allowances are available as follows for the year ending 31 December 2024:

	Additions	AIA	General pool	Total allowances
			£	£
Additions	Machinery	**1,110,000**		
Less AIA allowance		(1,000,000)		1,000,000
Transfer to general pool			110,000	
Additions for WDA	Car emissions 50 g/km		**25,000**	
Balance			**135,000**	
WDA 18%			(24,300)	24,300
Allowances for period				**1,024,300**
Balance c/f			**110,700**	

The machinery is allowable under AIA for new assets for a sole trader but just to the limit of £1,000,000. The balance of £110,000 is then transferred to the general pool for writing down at 18%. The car emissions of 50 g/km can be added to the general pool for writing down at 18%.

Within the general pool, there is a balance of £110,000 + £25,000 = £135,000 x 18% = £24,300 allowance.

The total allowances for the period are £1,000,000 + £24,300 = £1,024,300.

There is then a balance of £135,000 - £24,300 = £110,700 to be transferred to the following period from the general pool.

Long life assets

This section refers to items with a useful expected working life of at least 25 years from when they were purchased. The "working life" is from when it is first used to the time it is unusable, which may be with a different owner. An example would be a piece of farm machinery like a combine harvester.

They should be added to the special rate pool if the value of all the long-life items purchased in a single CAP adds up to £100,000. If their total value is less than £100,000 then they should be added to the general rate pool. The £100,000 limit should be pro-rated if the accounting period is less than 12 months.

For example, if the accounting period is 9 months, then the limit will be 9/12 x £100,000 = £75,000.

The assets which are added to the special rate pool between 1 April 2024 and 31 March 2025 can receive the allowance of **6%** WDA.

Integral features of a building

Although **buildings themselves do not qualify for capital allowances**, integral features do and examples of these are:

- Lifts, escalators and moving walkways
- Space and water heating systems
- Air-conditioning and air-cooling systems
- Hot and cold-water systems (not toilet and kitchen facilities)
- Electrical systems including lighting systems
- External solar shading

Integral features can be claimed on the special rate pool.

Capital allowance treatment of cars

Within the financial statements, motor vehicles are grouped together for analysis purposes. This will include cars, vans, lorries, motorbikes, etc.

For capital allowances purposes, vans, lorries and motorbikes are treated as general plant and machinery and are added to the general pool for normal AIA if applicable when purchased and WDA in future years.

We have already seen how cars which have emissions of 0g/km or are electric will receive the First Year Allowance at **100%** currently (FYA), but the treatment of other cars varies depending on their emissions.

Cars which have CO^2 emissions of between 1g/km and 50g/km are treated as additions which do not qualify for the FE, AIA or FYA, these will be added to the **general** pool and attract a WDA of **18%.**

Cars which have CO^2 emissions of above 50g/km are treated as additions which do not qualify for the FE, AIA or FYA, these will be added to the **Special Rate** pool and attract a WDA of **6%.**

The following tables are taken from the gov.uk website giving the rates applicable for claims for cars bought between April 2021 onwards. From the details in the table, you can determine which type of allowance is applicable to each type of car.

Cars bought from April 2021		
Description of Car	**Pool**	**What you can claim**
New and unused, CO^2 emissions are 0g/km (or car is electric)		**100%** FYA
New and unused, CO^2 emissions are between 1g/km and 50g/km	General rate	**18%** WDA
New or second hand, CO^2 emissions are above 50g/km	Special Rate	**6%** WDA
Second hand, CO^2 emissions are between 1g/km and 50g/km (or car is electric)	General rate	**18%** WDA

WDA's are therefore given for:

- Any new assets eligible for WDA's.
- The tax written down value (TWDV) which is the value of the balance in the general pool brought forward at the beginning of the accounting period.
- Less disposals of plant and machinery (covered later).

When calculating capital allowances, it is the date of purchase that determines what rate is to be used and when.

Single asset pools must be recorded separately and must not be pooled together. These will be covered later in the chapter.

It is not compulsory for a company to use its WDA and a decision may be based on what profits are available. If profits are low, it may be beneficial to carry forward the balance as a TWDV, which will then be available to be used against future higher profits in later years.

The following table can be useful for the categories and which pools they fall into for the WDA.

	Plant & Machinery (excluding cars)					Structures & Buildings
	Bought new	Bought 2nd hand	Assets held for leasing	General rate assets	Special rate assets	
Annual Investment Allowance (100% up to £1m)	✓	N/A	✓	✓	✓	N/A
Writing down allowances (18%)	✓	✓	✓	✓	N/A	N/A
Writing down allowances (6%)	✓	✓	✓	N/A	✓	N/A
Structures and Buildings Allowance (3% pa)	N/A					✓

Example 3.7

Ashe Limited started trading on 1 January 2024. In the first year, the company purchased the following items:

Plant and Machinery (purchased 1 June 2024)	£1,075,000
Car for Sales Manager with CO^2 emissions 45g/km (Purchased 1 May 2024)	£ 26,000

Determine the value of capital expenditure that Ashe Ltd can claim against AIA/FE and how much would be eligible for WDA after AIA.

	Additions	FE/AIA	General pool	Total allowances
		£	£	£
Additions	Machinery	**1,075,000**		
Less FE allowance		(1,075,000)		1,075,000
Transfer to general pool			0	
Additions for WDA	Car emissions 45 g/km		**26,000**	
Balance			26,000	
WDA 18%			(4,680)	4,680
Allowances for period				**1,079,680**
Balance c/f			**21,320**	

The car is not eligible for AIA so would need to be pooled for WDA as it is above the emissions limit for FYA 100% and below the emissions of 50 g/km for the special rate pool.

Activity 3.4

Beach Ltd started trading on 1 December 2023. In the first year, the company purchased the following items:

Qualifying plant and machinery (purchased 1 April 2024)	£1,000,000
Office Manager car with CO^2 emissions 100g/km (purchased 1 June 2024)	£15,000

How much can Beach Ltd claim against capital expenditure and how much if any would be eligible for WDA for the financial year ending 30 November 2024?

	Additions	FE/AIA	General pool	Special rate pool	Total allowances
		£	£	£	£
Additions					
Less allowance					
Transfer to general pool					
Additions for WDA					
Balance					
WDA 18%					
WDA 6%					
Allowances for period					
Balance c/f					

The decisions made will go on to affect the amount of corporation tax the business can save at the end of the year. Below we will look at the potential savings that can be made using the full expensing for an incorporated company in comparison to an unincorporated sole trader using the normal AIA.

Example 3.8

A sole trader purchases eligible qualifying main rate plant and machinery assets for the sum of £15,000,000 in the year 2024/25.

Claiming normal AIA (sole trader)	
	£
£1m AIA claimed	1,000,000
Balance of £14m written down at 18% p.a.	2,520,000
Total deduction in the first year	3,520,000
Total savings in Corporation tax @ 25%	880,000

A limited company purchases eligible qualifying main rate plant and machinery assets for the sum of £15,000,000 in the year 2024/25.

Claiming full expensing (limited company)	
	£
100% full expensing claimed	15,000,000
No balance left to write down	Nil
Total deduction in the first year	15,000,000
Total savings in Corporation tax @ 25%	3,750,000

It can be seen from the two scenarios that by claiming the 100% full expensing rate, the limited company are saving an extra £2,870,000 in corporation tax on these assets, this would then potentially encourage a company to invest in assets to save on their corporation tax bill.

It is likely that a sole trader with the ability to purchase assets at a value of £15,000.000 would change to a limited company as one of the benefits is the tax planning opportunities that it offers.

Preparation of computation for capital allowances

To prepare a calculation sheet for all the rates of allowances available it is important to set out a layout that can be followed so that no items are missed or duplicated.

There is no set format available or required but it is beneficial to itemise each individual element separately:

- FE/AIA
- FYA

- General Pool
- Special Rate Pool
- Total Allowances

You may not require all of the columns in a computation but after making a judgement on which columns are required you can take out any columns or add extra columns relevant to the computation that you are making.

The following is a template that can be used to assist in the computations for capital allowances. Note that when taking an AAT assessment, you will be given a blank template and will be required to complete the description rows with the additions and deductions yourselves based on the information given.

Additions	AIA	FE	FYA	General pool	Special rate pool	Total allowances
	£	£	£	£	£	£
TWDV b/f						
FYA additions						
FYA allowance						
Plant & Machinery						
AIA/FE allowance						
WDA additions						
Balance						
WDA 18% / 6%						
Allowances for period						
Balance c/f						

Any single assets would all require a further separate calculation column.

To prepare a computation, the approach should be a step-by-step one using the information provided in the question.

Example 3.9

On 1 January 2024, Helder Limited had a general pool for plant and machinery with a b/f Tax Written Down Value (TWDV) of £45,000. The special rate pool has a balance b/f of £15,000.

Within the year ending 31 December 2024, the following occurred:

- A packing machine was purchased in April 2024 for £320,000
- Specialised refrigeration equipment in May 2024 for £700,000
- A zero emissions goods vehicle was purchased in June 2024 for £26,000
- A car with CO^2 emissions of 188 g/km was purchased in July 2024 for £25,000

Using the template provided:

1. Enter the TWDV b/f balances from the last accounting period. These would be the c/f balances from the previous computation.

Additions	AIA	FE	FYA	General pool	Special rate pool	Total allowances
	£	£	£	£	£	£
TWDV b/f				**45,000**	**15,000**	

2. Identify the **new** asset additions and consider what capital allowances are available and what is applicable to the assets purchased. Ensure the purchase dates are within the correct rates for the allowances concerned.

The zero emissions goods vehicle is eligible for FYA at 100%. The FYA allowance is deducted from the FYA additions and as this is a 100% allowance, there is no balance to be transferred to any other pool. The allowance used of £26,000 is also shown in the total allowances end column.

The packing machine and refrigeration equipment are plant and machinery and are therefore eligible for FE/AIA. They are not eligible for FYA.

Under full expensing, the total allowances will be the 100% value of the plant and machinery.

A car with CO² emissions of 188 g/km was purchased in July. The emissions level is above the limit of 50 g/km and this vehicle will be required to be put into the special rate pool.

This addition is added to the additions for WDA at the 6% special rate.

Additions	AIA	FE	FYA	General pool	Special rate pool	Total allowances
	£	£	£	£	£	£
TWDV b/f				45,000	15,000	
FYA zero emissions goods vehicle			**26,000**			
FYA allowance			**(26,000)**			**26,000**
Machinery		**320,000**				
Plant		**700,000**				
FE/AIA allowance		**(1,020,000)**				**1,020,000**
Transfer to general pool				**0**		
WDA additions					**25,000**	

3. The columns can then be balanced. £45,000 for the general pool TWDV.
£15,000 special rate pool TWDV plus £25,000 additions gives a balance of £40,000 in the special rate pool.

Additions	AIA	FE	FYA	General pool	Special rate pool	Total allowances
	£	£	£	£	£	£
TWDV b/f				45,000	15,000	
FYA zero emissions goods vehicle			26,000			
FYA allowance			(26,000)			26,000
Machinery		320,000				
Plant		700,000				
FE/AIA allowance		(1,020,000)				1,020,000
Transfer to general pool				0		
WDA additions					25,000	
Balance				**45,000**	**40,000**	

4. Calculate the WDA at the relevant percentages:

- 18% for the main pool £45,000 x 18% = £8,100
- 6% for the special rate pool £40,000 x 6% = £2,400.

These figures are then also entered in the total allowances end column.

Balance				**45,000**	**40,000**	
WDA 18% / 6%				**(8,100)**	**(2,400)**	**10,500**

5. Add up all of the figures in the total allowances column to give the total allowances claimed in the period being £26,000 + £1,020,000 + £10,500 = £1,056,500.

Additions	AIA	FE	FYA	General pool	Special rate pool	Total allowances
	£	£	£	£	£	£
TWDV b/f				45,000	15,000	
FYA zero emissions goods vehicle			26,000			
FYA allowance			(26,000)			26,000
Machinery		320,000				
Plant		700,000				
FE/AIA allowance		(1,020,000)				1,020,000
Transfer to general pool				0		
WDA additions					25,000	
Balance				**45,000**	**40,000**	
WDA 18% / 6%				**(8,100)**	**(2,400)**	10,500
Allowances for period						**1,056,500**

6. Deduct the WDA 18% figures in the general and special rate pool columns to give the balance c/f to the next accounting period (TWDV). £45,000 - £8,100 = £36,900.

Deduct the WDA 6% special rate pool column to give the balance c/f to the next accounting period. £40,000 - £2,400 = £37,600.

Allowances for period						**1,056,500**
c/f total				**36,900**	**37,600**	

Activity 3.5

On 1 January 2024, Mango Limited had a main pool for plant and machinery with a b/f Tax Written Down Value (TWDV) of £37,500. The special rate pool has a balance b/f of £8,000.

Within the year ending 31 December 2024, the following occurred:

- A pressing machine was purchased in May 2024 for £497,000
- Specialised refrigeration equipment in July 2024 for £650,000
- A zero emissions goods vehicle was purchased in August 2024 for £31,000
- A car with CO^2 emissions of 125 g/km was purchased in September 2024 for £28,000

Complete the following template showing the addition of new assets against the relevant allowances and calculating the total allowances for the period and the total c/f to the following period.

Additions	AIA	FE	FYA	General pool	Special rate pool	Total allowances
	£	£	£	£	£	£
TWDV b/f						
FYA zero emissions goods vehicle						
FYA allowance						
Machinery						
Plant						
FE/AIA allowance						
Transfer to general pool						
WDA additions						
Balance						
WDA 18% / 6%						
Allowances for period						
c/f total						

Disposal of assets for capital allowances calculations

When a business sells or 'disposes of' an asset for which it had claimed capital allowances, the value must be included in the calculations for the accounting period in which it is sold. The amount of the proceeds received will be deducted from the value of the relevant pool b/f.

'Disposal' includes:

- Selling the asset
- Giving it away as a gift or transferring it to someone else
- Swapping it for something else
- Getting compensation for it – such as an insurance pay-out if it's been lost or destroyed
- Keeping it, but no longer using it in the business
- Using it outside of the business

The exception to this is donations to a charity or Community Amateur Sports Club (CASC). This is because these schemes receive benefits and reliefs from the government in different ways than a standard business.

Any disposals made during the year that are sold for more than the original cost are recorded by deducting the **lower of the original cost and the proceeds of sale** from the relevant pool.

That is, the deduction cannot be more than the original cost of the asset. The relevant pool will be the pool the asset was originally added to.

Example 3.10

Burch Ltd has a year ending 31 December 2024 and had the following transactions:

- TWDV Balance on the general pool of £35,000
- Plant purchased eligible for FE of £126,000
- Plant from the general pool sold with proceeds of £10,000 on an original cost of £8,000, purchased before 1 April 2023.

The calculation would be as follows:

Additions	FE/AIA	General pool	Total allowances
	£	£	£
TWDV b/f		35,000	
Plant	126,000		
FE/AIA allowance	(126,000)		126,000
Transfer to general pool		0	
Disposal		**(8,000)**	
Balance		**27,000**	
WDA 18%		(4,860)	4,860
Allowances for period			**130,860**
c/f total		**22,140**	

£8,000 is deducted from the main pool for the disposal which is the lower of the proceeds from the sale and original cost.

Capital allowances of £130,860 can be utilised.

Example 3.11

Blagthorne Ltd has the following information for the year ending 31 December 2024. All assets have been purchased and disposed of within the accounting period.

- **Balances TWDV b/f 1 January 2024:**

General Pool	£ 75,000
Special Rate Pool	£ 7,000

- **Additions January to December 2024:**

Zero emissions delivery vehicle	£ 30,000
Weighing Equipment	£115,000
Laptop	£ 1,500
Director's Car with CO^2 emissions 156g/km	£ 12,500
Office furniture	£ 27,000

- **Disposal of plant from main pool (purchased before 1 April 2023**. £ 6,000 (original cost £10,000)

Produce the calculation for capital allowances using the above information and the template provided.

Additions	FE/AIA	FYA	General pool	Special rate pool	Total allowances
	£	£	£	£	£
TWDV b/f			75,000	7,000	
FYA zero emissions vehicle		30,000			
FYA allowance		(30,000)			30,000
Weighing Equip	115,000				
Laptop	1,500				
Office furniture	27,000				
FE/AIA allowance	(143,500)				143,500
Transfer to general pool			0		
WDA additions				12,500	
Disposal			**(6,000)**		
Balance			**69,000**	**19,500**	
WDA 18% / 6%			(12,420)	(1,170)	13,590
Allowances for period					**187,090**
c/f total			**56,580**	**18,330**	

Office furniture, weighing equipment and the laptop all qualify for the FE and can be claimed at £143,500 purchase value.

The zero-emissions delivery vehicle is eligible for FYA at 100%.

The Director's car with CO^2 emissions of 156 g/km is added to the special rate pool as it is over 50g/km and is written down by 6%.

The disposal receipts are less than the original cost of the asset.

Activity 3.6

Horthorn Limited has the following non-current asset information for the accounting year ending 31 December 2024.

Balances b/f 1 January 2024	£
General Pool	158,100
Special Rate Pool	25,050
Additions:	
Office furniture	37,000
Machinery	164,000
Computer	3,000
Installing electric vehicle charging points	23,750
Managing Director's car with CO² emissions 186 g/km	32,250
Disposals:	
Director's car with CO² emissions 156 g/km	17,000
(Original cost £25,000 and purchased before 1 April 2023)	

All additions and disposals have occurred within the accounting period. From the above information and the layout provided calculate the total capital allowances eligible for Horthorn Limited and the balances to be carried forward to the next accounting period.

Additions	FE/AIA	FYA	General pool	Special rate pool	Total allowances
	£	£	£	£	£
TWDV b/f					
FYA electric points					
FYA allowance					
Machinery					
Computer					
Office furniture					
FE/AIA allowance					
Transfer to general pool					
WDA additions					
Disposal					
Balance					
WDA 18% / 6%					
Allowances for period					
c/f total					

Small pool write off

The general pool and the special rate pool are written down on a reducing balance basis and if there are no more additions will get smaller each year. In order to stop there being a calculation of the pool at an ever-decreasing amount, HMRC allows a business to write the pool off completely as soon as the TWDV brought forward is below £1,000.

This amount will be treated as a capital allowance.

Business ceases trading

Balancing charges can occur on the general pool throughout the life of the business whereas a balancing allowance only occurs in the general pool when a business ceases to trade. Balancing allowances are added to the capital allowance claim for the year, whilst balancing charges are deducted from the claim for the year.

Balancing allowances and balancing charges occur in the accounting period that a business ceases to trade. In the final chargeable accounting period (CAP) there are **no allowances given for FYA, AIA and WDA**.

Any assets purchased in this period will be added straight to the relevant pool. Any assets that had previously been purchased and claimed at 100% FYA will be added to the general pool for disposals.

If assets are not sold by the cessation date, then HMRC will accept "market value" on the last day of trading and this would then be the figure to use to calculate if there is a balancing allowance or balancing charge applicable.

Example 3.12

Hoak Ltd has a year-end of March. On 1 April 2024, the TWDV b/f in the main pool is £25,000. Hoak Ltd ceases to trade on 31 December 2024. Hoak Ltd will be required to calculate the final period.

The additions and disposals in the final period to 31 December 2024 are:

- 10 July 2024 — Plant purchased — £ 5,000
- 30 November 2024 — Disposal of plant — £32,200
  (originally purchased £48,000 May 2021)

	Additions/ Disposals	General pool	Total allowances
		£	£
TWDV b/f		25,000	
Additions	5,000		
Disposals	(32,200)		
Transfer to general pool		(27,200)	
Balancing allowance +			
Balancing charge -		**2,200**	(2,200)
Balance		**0**	
Allowances for period			**(2,200)**

Hoak Ltd has sold the plant for more than its value b/f in the main pool and this causes a balancing charge for capital allowances shown as a negative allowance in the total allowances column.

If the disposal proceeds were less than the value in the main pool this would create a balancing allowance in the calculation + (positive total).

Activity 3.7

Pyne Ltd cease trading on 31 October 2024. On 1 January 2024 the TWDV b/f in the main pool is £16,000. Within the period 1 January to 31 October, Pyne Ltd had the following additions and disposals:

- Plant purchased 5 February 2024 £8,750
- Plant disposal 19 September 2024 £23,500
  (original cost £29,000 purchased November 2023)

Calculate the final period for Pyne Ltd.

	Additions/ Disposals	General pool	Total allowances
		£	£
TWDV b/f			
Additions			
Disposals			
Transfer to general pool			
Balancing allowance +			
Balancing charge -			
Balance			
Allowances for period			

Opening and closing years of business (length of accounting period)

Earlier in the chapter, the difference between a period of account and an accounting period was given. As a reminder:

A "**period of account**" is the period of the company's financial accounts preparation and this could be longer than a 12-month period.

An "**accounting period**" is the period that Corporation Tax is chargeable and this **cannot** be longer than 12 months. Most of the time it coincides with the same period of account but when a company starts or ends trading within its business, this may not always be the case.

If, in an opening year of business, the period of account is longer than 12 months then this must be split into two accounting periods for CT and this also applies to the application of the capital allowances. The first calculation would cover the first 12 months, then the balance would be the second calculation.

When an accounting period is less than 12 months then the AIA and WDA are pro-rated accordingly to the nearest month.

However, FYAs are never pro-rated and are always given as the full 100% irrespective of the length of the accounting period.

Example 3.13

Whillo Ltd started trading on 1 November 2022 (prior to FE) and on that day purchased a binding machine costing £1,024,000.

The first period of account end date is 31 December 2023.

Calculate the capital allowances due for this first period of account:

a) The first chargeable accounting period for 12 months covers 1 November 2022 to 31 October 2023.

Additions	AIA	General pool	Total allowances
		£	£
Machinery	**1,024,000**		
AIA Allowance	(1,000,000)		1,000,000
Transfer to general pool		24,000	
Balance		24,000	
WDA 18%		(4,320)	4,320
Allowances for period			**1,004,320**
Balance c/f		**19,680**	

The full AIA (£1m in this period) is claimed within this first CAP with the WDA of 18% being applied to the main pool balance. TWDV c/f is £19,680 and the total capital allowances claimed for this first period is £1,004,320.

If this was entered into the adjusted trading profit calculation for the first 12 months (assuming a profit of £1,005,000 before capital allowances deductions) then it would appear in the first period ending 31 October 2023 as:

(The following is for example purposes only.)

Adjusted trading profit before deduction of capital allowances for period ending 31 October 2023	**1,005,000**
Less AIA claimed WDA claimed	 (1,000,000) (4,320)
Taxable profit	**680**

This taxable profit amount would then be the amount entered into the CT computation for the first period covering 1 November 2022 to 31 October 2023.

b) The second CAP for 2 months covers 1 November 2023 to 31 December 2023. There are no additions for this next period.

Additions	AIA	General pool	Total allowances
		£	£
TWDV b/f		19,680	
Balance		19,680	
WDA 18% x 2/12		**(590)**	**590**
Allowances for period			**590**
Balance c/f		**19,090**	

The WDA calculation is pro-rated to 2 months for this accounting period.

£19,680 x 18% = £3,542/12 = £295.17 x 2 = £590. TWDV c/f is £19,090 and the total capital allowances claimed for the second period is £590.

If the calculated adjusted trading profit before the deduction of capital allowances for the 2-month period had been £168,000 then the capital allowances would be shown as:

(The following is for example purposes only.)

Adjusted trading profit before deduction of capital allowances for period ending 31 December 2023	**168,000**
Less WDA claimed	 (590)
Taxable profit	**167,410**

This taxable profit amount would then be the amount entered into the CT computation for the second period covering 1 November 2023 to 31 December 2023.

Activity 3.8

Buckthorne Ltd usually prepares its financial statements to the end of April each year. In 2024, it changed the year-end to 31 December 2024 giving an 8-month period for preparing the accounts.

At the beginning of May 2024, the balance on the main pool was £26,400.

In November 2024 Buckthorne Ltd purchased plant valued at £750,000.

Calculate the capital allowances for the 8 months ending 31 December 2024 showing the TWDV c/f using the following layout. Use whole figures in your calculations.

Additions	AIA/FE	General pool	Total allowances
		£	£
TWDV b/f			
Plant			
Allowance			
Transfer to general pool			
Balance			
WDA 18%			
Allowances for period			
Balance c/f			

Activity 3.9

1) Poplur Limited commenced trading on 1 August 2024 and it has purchased the following assets in the 8-month period ending 31 March 2025.

- 30/8/2024 Office Equipment £8,500
- 21/11/2024 Production Machinery £83,200
- 22/12/2024 Alterations to floor necessary for production machinery installation £5,000

How much would qualify for the full expensing allowance for the period ending 31/3/2025?

a) £91,700

b) £96,700

c) £8,500

d) £88,200

2) Poplur Limited also purchased a motor car for £18,900 on 1 September 2024. It has CO^2 emissions of 45 g/km. It is used by the Sales Manager and 30% of the mileage is for private journeys.

How much WDA can be claimed for the vehicle for the period ending 31/3/2025?

a) £18,900

b) £3,402

c) £1,985

d) £1,134

Structures and buildings allowances

For construction contracts signed **on or after 29 October 2018** there may be relief available for building, buying or leasing a structure.

The structure must be used for the following qualifying activity:

- any trades, professions and vocations
- a UK or overseas property business (except for residential and furnished holiday lettings)
- managing the investments of a company
- mining, quarrying, fishing and other land-based trades such as running railways and toll roads.

The allowance can be claimed on construction costs, which include:

- fees for design
- preparing the site for construction
- construction works
- renovation, repair and conversion costs
- fitting out works

Residential premises will not qualify for the structures and buildings allowance, or parts of a building that are used for residential purposes with the remainder of the building used for commercial purposes.

From 1 April 2020, the rate is 3% over a period of 33 and 1/3 years.

If the business is subject to Corporation Tax, the claim can be made on 3% from 1 April 2020 on qualifying costs and the allowance period will end 33 and one-third years from the date the structure comes into use.

Example 3.14

A factory is built costing £800,000. All contracts for the work were entered into on 7 January 2022.

The factory was finished on 21 November 2022 and it began being used as an engineering premises for an engineering business on 1 January 2023. The accounts are prepared each year ending 31 December.

In the chargeable period to 31 December 2024 (366 days), they are able to claim 3% a year, for 91 days from 1 January 2024 to 31 March 2024 and 3% for 275 days from 1 April 2024.

£800,000 x 3% = £24,000.

If they had only been able to claim for part of a year, for example, 91 days then the calculation would be 91/366 (or 365 not a leap year) = 0.25 (round up) x £800,000 = £200,000 x 3% = £6,000 or a quarter of the year.

Claims can be made on the corporation tax return and there is also a requirement to produce an allowance statement for the structure for HMRC which must include:

- identification of the structure, descriptions and location
- date of earliest written contract for the construction work
- total qualifying costs
- date the structure was being used for a non-residential activity

For a purchased structure, allowances can only be claimed if a copy of the allowance statement from the previous owner is obtained.

Activity 3.10

Thompson Limited has a period of account that runs from 1 July to 30 June each year.

Thompson Limited constructed a qualifying building costing £1,000,000 which was brought into use on 1 October 2023.

What can Thompson Limited claim against Structures and Buildings allowance for the chargeable period the building is brought into use?

Summary of Chapter 3

- Capital allowances are given as a type of depreciation, to businesses, to replace depreciation in their tax calculations.
- A business can only claim capital allowances on assets that qualify as **plant and machinery**.
- Plant is defined by its '**function**' or '**setting**'.
- **Structures and Buildings Allowances** - For construction contracts signed on or after 29 October 2018 there may be relief available for building, buying or leasing a structure.
- **AIA** is a 100% allowance for qualifying expenditure (not including cars) to a maximum of £1,000,000 for FY2024**.** Any excess is then covered under the **WDA.**
- **FYA** is a 100% allowance for qualifying environmentally friendly cars and zero emissions goods vehicles as well as electric vehicle charging points and gas biogas and hydrogen refuelling equipment.
- **Full expensing Allowances** for qualifying purchases from 1 April 2023 for incorporated businesses.
- **Special Rate Pool** applies to items not pooled in the main pool, i.e.
    - Cars with CO^2 emissions exceeding 50g/km
    - Long life assets – with an expected life of 25 years or more
    - Integral features of a building or structure
    - Thermal insulation of buildings
- A **balancing allowance** is a + amount as it is a positive, an increase in allowances to the business.
- A **balancing charge** is a – amount as it is a negative, a reduction in allowances to the business.

When an accounting period is less than 12 months then the AIA and WDA are pro-rated accordingly to the nearest month for a limited company. However, FYAs are never pro-rated and are always given as the full 100% irrespective of the length of the accounting period.

Assessment 3

You are now required to log in to your ROGO account to complete your online assessment before progressing to the next chapter.

This page is left intentionally blank.

Chapter 4: Capital allowance differences for unincorporated businesses

By the end of this chapter, you should:

- Understand the differences in computing capital allowances for sole traders and partnerships as opposed to incorporated businesses.
- Be able to calculate private use assets for unincorporated businesses.
- Be able to compute capital allowances for sole traders and partnerships for different length accounting periods.
- Understand when a trading allowance is available and can be used.
- Understand the tax return forms for an individual.

Introduction

There are several differences between incorporated and unincorporated businesses when calculating taxation and the following is a reminder of the changes.

In a similar way to companies, a sole trader or partnership will still start with the net profit that is shown in the business accounts.

When adjusting trading profits the following are the differences that apply to an individual:

Full expensing does not apply to unincorporated businesses.

Private expenditure adjustments

Any expenses that are **private** and belong specifically to an owner of a business should be **disallowed** and **added back,** including any personal income tax or national insurance amounts.

If there is a business/personal split on the expense, it will just be the private element that is disallowed.

Salaries of owner

Any drawings or salary that a business owner takes is rather like paying a dividend to a shareholder in a limited company. This is not a business expense and must be **disallowed** and **added back** to profit.

Irrecoverable debts

A **specific** allowance for doubtful receivables usually applies to one particular customer and not to the whole receivables ledger and is normally calculated for limited companies only. This is because limited companies need to follow the rules of the Companies Act when producing their accounts, whereas unincorporated businesses are not bound by this act. A **specific** allowance for doubtful receivables is an allowable expense.

However, unincorporated businesses may contain a **genera**l allowance for doubtful receivables as well as Limited companies. Where a **general** allowance for doubtful receivables has been initially calculated (usually by a percentage of the total balance of the receivables ledger) this will be disallowed in the tax year it was produced. In following years, any increase in the general allowance will be **disallowed by being added back** and any decrease in the general allowance for doubtful receivables will be **disallowed and deducted.**

Example 4.1

Patrick runs a party planning business and his year end is 31 July 2024.

As at 1 August 2023, he had the following balances on the allowance for specific doubtful receivables of £92 and a general allowance for doubtful receivables of £130.

His new provisions for 31 July 2024 are:

- Specific provision £97
- General provision £112

There has also been an irrecoverable debt write-off on a non-trade debt of £100.

What allowable amounts would Patrick be able to claim against his profits?

There has been an increase in the specific provision of £5 and this is **allowable**.

There has been a decrease in the general provision of £18 and this is **disallowed.** As it is a decrease it will be deducted from the net profit.

The amount written off for the non-trade debt is **disallowed** and this will be added back to profit.

Charitable donations

For a limited company, any charitable donations not relieved as trade expenses are relieved as 'qualifying charitable donations'.

With a sole trader/partnership small local donations are allowed as trade expenses, donations through gift aid are not allowed as trade expenses, any other charitable donations are not allowed as trade expenses and they do not have the option for any other reliefs.

Income not included in the accounts but taxable as trading income

This normally applies in the instances where an owner takes goods for their own use. This should be **added back** to the accounting profit. The owner should be taxed at market value on the profit that would have been achieved (retail or wholesale).

Expenditure not in the accounts but allowable

Any business expense that may have been paid for by the owner can be deducted as a trade expense if it meets the wholly and exclusively used in the trade test.

This adjustment does not apply to an incorporated business.

Private use of assets

There may be times when a business owner uses an asset (such as a car) for private use as well as business use. If an asset has some degree of private use, it cannot be placed into the general pool or the special rate pool.

Instead, the asset is recorded in a separate **private asset pool** and written down at the appropriate rate. The value of the capital allowance which the owner can claim would be pro-rated by the proportion of the car that is used for business purposes.

If the asset is being used privately by an employee, there is no restriction on the allowances being claimed by the owner.

Example 4.2

Stuart bought himself a new car in April 2024 costing £30,000 which he uses for his business 70% of the time. The car has emissions of 170g/km.

How can capital allowances be claimed on this car?

Normally this would be placed into the special rate pool (as emissions are more than 50g/km), but as there is some degree of private usage it must be placed into its own pool – effectively each private use asset must have its own column in the capital allowances calculation we looked at earlier.

The car is still written down by the full percentage (£1,800) however Stuart can only claim 70% (£1,260) as a Capital Allowance for tax purposes. The reason for this is so that the amount of capital allowances which relate to the car can be identified and pro-rated and the private use pool reduced accordingly.

Additions	General pool	Private use pool	Total allowances	
	£	£	£	
TWDV b/f				
WDA additions		30,000		
Balance		**30,000**		
WDA 6%		**(1,800)**	**70%**	**1,260**
Allowances for period				**1,260**
Balance c/f		**28,200**		

Activity 4.1

As at 1 May 2024, Todd, owner of a sole trader business has the following Tax Written Down Value (TWDV):

- Car with CO² emissions 175 g/km (25% private use) £22,000
- Car with CO² emissions 45 g/km (25% employee use) £15,000

Additions	General pool	Private use pool	Total allowances
	£	£	£
TWDV b/f			
Balance			
WDA 18%/6%			
Allowances for period			
Balance c/f			

Lengths of accounting periods

As mentioned in the previous chapter an accounting period for a limited company under corporation tax rules cannot be any greater than 12 months. This is not the case for a sole trader/partnership and if an unincorporated business has a shorter or longer period than 12 months the calculation would be scaled up or down accordingly.

The exception to this is the first year allowance, as these are always 100% of the asset value and therefore the period length is irrelevant.

Example 4.3

Kenny Portillo started trading in his sole trader business on 1 March 2023. On commencement of trading, he spent £30,000 on qualifying plant and a car for an employee for delivery purposes at a cost of £16,000 with CO^2 emissions of 45 g/km.

a) What would be the allowances he could claim for the first two accounting periods if he prepared his first accounts to 31 December 2023 and then annually on this date afterwards?

First accounts – 10 months March to December 2023.

Additions	AIA	General pool	Total allowances
	£	£	£
Plant	30,000		
AIA allowance	(30,000)		30,000
Transfer to general pool		0	
WDA additions		16,000	
Balance	**0**	**16,000**	
WDA 18% x 10 / 12		(2,400)	2,400
Allowances for period			**32,400**
c/f total		**13,600**	

The AIA of £1,000,000 would be scaled down to 10 months being £833,333 applicable but only £30,000 is required.

The WDA on the car is scaled down to 10 months £16,000 x 18% = £2,880 / 12 x 10 = £2,400.

Second year – 12 months to 31 December 2024

Additions	AIA	General pool	Total allowances
	£	£	£
TWDV		13,600	
Balance		**13,600**	
WDA 18%		(2,448)	2,448
Allowances for period			**2,448**
c/f total		**11,152**	

The full 12 months can be claimed on the WDA of 18% in year 2.

b) What would be the allowances he could claim in the first two years if his first accounts were prepared to 30 June 2024 and then annually on this date afterwards?

First accounts 16 months – March 2023 to June 2024

Additions	AIA	General pool	Total allowances
	£	£	£
Plant	30,000		
AIA allowance	(30,000)		30,000
Transfer to general pool		0	
WDA additions		16,000	
Balance		**16,000**	
WDA 18% x 16 / 12		(3,840)	3,840
Allowances for period			**33,840**
c/f total		**12,160**	

The AIA of £1,000,000 would be scaled up to 16 months being £1,000,000 + (£1,000,000 x 4 / 12 = 333,333) = £1,333,333 maximum over the period. Only £30,000 is required.

The WDA on the car is scaled up to 16 months £16,000 x 18% = £2,880 / 12 x 16 = £3,840.

Second year – 12 months to 30 June 2025

Additions	AIA	General pool 18%	Total allowances
£	£	£	£
TWDV		12,160	
Balance		**12,160**	
WDA 18%		(2,189)	2,189
Allowances for period			**2,189**
c/f total		**9,971**	

Activity 4.2

Esha Kouma commenced trading on 1 June 2023 and prepares her first accounts to the end of September 2024.

Within August 2023 she purchased office furniture costing £5,400 and a car with CO^2 emissions of 115 g/km costing £22,000.

a) Complete the capital allowances calculations for this first accounting period.

Additions	AIA	General pool	Special rate pool	Total allowances
	£	£	£	£
Furniture				
AIA allowance				
Transfer to general pool				
WDA additions				
Balance				
WDA 6%				
Allowances for period				
Balance c/f				

b) What would be the total capital allowances available under AIA for the period?

£1,000 Personal trading allowance

There is a tax-free £1,000 allowance for taxpayers with very low levels of income from trading (sole traders but not partnerships). Essentially the allowance means that individuals who have low earnings from trading or casual income can earn up to the £1,000 allowance and not pay tax on those earnings.

The allowance is also available to those people who earn more than £1,000 in each category (before the deduction of expenses), in which case those people will be able to earn the first £1,000 tax-free **instead** of claiming any expenses.

The allowance is aimed at people who may make relatively small profits from selling goods on eBay, selling at car boot sales, making and selling cakes or having odd jobs doing gardening, babysitting or similar work – **but who would not necessarily class it as a "business"**.

Anyone whose earnings are less than £1,000 a year will not need to fill in a tax return to declare any of this income but people earning over £1,000 will need to declare those earnings and deduct the £1,000 allowance from the income, any income above the allowance would then be taxable.

If a sole trader has income less than £1,000 but expenses are higher, the sole trader can decide whether to claim the trading allowance or get relief from trading losses. (Covered later in the course.)

Example 4.4

Jemima makes and sells cakes from her own home for friends, colleagues at work and family.

In which of the following circumstances would it be beneficial for Jemima to deduct the trading allowance, not need to declare it, or recognise a trading loss?

a) Jemima has income of £1,200 and expenses of £500.

> She should choose to deduct the trading allowance as this will make her profit £200 instead of £700, so the tax would be lower.

b) Jemima has income of £750 and expenses of £300.

> She will not need to declare it as her income is less than £1,000.

c) Jemima has income of £600 and expenses of £780.

> She should recognise a trading loss as her expenses are higher than her income.

Tax forms for self-employment

The forms you are likely to come across as a self-employed individual are:

SA100 – is the form used for the personal details of individuals who need to complete returns for employment, self-employment, partnerships, capital gains, property income etc, you will complete this form to notify HMRC of any interest and dividends as well as UK Pension.

SA102 – this form is required if you are **employed** but have benefits in kind and employment expenses above £2,500.

SA103 – is the form a **self-employed** person needs to complete showing their business income and allowable expenses, if you have income less than **£85,000** per year you can use the 'SA103 short form', however in some cases, HMRC may decide that you need to complete the SA200 instead.

If your income is higher than £85,000 then you will need to complete the 'SA103 full form'.

SA105 – if you have UK Property Income you could be classed as a landlord and need to complete this form.

SA108 – if you have any capital gains in the year you will need to complete this form.

SA104 – this form relates to a partnership business. Each partner is required to complete this form to record their own personal income.

SA800 – the 'designated partner' of a partnership will need to complete this **before** each individual partner can complete their own tax returns SA104.

CIS 305 – to be completed by the subcontractor if the business operates as a subcontractor for the Construction Industry Scheme.

64-8 – to be completed if the business employs a tax agent.

SA1 – this is the online form to register for Self-Assessment.

SA200 – HMRC may request you to complete this form, it is a simpler version of the SA100, and it contains a limited number of questions so only those who have relatively straightforward tax affairs such as an Employee/Pensioner with Limited Investment Income or an Employee who has taxable benefits/expense payments or self-employed persons with a turnover of less than £85,000. ***You will not be able to access this form online.***

SA106 – to be completed if an individual has foreign income to report.

SA109 – used if you have foreign income and claiming the remittance basis.

The tax return

Any taxpayer who falls within the scope of self-assessment must complete the appropriate sections of a tax return and submit it to HMRC along with the payment of any outstanding tax.

The paper tax return is made up of the 'Return' (*Form SA100*) which collects information about the taxpayer's personal details, and income from interest and dividends, pensions, charitable donations and other information about the taxpayer's situation. Some taxpayers may be required to complete the Short Return (*Form SA200)* if they have been notified by HMRC.

In addition to the tax return, taxpayers must also complete a number of Supplementary Pages, in which they record details of their income from various sources. The taxpayer need only complete the pages which are relevant to him or her. So, for example, an individual taxpayer with no employment income for the tax year would not complete the supplementary page for employment. However, a taxpayer with income from three different employers would need to complete three sets of supplementary pages for employment.

A similar structure is followed in the online return, where the taxpayer selects which types of income they have had and is directed to the appropriate sections of the online return.

An individual with relatively simple tax affairs who files on paper rather than online may be able to receive the short tax return instead of the full Self-Assessment tax return. For example, this could apply to a sole trader with a turnover below £85,000 and with straightforward investment income, other employment income (e.g. a part-time job) or a reasonably small amount of income from property.

The short tax return is four pages long and is around one-third the size of an average self-assessment tax return with supplementary pages. The guidance is also much shorter and simpler. There is no need to calculate the tax on the form, but there is a two-page simple calculation to give you a rough idea of the tax liability.

Filing dates are the same as for the full self-assessment return.

The short tax return is normally issued automatically based on the information in the previous year's return. However, individuals must tell HMRC if their circumstances change. The short tax return **cannot** be downloaded – individuals can only use the short tax return if HMRC asks them to.

The following are the pages applicable to SA103 full (for the previous tax year as 2024-25 not available at the time of writing):

HM Revenue & Customs

Self-employment (full)

Tax year 6 April 2023 to 5 April 2024 (2023–24)

Please read the 'Self-employment (full) notes' to check if you should use this page or the 'Self-employment (short)' page.

For help filling in this form, go to www.gov.uk/taxreturnforms and read the notes and helpsheets.

Your name

Your Unique Taxpayer Reference (UTR)

Business details

1 **Business name** – unless it's in your own name

2 **Description of business**

3 **First line of your business address** – unless you work from home

4 **Postcode of your business address**

5 **If the details in boxes 1, 2, 3 or 4 have changed in the last 12 months, put 'X' in the box and give details in the 'Any other information' box**

6 **If your business started after 5 April 2023, enter the start date** DD MM YYYY

7 **If your business ceased after 5 April 2023 but before 6 April 2024, enter the final date of trading** DD MM YYYY

8 **Date your books or accounts start** – the beginning of your accounting period DD MM YYYY

9 **Date your books or accounts are made up to or the end of your accounting period** – read the notes if you have filled in box 6 or 7 DD MM YYYY

10 **If you used cash basis, money actually received and paid out, to calculate your income and expenses, put 'X' in the box**

Other information

Boxes 11 and 12 are not in use

13 **If special arrangements apply, put 'X' in the box**

14 **If you provided the information about your 2023–24 profit on last year's tax return, put 'X' in the box**

Business income

15 **Your turnover** – the takings, fees, sales or money earned by your business

£ .00

16 **Any other business income not included in box 15**

£ .00

16.1 **Trading income allowance** – read the notes

£ .00

SA103F 2024 Page SEF 1 HMRC 12/23

Business expenses

Please read the 'Self-employment (full) notes' before filling in this section.

Total expenses	Disallowable expenses
If your annual turnover was below £85,000, you may just put your total expenses in box 31	Use this column if the figures in boxes 17 to 30 include disallowable amounts
17 Cost of goods bought for resale or goods used £ .00	32 £ .00
18 Construction industry – payments to subcontractors £ .00	33 £ .00
19 Wages, salaries and other staff costs £ .00	34 £ .00
20 Car, van and travel expenses £ .00	35 £ .00
21 Rent, rates, power and insurance costs £ .00	36 £ .00
22 Repairs and maintenance of property and equipment £ .00	37 £ .00
23 Phone, fax, stationery and other office costs £ .00	38 £ .00
24 Advertising and business entertainment costs £ .00	39 £ .00
25 Interest on bank and other loans £ .00	40 £ .00
26 Bank, credit card and other financial charges £ .00	41 £ .00
27 Irrecoverable debts written off £ .00	42 £ .00
28 Accountancy, legal and other professional fees £ .00	43 £ .00
29 Depreciation and loss or profit on sale of assets £ .00	44 £ .00
30 Other business expenses £ .00	45 £ .00
31 Total expenses (total of boxes 17 to 30) £ .00	46 Total disallowable expenses (total of boxes 32 to 45) £ .00

SA103F 2024 Page SEF 2

Net profit or loss

47 **Net profit** – if your business income is more than your expenses (if box 15 + box 16 minus box 31 is positive)

£ . 0 0

48 **Or, net loss** – if your expenses are more than your business income (if box 31 minus (box 15 + box 16) is positive)

£ . 0 0

Tax allowances for vehicles and equipment (capital allowances)

There are 'capital' tax allowances for vehicles, equipment and certain buildings used in your business (do not include the cost of these in your business expenses). Please read the 'Self-employment (full) notes' and use the examples to work out your capital allowances.

49 **Annual Investment Allowance**

£ . 0 0

50 **Capital allowances at 18% on equipment, including cars with lower CO2 emissions**

£ . 0 0

51 **Capital allowances at 6% on equipment, including cars with higher CO2 emissions**

£ . 0 0

52 **Zero-emission goods vehicle allowance**

£ . 0 0

52.1 **Zero-emission car allowance**

£ . 0 0

53 **The Structures and Buildings Allowance**

£ . 0 0

53.1 **Freeport and Investment Zones Structures and Buildings Allowance**

£ . 0 0

54 **Electric charge-point allowance**

£ . 0 0

55 **100% and other enhanced capital allowances**

£ . 0 0

56 **Allowances on sale or cessation of business use (where you've disposed of assets for less than their tax value)**

£ . 0 0

57 **Total capital allowances (total of boxes 49 to 56)**

£ . 0 0

Box 58 is not in use

59 **Balancing charge on sales of assets or on the cessation of business use (including where Business Premises Renovation Allowance has been claimed) for example, where you've disposed of assets for more than their tax value**

£ . 0 0

Calculating your taxable profit or loss

You may have to adjust your net profit or loss for disallowable expenses or capital allowances to arrive at your taxable profit or your loss for tax purposes. Please read the 'Self-employment (full) notes' and fill in the boxes below that apply.

60 **Goods and services for your own use**

£ . 0 0

61 **Total additions to net profit or deductions from net loss (box 46 + box 59 + box 60)**

£ . 0 0

62 **Income, receipts and other profits included in business income or expenses but not taxable as business profits**

£ . 0 0

63 **Total deductions from net profit or additions to net loss (box 57 + box 62)**

£ . 0 0

64 **Net business profit for tax purposes (if box 47 + box 61 minus (box 48 + box 63) is positive)**

£ . 0 0

65 **Net business loss for tax purposes (if box 48 + box 63 minus (box 47 + box 61) is positive)**

£ . 0 0

SA103F 2024 Page SEF 3

Calculating your taxable profit or loss (continued)

Basis period reform simplifies the tax rules for the self-employed and partners so that a business's profit or loss for a tax year is measured in the tax year itself, regardless of its accounting dates or whether a business has recently started trading. This removes the complex basis period rules and stops the profits being taxed twice, as may have occurred under the old rules (overlap relief).

You may be affected by basis period reform if you had an accounting date that was not on or between 31 March and 5 April in the 2022–23 tax year. If you do not have a transition profit or loss to report, you only need to consider completing boxes 66 to 73, 74, 75 and 76. Please read the 'Self-employment (full) notes' and fill in the boxes below that apply.

66 **Date your basis period began** DD MM YYYY

67 **Date your basis period ended** DD MM YYYY

68 **If your basis period is not the same as your accounting period, enter the adjustment needed to arrive at the profit or loss for the basis period** – if the adjustment needs to be taken off the profit figure, put a minus sign (–) in the box – do not include any transition profit or loss in this box, see box 73.1

£ · 0 0

69 **Overlap relief not previously deducted on a change of accounting date** – do not include overlap relief in this box if you have a transition profit or loss, see box 73.2

£ · 0 0

Box 70 is not in use

71 **Adjustment for change of accounting practice**

£ · 0 0

72 **Averaging adjustment (only for farmers, market gardeners and creators of literary or artistic works)** – if the adjustment needs to be taken off the profit figure, put a minus sign (–) in the box

£ · 0 0

73 **Adjusted profit for 2023–24** – see the working sheet in the notes

£ · 0 0

Only complete boxes 73.1 to 73.4 if you have a basis period transition profit or loss – read the notes

73.1 **Profit or loss of the transition part of the basis period**

£ · 0 0

73.2 **Overlap relief used on the transition part of the basis period this year**

£ · 0 0

73.3 **Spread of the transition profit treated as arising in this tax year** – read the notes

£ · 0 0

73.4 **Loss brought forward from earlier years set off against this year's spread of the transition profit (up to the amount in box 73.3)**

£ · 0 0

74 **Loss brought forward from earlier years set off against this year's adjusted profit**

£ · 0 0

75 **Any other business income not included in boxes 15, 16 or 60**

£ · 0 0

76 **Total taxable profits from this business** – see the working sheet in the notes, do not include the amount in box 73.3

£ · 0 0

Losses

If you've made a net loss for tax purposes (in box 65), or if you've losses from previous years, read the 'Self-employment (full) notes' and fill in boxes 77 to 80, as appropriate.

77 **Adjusted loss for 2023–24** – see the working sheet in the notes

£ · 0 0

78 **Loss from this tax year set off against other income for 2023–24**

£ · 0 0

79 **Loss to be carried back to previous years and set off against income (or capital gains)**

£ · 0 0

80 **Total loss to carry forward after all other set-offs** – including unused losses brought forward

£ · 0 0

SA103F 2024 Page SEF 4

Class 2 and Class 4 National Insurance contributions (NICs)

If your total profits from all self-employment and partnerships for 2023–24 are less than £6,725 you do not have to pay Class 2 National Insurance contributions, but you may want to pay voluntary (box 100) to protect your rights to certain benefits.

100 **If your total profits for 2023–24 are less than £6,725 and you choose to pay Class 2 NICs voluntarily, put 'X' in the box**

101 **If you're exempt from paying Class 4 NICs, put 'X' in the box**

102 **Adjustment to profits chargeable to Class 4 NICs**

£ .00

Any other information

103 **Please give any other information in this space**

SA103F 2024 Page SEF 6

Example 4.5

Halima is a sole trader who owns a grocery store on the High Street.

She has the following profit or loss account.

Turnover	£103,000
Cost of sales	£22,540
Gross profit	£ 80,460
Expenses	
Depreciation	£ 3,790
Motor expenses	£18,485
Wages	£25,360
Drawings	£ 5,000
	£ 52,635
Net profit	£ 27,825

A. Halima purchased a new van at a cost of £15,500 which was included in the motor expenses.

B. Halima also has a general pool with a TWDV balance of £4,987. She wishes to claim the maximum capital allowances available for the year.

C. Halima purchased £250 worth of goods specifically for private use, which is included in the cost of sales.

Required: show which boxes would need to be completed to record her business income and expenses.

You would first enter her name and unique tax reference in the relevant boxes on page 1 along with the business details such as business name.

Box 15: £103,000	Sales income
Box 17: £22,290	Cost of sales less items purchased for personal use £250
Box 19: £25,360	Wages
Box 20: £2,985	Motor expenses less the £15,500 van as this will be a capital allowance
Box 29: £3,790	Depreciation
Box 44: £3,790	Depreciation as disallowable
Box 31: £54,425	Total expenses
Box 46: £3,790	Total disallowable expenses
Box 47: £48,575	Net profit

We then need to complete the tax allowances for vehicles and equipment (capital allowances).

Box 49: £15,500	Van purchase
Box 50: £898	Written down allowance rounded up to whole pounds
Box 57: £16,398	Total capital allowances for the year
Box 63: £16,398	Total deductions to net profit
Box 64: £35,967	Net profit after adjustments

a) AIA can be claimed on vans as these are specifically for business use.

b) She can claim written down allowances on £4,987 at 18% = £897.66 (always round to whole pounds) so this would be £898.

c) As the items **were purchased** specifically for private use then you would deduct the amount from the cost of sales box 17.

However; If you take goods or stock out of the business for private use, you need to enter the normal sale price in box 60. The amount then needs to be added to the net profit.

Summary of Chapter 4

- Capital allowance restrictions for private use of business assets
- FYA are always given fully to individuals irrespective of the length of the accounting period.
- For an unincorporated business that has a shorter or longer period than 12 months, the calculation would be scaled up or down accordingly.
- £1,000 personal allowance is a benefit to an individual in qualifying circumstances

Assessment 4

You are now required to log in to your ROGO account to complete your online assessment before progressing to the next chapter.

This page is left intentionally blank

Chapter 5: Taxable profits chargeable for incorporated businesses

By the end of this chapter, you should:

- Be able to calculate taxable total profits from given trading income, property income, investment income, chargeable gains and qualifying charitable donations for the following periods:
    - Longer than 12 months
    - Shorter than 12 months
    - Equal to 12 months
- Know how to deal with the treatment of dividends paid, dividend income, royalties received and paid, and interest received and paid.
- Be able to deal with property income and expenses.
- Be able to deal with qualifying charitable donations.
- Calculate corporation tax payable at the relevant rates.
- Complete elements of a corporation tax return.

Introduction

In the previous two chapters the calculations for capital allowances for both unincorporated and incorporated businesses were followed which fulfils **Step 5** of the template for adjusted trading profit, also referred to as **trading income**.

Steps	Adjustment of Profits	£
1	Net profit before tax as per accounts	**X**
	Add	
2	Disallowable expenses	X
3	Income not included in the accounts but taxable as trading income	X
		X
	Deduct	
4	Income in the accounts not taxable as trading income, e.g. property rental income	(X)
	Adjusted trading profit before deduction of capital expenses	**X**
5	Expenditure deductible from trading profits, e.g. capital allowances	(X)
6	**Adjusted trading profit (trading income)**	**X**

The next calculation carries on from Step 6, from the adjusted trading profit figure after capital allowances have been deducted.

Taxable total profits (TTP) are the profits that the limited company must pay Corporation Tax on, at the relevant rate for the accounting period.

The different types of **other income** are then looked into and there are further adjustments to the adjusted trading profit to be made for the following items of other income to achieve the TTP (Taxable Total Profits).

These items have been previously added or deducted within the adjusted trading profit calculation and they are now required to be dealt with separately under the TTP corporation tax computation:

- Non-trade interest
- Property or rental income
- Chargeable Gains
- Qualifying Charitable Donations

Note: Unlike a sole trader there is never any adjustment for the private use of assets for a Limited Company and a Limited company period of account can be longer than a 12-month period even if the accounting period for CT **must not be any longer than** 12 months. Calculating for a longer period of account will be dealt with later in this chapter.

The following is a starting template for the calculation of corporation tax which will be followed as the chapters continue. The first entry on the CT computation is the adjusted trading profit figure (from Step 6 of the adjusted trading profit template) which is referred to as trading income in the CT template.

This template will be added to as we progress through the calculations:

Corporation Tax computation for 12 months ended 20XX	
Trading income	**X**
Add:	
Non-trade Interest	X
Other Income	X
Property Income	X
Chargeable gains	X
Total profits	X
Less:	
Qualifying charitable donations	(X)
Taxable total profits (TTP)	X

Treatment of dividends paid

Dividends paid **may not** be deducted from Taxable Total Profits.

Dividends are not classified as a business expense for Corporation Tax – and companies should not pay out a dividend if the company does not have enough profit after tax available to cover the dividend amount.

Companies do not pay tax on dividend payments but the receivers (shareholders) may have to pay tax on the dividends they receive through their own personal tax affairs.

Treatment of dividend income

Dividend income received is not assessable under Corporation Tax. Dividend income should not have been included within net accounting profits in the business accounts anyway. If it has been incorrectly included in net profits then it should have been deducted when calculating the adjusted trading profits figure.

Dividend income is income received from another company which would have already had Corporation Tax applied to the profits within that business and would not be required to have it applied again.

Treatment of royalties received and paid

Royalties are normally associated with the use of patents and these amounts should have been accounted for in the accounts on an accrual basis, and if so, there would be no adjustment to be made to either royalties payable or receivable.

Royalties received are taxed as trading profits and royalties paid are deducted as an expense against trading profits, so would already be included in the net profit before tax.

One thing that may be required to be adjusted is if the Limited Company receives or pays royalties to an individual rather than to another Limited Company. All royalties received and paid are usually gross. However, patent royalties received and paid to individuals are calculated net of basic rate tax. However, Corporation Tax computations must be shown gross.

The calculation to gross up the net royalties would be:

Patent royalty net x 100/80

Example 5.1

Sathurn Limited has received the following royalty receipts from:

Nepdoon Ltd	£2,700 (gross amount, no tax deducted)
Mr Jack Daniels	£1,400 (net amount, tax deducted)

The amount from Nepdoon Ltd has been received gross as it is from another limited business. However, the amount from Mr. Jack Daniels, an individual, needs to be grossed up.

£1,400 x 100/80 = £1,750 gross

Therefore, the amounts shown in the accounts should be £2,700 + £1,750 = **£4,450.**

Treatment of interest received and paid

When calculating corporation tax for a company, interest received and paid is also known as a loan "relationship" and will also include any costs relating to the loan.

The key definition of a loan relationship is:

- it is a money debt;
- it arises from a transaction for the lending of the money

The treatment for CT with interest received and paid depends on whether it is from a Trading or Non-Trading loan relationship.

Trading loans

Interest paid on trading loans is an **allowable** deduction from trading profits and therefore there is no action to be taken as it should be in the statement of profit or loss already as an expense which has reduced the profit.

It is highly unlikely that there will be any interest received on trading loans but if this is the case then this would have already been included in the statement of profit or loss as income which increases profit so no action would need to be taken.

Non-trading loans

Interest paid on **non-trading loans** was **disallowed** for adjusted trading profits (added back). It is then part of the calculation in TTP and is an allowable deduction to be made against any non-trade interest income.

An example of this would be a loan to purchase a property to be used for rental purposes by the company. This interest expense can be used to relieve tax that will be incurred on non-trading interest income.

Non-trading interest income (received) was a deduction for adjusted trading profits. Non-trading interest income would involve interest received on business bank deposits or building society accounts. This interest is chargeable to CT at the applicable rate after deducting interest paid, as above. All interest is calculated on the accruals accounting basis where figures should be for amounts due and not just received or paid. Within calculations, you may see this taxable income being referred to as an NTL-R credit. (Non-trading loan relationship credit).

The annual accounts should normally show the interest figures as an accrued amount anyway but if this is not the case then an adjustment will be required to ensure the correct amount is applied to the correct period of account.

Example 5.2

Gupiter Limited has a business bank deposit account that was opened at the beginning of their accounting year 1 April 2024.

The following interest payments have been received for the bank account:

30 June 2024 — £750.00 (3 months Apr, May, June)
31 December 2024 — £1,500.00 (6 months July-December)
30 June 2025 — £2,000.00 (6 months January – June)

What would be the non-trade interest income to be included in the CT return for the accounting period ending 31 March 2025?

The interest received in June 2025 would need to be accrued for the element up to the end of March 2025, the end of the accounting year:

£2,000/6 months x 3 months (Jan-March) = £1,000.

£750 + £1,500 + £1,000 = £3,250 non-trade interest income to be included in the CT computation.

Example 5.3

Marz Ltd has calculated a trading income of £47,000 before calculating Taxable Total Profits (TTP) for the period of account 1 January 2024 to 31 December 2024.

The following amounts of interest have been **received** on the bank deposit account:

March 2024 received £500
June 2024 received £550
September 2024 received £700
December 2024 received £875

The following amounts of interest have been paid on a non-trading bank loan:

June 2024 paid £1,750

The total amount of interest paid can be offset against the total receipts of interest.
£500 + £550 + £700 + £875 = £2,625 - £1,750 = **£875 net non-trade interest**.

The balancing figure can be entered into the CT computation.

Corporation Tax computation for 12 months ended December 2024	
	£
Trading income	47,000
Add:	
Non-trade Interest	**875**

Property Income

As mentioned in the underpinning knowledge section, property income is dealt with under the CT computation, as it was taken out of the adjusted trading profit calculation because it is not part of trading income.

A business with property income should deduct all relevant property expenses from the property income amount to achieve its own individual property profit or loss figure. This figure will then be used in the CT computation.

Limited companies are subject to CT on net rental profits and do not obtain relief of a tax-free allowance (unlike basic rate taxpayers).

To calculate net profits for property income, the expenses must be incurred "wholly and exclusively" for the purposes of the rental property. Property income is also taxed on an accrual basis. Capital receipts and expenditure are excluded.

Under a Limited Company, mortgage interest expense can be offset against property income in the calculation of net property income.

Property expenses

Allowable expenditure is revenue in nature and incurred on the day-to-day running of the property and excludes expenditure on purchasing the property or enhancing it in any way.

Property expenses would include items like:

- Buildings insurance
- Maintenance and repairs (not improvements)
- Council tax
- Utility bills
- Property letting fees

You will not be expected to calculate property income for a business within this course and will be given a figure for net property income in any assessments.

Example 5.4

Marz Limited from Example 5.3 also received rental income from another business that rents part of their premises within their building. Rental income net of expenses was calculated at £9,750 for the period 1 January 2024 to 31 December 2024.

This property income figure can now be included within the CT computation.

Corporation Tax computation for 12 months ended December 2024	
	£
Trading income	47,000
Add:	
Non-trade Interest	875
Property income	**9,750**

The next section on the CT computation template is chargeable gains – this is quite a complex area and there is a whole chapter **(Chapter 8**) dedicated to this within this course. The computations for chargeable gains will be done on a separate basis similar to how capital allowances were accounted for, so for now we will just use a given figure of £16,500 that has been provided for this example for Marz Ltd. Total profits can now be added - £47,000 + £875 + £9,750 + £16,500 = £74,125.

Corporation Tax computation for 12 months ended December 2024	
	£
Trading profit (trading income)	47,000
Add:	
Non-trade Interest	875
Property Income	9,750
Chargeable gains	**16,500**
Total profits	**74,125**

Qualifying charitable donations

This is the last calculation in the CT computation for taxable total profits.

As referred to in Chapter 2, although qualifying charitable donations are always disallowed in the adjustment of profits calculation they are however, allowable for corporation tax purposes under qualifying charitable donations where tax relief is given. These donations are paid gross and can be deducted when calculating TTP.

Local charity donations are treated as a form of advertising as these donations improve the image of the business within the local community. The local charity donation is allowable as an expense for tax purposes and would be dealt with as an expense within the accounts.

Qualifying charitable donations are not accounted for on an accruals basis like interest but instead are accounted for in a Corporation Tax accounting period when they are paid.

In our example for Marz Limited, a donation for a national charity has been made on 31 September 2024 for £3,000.

This can now be included in the Corporation Tax computation template.

Corporation Tax computation for 12 months ended December 2024	
	£
Trading profit (trading income)	47,000
Add:	
Non-trade Interest	875
Property Income	9,750
Chargeable gains	16,500
Total profits	74,125
Less:	
Qualifying charitable donations	**(3,000)**
Taxable total profits (TTP)	**71,125**

Taxable total profits are now £**71,125.**

Always ensure you remember to include total taxable income and gains, i.e. trading income, property income, interest income and net chargeable gains.

Chargeable gains

As mentioned earlier, there is a section within the computations for TTP that includes chargeable gains and these will be covered in detail later in the course. However, at this stage, it will be beneficial to understand that when the gains and losses on asset disposals have been calculated they will be put into a summary of the position to enable the net chargeable gains/losses to be entered into the corporation tax calculations. The following is an example template of 3 gains and 1 loss from disposal of assets less any capital losses b/f from previous years. If the summary shows a net chargeable loss, then this will be dealt with later in the course.

Summary of net chargeable gains	£
1) Chargeable gain	X
2) Chargeable gain	X
3) Chargeable gain	X
Gross chargeable gains current CAP period	**X**
4) Allowable loss	(X)
Net chargeable gains/(losses) current CAP period	**X**
Less: Capital losses b/f previous period	(X)
Net chargeable gains	**X**

Calculating taxable total profits (TTP)

In Chapter 2 the steps were taken to adjust net accounting profit to adjusted trading profit **before** capital allowances.

Chapter 3 covered capital allowances for limited companies, which then gave us the adjusted trading profit figure **after** capital allowances were applied.

Within this chapter, we have followed on from the trading profit figure to calculate the taxable total profits (TTP).

These steps can now all be followed in a complete calculation of a Limited Company corporation tax calculation.

Example 5.5

Veenus Limited is a small business that produces mystical and gothic garden ornaments and accessories and has the following results for the year ending 31 March 2025 after all year-end adjustments have been made to the accounts.

Veenus Limited statement of profit or loss year ending 31 March 2025		
	£	£
Gross trading profit		156,883
Other income		4,800
Less:		
Trade expenses	127,281	
Other charges	14,060	(141,341)
Net profit before taxation		**20,342**

Other information:

- In January 2025 the company purchased a new machine for a coating process for the ornaments side of the business at a cost of £15,000 plus VAT.
- Other charges contain:
  - a late payment fine to HMRC of £250.00
  - Donation to local charity of £50 for advertising some of Veenus Limited's products
  - Entertaining clients amounts to £600.00
  - Depreciation charges £13,160
- Other income refers to property income of £400.00 per month

a) Calculate the adjusted trading profit from the net profit from the accounts.

Adjustment of Profits	**£**
Net Profit before tax as per accounts	**20,342**
Add	
Depreciation Late fine Entertaining clients	13,160 250 600
	34,352
Deduct	
Property income	(4,800)
Adjusted trading profit before deduction of capital expenses	**29,552**
Capital allowances	(15,000)
Adjusted trading profit (trading income)	**14,552**

The donation to a local charity is allowable.

b) Complete the calculation for the Corporation tax computation.

Corporation Tax computation for 12 months ended 31 March 2025	
	£
Trading income	14,552
Add:	
Non-trade Interest	0
Property Income	4,800
Chargeable gains	0
Total profits	**19,352**
Less:	
Qualifying charitable donations	0
Taxable total profits (TTP)	**19,352**

Property income is deducted within the calculations of adjusted trading profit but then added back within the corporation tax computation.

Veenus Limited have taxable total profits of £19,352.

Activity 5.1

Tightan Limited has the following information available for the year ending 31 December 2024.

Adjusted trading profit before capital allowances	£250,300
Capital allowances calculated	£13,000
Rental income (net of expenses)	£16,000
Interest payable on purchase of property bank loan (accrued)	£2,000
Building Society interest received (accrued)	£10,000
Donation to national charity	£7,000

Calculate the taxable total profits for the year ending 31 December 2024 using the templates below:

Adjusted trading profit before deduction of capital allowances	
Less Expenditure deductible from trading profits e.g. capital allowances	
Adjusted trading profit	

Corporation Tax computation for 12 months ended December 2024	
	£
Trading profit (trading income)	
Add:	
Non-trade Interest	
Property Income	
Chargeable gains	
Total profits	
Less:	
Qualifying charitable donations	
Taxable total profits (TTP)	

Applying relevant corporation tax rates

The start of a year for the application of Corporation Tax Rates is 1 April until the following 31 March.

For Financial Year 2024 or FY24 (CAP or chargeable accounting period) for all taxable profits the applicable main rate is **25%** for companies with profits over £250,000.

In example 5.5 for Veenus Ltd above, the year end is 31 March 2025 which is referred to as FY**2024** as the start of the year is 1 April **2024**.

Rates for Corporation Tax years starting 1 April

There are different rates for ring fence companies.

Rate	2024	2023	2022	2021	2020	2019	2018	2017
Small profits rate (companies with profits under £50,000)	19 %	19%	—	—	—	—	—	—
Main rate (companies with profits over £250,000)	25%	25%	—	—	—	—	—	—
Main rate (all profits except ring fence profits)	—	—	19%	19%	19%	19%	19%	19%
Marginal Relief lower limit	£50,000	£50,000	—	—	—	—	—	—
Marginal Relief upper limit	£250,000	£250,000	—	—	—	—	—	—
Standard fraction	3/200	3/200	—	—	—	—	—	—

As the applicable rate for FY2024 for profits under £50,000 is 19%, Veenus Limited's tax liability would be **£19,352** taxable profits x 19% tax rate = **£3,676.88.**

Example 5.6

Starz Ltd has provided the following information from their financial reports for the year ending 31 December 2024.

Income	
Net property income	£18,800
Dividend income received from UK business	£4,500
Trading Income	£650,000
Bank deposit interest received	£6,300

Expenditure	
Interest on bank loan to purchase property	£3,300
QCDs	£2,500
Dividends paid	£22,000
Chargeable gain in period	£70,000
Capital losses b/f from previous years	£16,500

Calculate the company's corporation tax for the year ending 31 December 2024 by completing the following templates. A '0' is entered into any boxes that do not require an entry.

INCOME

Corporation Tax computation for 12 months ended December 2024	
	£
Trading income	650,000
Add:	
Non-trade Interest	3,000
Non-exempt dividends	0
Property Income	18,800

The interest from non-trading loan relationships consists of the £6,300 bank deposit interest received less the £3,300 interest on the bank loan to purchase the property.

Dividend income from UK business and Dividends paid are not applicable therefore a '0' is entered into this box.

Summary of net chargeable gains	£
Gross chargeable gains current CAP period	**70,000**
Less: Capital losses b/f previous period	16,500)
Net chargeable gains	**53,500**

Net chargeable gains are gross chargeable gains less the allowable losses including losses b/f of £16,500. This figure can then be entered into the CT computation.

Corporation Tax computation for 12 months ended December 2024	
	£
Trading income	650,000
Add:	
Non-trade Interest	3,000
Non-exempt dividends	0
Property Income	18,800
Chargeable gains	53,500
Total profits before qualifying donations	725,300

DEDUCTIONS AND RELIEFS

Total profits before Qualifying Donations	725,300
Less QCDs	(2,500)
Taxable Total Profits	**722,800**

Profits before QCDs is £671,800 total income + £53,500 net chargeable gains = £725,300.

QCDs are then deducted giving total profits chargeable to Corporation Tax of £722,800.

Calculation of tax (apportion the profits on a monthly basis)

	Financial Year (yyyy)		Amount of Profit £		Rate of tax %		Tax £
	2023		180,700		25		45,175
	2024		542,100		25		135,525

2023 – 3 months 1 January to 31 March 2024
£722,800 / 12 x 3 = £180,700 x 25% (FY2023) = £45,175

2024 – 9 months 1 April 2024 to 31 December 2024
£722,800 / 12 x 9 = £542,100 x 25% = £135,525

Activity 5.2

Europa Limited has the following results for the year ending 31 March 2025:

Trading income	£260,000
Dividends paid UK	£20,000
Chargeable gain	£8,000
Net non-trading interest	£3,750

Calculate the Corporation tax liability for the year ending 31 March 2025

Corporation Tax computation for 12 months ended 31 March 2025	
	£
Trading income	
Add:	
Non-trade Interest	
Property Income	
Chargeable gains	
Total profits	
Less:	
Qualifying charitable donations	
Taxable total profits (TTP)	
Tax rate	
Tax liability	

Marginal relief for profits between £50,000 and £250,000

To calculate a marginal relief tax, you need to multiply the marginal relief fraction of 3/200 by the difference of the upper limit of £250,000 and the company's profits.

For example, if a company's taxable profits for a 12-month accounting period are £80,000, you would use the calculation of 3/200 x (£250,000 - £80,000) = £2,550 marginal relief.

Therefore £80,000 x 25% corporation tax = £20,000 les the marginal relief of £2,550 = £17,450 corporation tax payable.

For any accounting period less than 12 months, the thresholds will be reduced proportionately, e.g. for a 6-month period, the lower limit would be £25,000 and the upper limit would be £125,000.

Marginal relief came into use from 1 April 2023.

If a company has associated companies (significantly controlled) then the limits are divided by the total amount of companies. For example, one associated company would reduce the limits to £125,000 upper limit and £25,000 lower limit.

Activity 5.3

Slater Ltd has prepared accounts for the 16 month period to 30 June 2024. After completion of the calculations for taxable total profits, the profits chargeable to corporation tax are £447,600.

Calculate the corporation tax liability for Slater Limited for the two accounting periods.

First 12 months:

Following 4 months:

Example 5.7

TMCF Ltd has taxable total profits of £112,000 for the year ended 31 March 2025 and has one associated company.

TMCF Ltd can claim marginal relief as profits are between the lower and upper limits. However, as there is one associated company, the marginal relief is divided by 2 which means the upper limit becomes £125,000 and the lower limit becomes £25,000.

The calculation becomes 3/200 x (£125,000 - £112,000) = £195

£112,000 x 25% = £28,000 - £195 marginal relief = £27,805 corporation tax payable for the period ended 31 March 2025.

Periods of account that are longer or shorter than 12 months

In Chapter 3, information was given regarding company accounts covering a period of longer than 12 months. If the financial accounts do cover a longer period, two chargeable accounting periods (CAPs) are required for corporation tax, one for the first 12 months and the second one for the balancing period (shorter period).

When this occurs, there are some changes to the allocation of items within the TTP calculation for other income, chargeable gains and qualifying charitable donations.

Trading income before capital allowance deduction	•Time apportioned
Capital allowances and balancing charges	•Separate capital allowances computation
Property income	•Time apportioned
Non-trade interest	•Accrued period calculated then time apportioned
Chargeable gains	•Separate disposals calculation within period when asset is sold
Qualifying charitable donation	•Payment period

Example 5.8

Moone Limited has financial accounts covering a 16-month period ending 31 July 2024.

Within this 16-month period the following has occurred:

	Date	£
Adjusted trading profit	31/07/24	375,000
Capital allowances	01/04/23 to 31/03/24	15,000
Capital allowances	01/04/24 to 31/07/24	4,000
Building Society interest receipt (£1,900 refers to year ending 31/03/23)	31/05/24	2,500
Building Society interest receipt	31/05/24	2,700
Building Society interest receipt accrual	31/07/24	300
Property Income	31/07/24	10,400

Chargeable gain	30/06/23	17,000
Chargeable gain	31/03/24	24,000
QCD paid	31/01/24	4,000
QCD paid	30/06/24	3,000

To calculate the correct amounts for the two individual CAPs you need to determine the months and years that the two periods cover from 1 April 2023 to 31 July 2024.

The easiest way to start this is to produce a timeline for reference:

2023									**2024**						
1	2	3	4	5	6	7	8	9	10	11	12	13	14	15	16
A	M	J	J	A	S	O	N	D	J	F	M	A	M	J	J
12 months April to March												4 months Apr-Jun			

Workings:

1) Adjusted trading profits before capital allowances are allocated on a **time apportioned basis.**

The total figure for the 16-month period is £375,000. Divide this by the 16 months and split over 12 months **(£281,250**) and 4 months **(£93,750**).

Deducted from these figures are the capital allowances, £15,000 to be deducted from the 12-month period and £4,000 to be deducted from the 4-month period.

12 months = £281,250 - £15,000 = **£266,250**
4 months = £93,750 - £4,000 = **£89,750**

These figures can now be entered into the CT computation template:

Corporation Tax computation		
	£	**£**
	01/04/23 to 31/03/24	01/04/24 to 31/07/24
Trading income	**266,250**	**89,750**

2) Non-trade interest is calculated on an **accrual basis** and then a time apportioned basis split to the relevant periods.

Receipt 31/05/24 included an amount of £1,900 for the previous year which will need deducting.

£2,500 - £1,900 = £600
Receipt 31/05/24 = £2,700
Accrual 31/07/24 (June and July) = <u>£300</u>
Total Building Society interest = £3,600/16 x 12 = **£2,700** first period
x 4 = **£900** second period

These figures can now be entered into the CT computation:

Corporation Tax computation		
	£	**£**
	01/04/23 to 31/03/24	01/04/24 to 31/07/24
Trading profit (trading income)	266,250	89,750
Add:		
Non-trade Interest	**2,700**	**900**

3) Property income is **time apportioned**. £10,400/16 x 12 = **£7,800**
x 4 = **£2,600**

These figures can now be entered into the CT computation:

Corporation Tax computation		
	£	**£**
	01/04/23 to 31/03/24	01/04/24 to 31/07/24
Trading profit (trading income)	266,250	89,750
Add:		
Non-trade Interest	2,700	900
Property Income	**7,800**	**2,600**

4) Gains are allocated to the **period in which the disposal occurred**;

30/06/23 £17,000 is the third month in the first 12-month period
31/03/24 £24,000 is the last month in the first 12-month period
Therefore £17,000 + £24,000 = **£41,000** is entered in the first CAP

This figure can now be entered in the CT computation and the profits can be totalled:

Corporation Tax computation		
	£	**£**
	01/04/23 to 31/03/24	01/04/24 to 31/07/24
Trading profit (trading income)	266,250	89,750
Add:		
Non-trade Interest	2,700	900
Property Income	7,800	2,600
Chargeable gains	**41,000**	**0**
Total profits	**317,750**	**93,250**

5) QCDs are allocated to the **relevant period that they are paid**.

31/01/24 paid £4,000 would be allocated to the first 12-month CAP
30/06/24 paid £3,000 would be allocated to the second 4-month CAP

Corporation Tax computation		
	£	**£**
	01/04/23 to 31/03/24	01/04/24 to 31/07/24
Trading profit (trading income)	266,250	89,750
Add:		
Non-trade Interest	2,700	900
Property Income	7,800	2,600
Chargeable gains	41,000	0
Total profits	317,750	93,250
Less:		
Qualifying charitable donations	(4,000)	(3,000)
Taxable total profits (TTP)	**313,750**	**90,250**

Activity 5.4

Cuting Limited has accounts prepared for a 15-month period running from 1 April 2023 to 30 June 2024.

	Date	£
Adjusted trading profit	30/06/24	480,000
Capital allowances	01/04/23 to 31/03/24	25,000
Capital allowances	01/04/23 to 30/06/24	7,500
Building Society interest receipt (£1,500 refers to year ending 31/3/23)	31/05/23	3,000
Building Society interest receipt	31/05/24	2,800
Building Society interest receipt accrual	30/06/24	500
Property Income	30/06/24	18,800
Chargeable gain	31/05/23	16,500
Chargeable gain	31/03/24	19,000
QCD paid	31/12/23	3,000
QCD paid	31/03/24	3,000
QCD paid	30/06/24	2,000

Calculate the two CAPs for the 15-month period based on the relevant apportionment rules.

Corporation Tax computation		
	£	£
	01/04/23 to 31/03/24	01/04/24 to 30/06/24
Trading income		
Add:		
Non-trade Interest		
Property Income		
Chargeable gains		
Total profits		
Less:		
Qualifying charitable donations		
Taxable total profits (TTP)		

Completing elements of a corporation tax return

For accounting periods starting on or after 1 April 2015, the full Company Tax return (CT600) along with the (CT600) supplementary pages should be used. A Company Tax Return is not just the CT600 but includes the company's financial statements and tax computations worksheets.

You need to file a company tax return if your company gets a 'notice to deliver a company tax return' (form CT03) from HMRC irrespective of whether the company has made a loss, or if there is no Corporation Tax to pay.

All Limited companies must complete a Company Tax Return and the return must be sent to HMRC within the correct period of time (covered in Chapter 11).

All companies **must** file their CT Return online with HMRC along with the accounts and CT calculations (there are a few limited exceptions from online filing).

Corporation Tax is paid at the rate applicable to the "accounting period" for CT.

The following is the link to the paper version CT600 (2024) Version 3 which gives all the relevant boxes for completion.

https://www.gov.uk/government/publications/corporation-tax-company-tax-return-ct600-2015-version-3

The guide for completing a Company Tax Return can be found at the following link.

https://www.gov.uk/government/publications/corporation-tax-company-tax-return-guide

For the purposes of this course, we will only be following and completing the sections of the CT return CT600 (2024) version 3 that are applicable to the calculations we have been making throughout the previous chapters.

When the Taxable Total Profit calculation has been completed then the figures can be used to complete the boxes on the CT return.

Example 5.9

Taking the details from Veenus Limited Example 5.5, the following details from the adjustment of profits and corporation tax computation would go on the Company tax return as follows:

Adjustment of Profits	**£**
Net Profit before tax as per accounts	**20,342**
Add	
Depreciation Late fine Entertaining clients	13,160 250 600
	34,352
Deduct	
Property income	(4,800)
Adjusted trading profit before deduction of capital expenses	**29,552**
Capital allowances	(15,000)
Adjusted trading profit (trading income)	**14,552**

Corporation Tax computation for 12 months ended 31 March 2025	
	£
Trading income	14,552
Add:	
Non-trade Interest	0
Property Income	4,800
Chargeable gains	0
Total profits	**19,352**
Less:	
Qualifying charitable donations	0
Taxable total profits (TTP)	**19,352**

Details of the company and the period of the return are completed on Page 1 of the return:

HM Revenue & Customs

Company Tax Return

CT600 (2024) Version 3

for accounting periods starting on or after 1 April 2015

Your Company Tax Return

If we send the company a 'Notice' to deliver a Company Tax Return it has to comply by the filing date or we charge a penalty, even if there is no tax to pay.

A return includes a Company Tax Return form, any supplementary pages, accounts, computations and any relevant information. The CT600 Guide tells you how the return must be formatted and delivered. It contains general information you may need to deliver your return, links to more detailed advice and box-by-box guidance for this form and the supplementary pages.

The forms in the CT600 series set out the information we need and provide a standard format for calculations.

Company information

1	Company name	Veenus Limited
2	Company registration number	46824687
3	Tax reference	1234567890
4	Type of company	0

Northern Ireland (NI)

Put an 'X' in the appropriate boxes below

5	NI trading activity	
6	SME	
7	NI employer	
8	Special circumstances	

About this return

This is the tax return for the company named above, for the period below

30	from DD MM YYYY	01 04 2024
35	to DD MM YYYY	31 03 2025

Put an 'X' in the appropriate boxes below

40	A repayment is due for this return period	
45	Claim or relief affecting an earlier period	
50	Making more than one return for this company now	
55	This return contains estimated figures	
60	Company part of a group that is not small	
65	Notice of disclosable avoidance schemes	
	Transfer pricing	
70	Compensating adjustment claimed	
75	Company qualifies for SME exemption	

CT600(2024) Version 3 Page 1 HMRC 04/24

There are boxes on Page 2 that detail the turnover and trading profits of the company, which would be taken from the financial statements and the adjusted trading profits calculation.

Tax calculation - Turnover

Box	Description	£
145	Total turnover from trade	327353.00
150	Banks, building societies, insurance companies and other financial concerns - put an 'X' in this box if you do not have a recognised turnover and have not made an entry in box 145	

Income

Box	Description	£
155	Trading profits	14552.00
160	Trading losses brought forward set against trading profits	.00
165	Net trading profits – box 155 minus box 160	14552.00
170	Bank, building society or other interest, and profits from non-trading loan relationships	.00
172	Put an 'X' in box 172 if the figure in box 170 is net of carrying back a deficit from a later accounting period	

CT600(2024) Version 3 Page 2 HMRC 04/24

Page 3 itemises any other income, like income from a property.

Income - continued

Box	Description	£
175	Annual payments not otherwise charged to Corporation Tax and from which Income Tax has not been deducted	.00
180	Non-exempt dividends or distributions from non-UK resident companies	.00
185	Income from which Income Tax has been deducted	.00
190	Income from a property business	4800.00
195	Non-trading gains on intangible fixed assets	.00
200	Tonnage tax profits	.00
205	Income not falling under any other heading	.00

Page 4 gives details of the actual tax calculation on how much profit has to be taxed and at what rate.

Tax calculation

326	Number of associated companies in this period	
327	Number of associated companies in the first financial year	
328	Number of associated companies in the second financial year	
329	Put an 'X' in box 329 if the company is chargeable at the small profit rate or is entitled to marginal relief	

Enter how much profit has to be charged and at what rate

	Financial year (yyyy)		Amount of profit		Rate of tax %		Tax
330	2024	335	£ 19352	340	25	345	£ 4838.00 p
		350	£	355		360	£ p
		365	£	370		375	£ p
380		385	£	390		395	£ p
		400	£	405		410	£ p
		415	£	420		425	£ p

CT600(2024) Version 3 Page 4 HMRC 04/24

Pages 5, 6 and 7 carry on with details of any other taxes, deductions, reliefs, etc.

Page 8 details enhanced expenditure and research and developments.

Page 9 covers the details of capital allowances and balancing charges calculations.

Information about capital allowances and balancing charges/disposal values

Allowances and charges in the calculation of trading profits and losses

		Capital allowances		Balancing charges
Annual investment allowance	690	£ 15000		
Full expensing	688	£	689	£
Machinery and plant – super-deduction	691	£	692	£
Machinery and plant – special rate allowance	693	£	694	£
Machinery and plant – special rate pool	695	£	700	£
Machinery and plant – main pool	705	£	710	£
Structures and buildings	711	£		
Business premises renovation	715	£	720	£
Other allowances and charges	725	£	730	£

Page 10 covers qualifying expenditure.

Page 11 refers to overpayments and repayments.

Page 12 deals with bank account details for payment and the declaration that the return is correct and complete.

Bank details (for a person to whom a repayment is to be made)

920	**Name of bank or building society**	Lloyds Bank
925	**Branch sort code**	3 0 9 5 4 7
930	**Account number**	0 2 6 7 4 9 4 1
935	**Name of account**	Veenus Limited
940	**Building society reference**	

Payments to a person other than the company

945 **Complete the authority below if you want the repayment to be made to a person other than the company**
I, as (enter status - for example, company secretary, treasurer, liquidator or authorised agent)

950 **of** (enter company name)

955 **authorise** (enter name)

960 **of address** (enter address)

965 **Nominee reference**

to receive payment on company's behalf

970 **Name**

Declaration

Declaration
I declare that the information I have given on this Company Tax Return and any supplementary pages is correct and complete to the best of my knowledge and belief.

I understand that giving false information in the return, or concealing any part of the company's profits or tax payable, can lead to both the company and me being prosecuted.

975 **Name**
Veronica Veenus

980 **Date** DD MM YYYY
31 12 2025

985 **Status**
Director

CT600(2024) Version 3 Page 12 HMRC 04/24

There are a lot of boxes within the Corporation Tax Return that are not covered by this course and will remain blank. You should not have to complete actual corporation tax boxes within an actual assessment.

Summary of Chapter 5

- Taxable total profits (TTP) are the profits that the company must pay Corporation Tax on at the relevant rate for the accounting period.

- Dividends paid **may not** be deducted from Taxable Total Profits.

- **UK Dividends received** are not taxable.

- **Royalties received** are taxed as trading profits and royalties paid are deducted as an expense against trading profits.

- **Interest received and interest paid** is also known as a loan "relationship" and will also include any costs relating to the loan.

- Interest paid on trading loans is an allowable deduction from trading profits.

- **Non-trading** loan relationships are 'pooled' together to achieve non-trading loan relationship debits or credits.

- A business with property income should deduct all relevant property expenses from the property income amount to achieve its own individual property profit or loss figure.

- **QCDs** are allowable for corporation tax purposes under qualifying charitable donations where tax relief is given.

- The start of a year for the application of Corporation Tax Rates is **1 April until the following 31 March.**

- If the financial accounts cover longer than 12 months, two chargeable accounting periods (CAPs) are required, one for the first 12 months and the second one for the balancing period.

- For accounting periods starting on or after 1 April 2015, the full Company Tax return (CT600) along with the (CT600) supplementary pages should be used.

Assessment 5

You are now required to log in to your ROGO account to complete your online assessment before progressing to the next chapter.

This page is left intentionally blank

Chapter 6: Profits, losses and NICs for unincorporated businesses

By the end of this chapter, you should:

- Be able to calculate the business profits to be included in each tax year using the tax year basis.
- Be able to allocate profits between partners.
- Understand the type of income that Class 4 NICs are payable on.
- Be able to calculate Class 4 NICs.

Introduction

An unincorporated business can make up its accounts **for any period** and this is the starting point used for the adjustment of profits and capital allowances calculations that have been covered in previous chapters.

With income tax for unincorporated businesses, this is calculated on the tax year which runs from 6 April to the following 5 April. Therefore, for 24/25 this would be 6 April 2024 to 5 April 2025.

Every year, therefore, on 6 April a new set of tax regulations, rates and allowances come into force.

However, it is necessary to be able to take calculated taxable trading profits and **connect them to a particular tax year.**

A difficulty arises where the business's financial year does not run from 6 April to 5 April – businesses can have any financial year they choose, and most will choose to run from the day they start trading until twelve months later. It is also possible for businesses to have an accounting period which is either longer or shorter than twelve months. This means that it can be difficult to determine which profits made in a particular financial period should be matched to which tax year's rates.

Up until tax year 23/24, there were rules called basis periods that were used for reporting business tax information to HMRC on a tax year basis regardless of the accounting period. The **tax year 2023/24 was a transitional year for switching over to the new tax year basis.** This was a very complicated set of rules and measures have now been put in place for a simplification of these rules called **Basis period reform** (BPR).

From 6 April 2024, a new 'tax year basis' of assessment will apply to the trading profits of unincorporated businesses, such as sole traders and partners subject to income tax. Businesses that have already produced their accounts up to 31 March or 5 April or any of the intervening dates will not see any change and will not be affected.

Any unincorporated businesses having a year-end other than 31 March to 5 April (or any date in between) will be required to apportion amounts from two sets of accounts to calculate their profits arising in the tax year (6 April to 5 April).

This could mean that there is less time for preparation and submission of a tax return by the 31 January deadline (online).

Example 6.1

Maisie & Millie opened a new business as a partnership on 1 October 2020, making hand-made chocolates. They make accounts up each year to the year ending 30 September.

According to which Finance Act/s will Maisie and Millie's profits for the financial year 1 October 2024 - 30 September 2025 be taxed?

The profits for the period from 1 October 2024 to 5 April 2025 will be taxed according to the Finance Act which is in operation for that financial period – i.e. Finance Act 2024 (which runs from 6 April 2024 to 5 April 2025).

The profits for the period from 6 April 2025 to 30 September 2025 will be taxed according to the Finance Act which is in operation for that financial period – i.e. Finance Act 2025 (which runs from 6 April 2025 to 5 April 2026).

Example 6.2

Eleanor is self-employed and has a 30 June accounting end date. For her 2024/25 tax return, she must prepare her accounts for the two accounting years 1 July 2023 – 30 June 2024 and 1 July 2024 – 30 June 2025.

1/7/2023 – 30/6/2024 (leap year) profits £30,012 / 366 days = £82 per day.

1/7/2024 – 30/6/2025 profits £32,850 / 365 days = £90 per day.

Profits must then be apportioned from these two sets of accounts on a pro-rata basis into the 2024/25 tax year that is being reported.

6/4/2024 to 30/6/2024 = 86 days @ £82 per day = £7,052 profits.

1/7/2024 to 5/4/2025 = 280 days @ £90 per day = £25,200 profits.

Total pro-rated profits = £7,052 + £25,200 = £32,252 for tax year 2024/25.

In these circumstances, it may be that there is not enough opportunity and time to finalise the profits for the second accounting period before the tax filing deadline. In these instances, it will be necessary to use estimates from the 2025 accounts. Then after 31 January 2026, after finalisation of the 2025 accounts, the 2024/25 tax return may need to be amended to the figures for the finalised 2025 accounts if they are different from the estimated figures. You have until 31 January 2027 to amend the tax return.

Activity 6.1

Jake is self-employed and has a 31 December accounting date. Which of the following will he be required to make his accounts up to to be able to complete his 2024/25 tax return?

a) 1 January 2024 to 31 December 2024 and 1 January 2025 to 31 December 2025.

b) 6 April 2024 to 5 April 2025 and 6 April 2025 to 5 April 2026.

c) 1 January 2023 to 31 December 2023 and 1 January 2024 to 31 December 2024.

d) 6 April 2023 to 5 April 2024 and 6 April 2024 to 5 April 2025.

Partnerships

A partnership is a relationship between two or more persons working together for the purpose of running a business. Each person contributes money, property, labour or skill, and expects to share in the profits or losses of the business.

Partners will often draw up an agreement in writing called Articles of Partnership, Partnership Agreement or Partnership Deed. This sets down how the partnership is to work and also the rights and obligations of each partner.

In the absence of such an agreement or where the agreement is silent, **all partners are bound by the Partnership Act 1890**.

- All profits/losses should be shared equally
- No interest is to be paid on capital
- No interest is to be charged on drawings

A partnership agreement can be changed at any time as long as all the partners agree to do so.

Tax responsibilities for partnerships

Partnerships must prepare annual accounts to show income, expenses, gains, losses, etc, from their business. Partnerships do not pay income tax as an entity; instead, each individual partner will be taxed on their own share of the business partnership profits. Effectively, each partner is treated as running a sole trader business for tax purposes.

The partnership first needs to choose a 'nominated' partner to register the partnership and complete their tax returns online at: www.hmrc.gov.uk

When the nominated partner registers the partnership, they will automatically register themselves for self-assessment.

Any new partnership must register the partnership or individual partners by the 5 October in their business's second tax year. Penalties can be charged for failure to do this.

Example 6.3

Mark and Glenda begin a partnership business on 18 May 2024.

The partnership must register with HMRC before 5 October 2025.

The 'nominated partner' will be the person who is responsible for managing the tax returns of the "partnership" itself by completing SA800 and keeping the business records.

HM Revenue and Customs (HMRC) will usually write (or email) to the partnership in April or May telling them to send a completed partnership tax return by:

- 31 October 2025 (if you have previously submitted paper forms and HMRC allow you to continue doing so)
- 31 January 2026

New partnerships must submit their returns online.

Once the partnership tax return has been completed, the partnership must then let each partner know their share of the profits and losses. This is to ensure that each partner can:

- Complete their own personal Self-Assessment Tax Return SA104.
- Pay Income Tax **on their share of the partnership's profits.**
- Pay National Insurance.

The partnership will also have to register for VAT if they expect their income to be more than the threshold of £90,000 for the tax year 2024/2025.

HMRC should be notified of changes to the partnership, including:

- If a partner joins or leaves
- If a partner dies or is made bankrupt
- Change of a partner's name or address
- Changing the nominated partner
- Closing the partnership.

Allocation of partnership profits

Profits are allocated to the partners using their profit share ratio (PSR) as agreed between them in their partnership agreement.

Example 6.4

Cain and Able are in partnership, under their partnership agreement they share profits at a ratio of 3:2.

Their **adjusted** net profit from the partnership tax return is £118,500.

What is the profit share for each partner?

Cain will receive a profit of £118,500 / 5 x 3 = **£71,100**

Able will receive a profit of £118,500 / 5 x 2 = **£47,400**

However, this can be further complicated if the partnership agreement allows interest on drawings to be charged to the partners, interest on capital being received by the partners or a salary is paid to a partner.

The profit allocation will always be based on the amount of profit remaining **after** these adjustments are made (after the appropriation account).

Example 6.5

Xander and Richard have net profits after adjustments of £142,000; according to the profit share ratio, profit is to be shared 5:3 respectively.

The partnership agreement states that Xander is to receive a salary of £22,000 and Richard is to receive a salary of £15,000. The partnership agreement also states interest on capital is to be paid at a rate of 2%.

Xander's capital balance throughout the year was £10,000 and Richard's was £4,000.

Calculate the profit share, and total partnership income, for each partner.

Xander receives income of £22,000 and interest on his capital (£10,000 x 2% = £200) = £22,200 before profit sharing.

Richard receives income of £15,000 and interest on his capital (£4,000 x 2% = £80) = £15,080 before profit sharing.

The profits available to be shared are therefore £142,000 - £22,200 - £15,080 = £104,720.

These profits are shared:

Xander = £104,720 /8 x 5 = £65,450
Richard = £104,720 /8 x 5 = £39,270

Appropriation Account	Total £	Xander	Richard
Profit/ (loss) for the year	**142,000**		
Less appropriation of profits			
Partner's salaries	37,000	22,000	15,000
Interest on capital	280	200	80
Profit available for distribution	**104,720**		
Profit Share			
Xander	65,450		
Richard	39,270		
Total profit distributed	**104,720**		

The total income received by each partner for tax purposes would be:

- Xander = Share of profits after appropriation £65,450 + Salary £22,000 plus interest on Capital £200 = **£87,650**
- Richard = Share of profits after appropriation £39,270 + Salary £15,000 plus interest on Capital £80 = **£54,350**

Note that £87,650 + £54,350 = £142,000 (the total partnership profits).

Any partnership losses will be divided by the partners using the profit share ratio and entered in the individual partner's details.

Once the nominated partner has completed the Tax return SA800, he will be required to complete a statement showing the partnership's profits and losses for each individual partner. The nominated partner will need to ensure each partner receives a copy of the statement. Each partner can then complete their own personal tax return.

Example 6.6

Example of SA800 tax return 2024 (2025 not available at time of writing).

HM Revenue & Customs

Partnership Tax Return 2024
for the year ended 5 April 2024 (2023–24)

Tax reference

Date

HM Revenue and Customs office address

Telephone

Issue address

For Reference

This notice requires you by law to send us a tax return giving details of income and disposals of chargeable assets, and any documents we ask for, for the year 6 April 2023 to 5 April 2024.

You can file the tax return using either:

- this form and any supplementary pages you need
- the internet (you'll need to buy commercial software). Most people file online. If you file online you'll receive an instant online acknowledgement telling you that we've received your tax return safely. To file online, go directly to our official website by typing www.gov.uk/file-your-self-assessment-tax-return into your internet browser address bar. Do not use a search website to find HMRC services online

Make sure that your tax return, and any documents asked for, reach us by:

- **31 October 2024** if you complete a paper tax return
- **31 January 2025** if you file online

Please see the Partnership Tax Return Guide for filing dates if this notice was given after 31 July 2024 or if the partnership includes a company as a partner.

Each partner who was a member of the partnership during the return period is liable to automatic penalties if the Partnership Tax Return does not reach us by the relevant filing date shown above. They'll have to pay interest and may have to pay a late payment penalty on any tax they pay late.

We check all tax returns and there are penalties for supplying false or incomplete information.

Who should send the Partnership Tax Return?
If this Partnership Tax Return has been issued in the name of the partnership, then the partner nominated by the other members of the partnership during the period covered by the tax return is required by law to complete it and send it back to us. If the partners are unable to nominate someone, they should ask us to nominate one of them.

If this Partnership Tax Return has been issued in the name of a particular partner, that partner is required by law to send it back to us.

The Partnership Tax Return – your responsibilities
We've sent you pages 1 to 8 of the tax return for the most common types of partnership income. You might need other supplementary pages, which we have not sent you, for other types of income and disposals.

You are responsible for making sure that you have the right pages. Answer the questions on page 2 of this form to find out if you have the right ones.

You should make sure that the information needed by individual partners to complete their personal tax returns is given to them as quickly as possible (some partners may want to send their own returns by 31 October 2024).

If you need help:

- refer to the Partnership Tax Return Guide, go to www.gov.uk/taxreturnforms
- phone the number above – we can answer most questions by phone
- when the office is closed, phone our helpline on 0300 200 3310 for general advice
- go to www.gov.uk/self-assessment-tax-returns

SA800 2024 PARTNERSHIP TAX RETURN: PAGE 1 12/23

Partnership business and investment income for the year ended 5 April 2024

Answer Questions 1 to 6 on this page and Question 7 on page 8 to check that you have the pages you need to make a complete return of partnership income and related information for the year ended 5 April 2024. If you answer 'Yes', you must make sure that you have the right pages and then fill in the relevant boxes. If not, go to the next question.

To get the appropriate supplementary pages and notes that will help you fill in this form, go to www.gov.uk/taxreturnforms

Check to make sure that you have the right supplementary pages (including the Partnership Savings pages – see Question 7) and then tick the box below

Q1 Did the partnership receive any rent or other income from UK property (read the Partnership Tax Return Guide if you've furnished holiday lettings)? Yes [ ] — UK PROPERTY [ ]

Q2 Did the partnership have any foreign income? Yes [ ] — FOREIGN [ ]

Q3 Did the partnership business include a trade or profession at any time between 6 April 2023 and 5 April 2024? Yes [ ] — If yes, complete boxes 3.1 to 3.117 on pages 2 to 5 as appropriate.

Q4 Did the partnership dispose of any chargeable assets? Yes [ ] — CHARGEABLE ASSETS [ ]

Q5 During the return period has the partnership included any member who is:

- a company Yes [ ]
- not resident in the UK Yes [ ]

If yes, read the Partnership Tax Return Guide about filling in the Partnership Statement, go to www.gov.uk/taxreturnforms

- a partner in a business controlled and managed abroad and who is not domiciled in the UK or is not ordinarily resident in the UK? Yes [ ] — If yes, read the Partnership Tax Return Guide.

Q6 Are you completing this tax return on behalf of a European Economic Interest Grouping (EEIG)? Yes [ ] — If yes, read the Partnership Tax Return Guide.

Q6.1 During the return period, did the partnership export goods and or services to individuals, enterprises or other organisations outside the UK?

- goods Yes [ ]
- services Yes [ ]
- neither Yes [ ]

If yes, read the Partnership Tax Return Guide.

Trading and professional income for the year ended 5 April 2024

You have to fill in a set of boxes for each trade carried on by the partnership and you may have to fill in a separate set if partnership accounts were made up to more than one date in the year ended 5 April 2024. Check the rules in the Partnership Tax Return Guide.

Partnership details

Name of business

3.1 [ ]

Description of partnership trade or profession

3.2 [ ]

Accounting period – read the Partnership Tax Return Guide, go to www.gov.uk/taxreturnforms

Start 3.4 [/ /] End 3.5 [/ /]

- Date of commencement (if after 5 April 2023) 3.7 [/ /]
- Date of cessation (if before 6 April 2024) 3.8 [/ /]
- Tick box 3.9 if you used the 'cash basis', money actually received and paid out, to calculate your income and expenses – read the guide 3.9 [ ]
- Tick box 3.10 if you do not need to complete boxes 3.14 to 3.93 and boxes 3.99 to 3.115 3.10 [ ]
- Tick box 3.11 if the partnership's accounts do not cover the period from the last accounting date (explain why in the 'Additional information' box, box 3.116 on page 3) 3.11 [ ]

Boxes 3.12 and 3.13 are not used

SA800 2024 PARTNERSHIP TAX RETURN: PAGE 2

Trading and professional income for the year ended 5 April 2024 – continued

Capital allowances – summary

	Capital allowances	Balancing charges
• Annual Investment Allowance (include any balancing charges in box 3.17 below)	3.13A £	
• Zero-emission goods vehicle allowance	3.14 £	3.15 £
• Capital allowances at 18% on equipment, including cars with lower CO2 emissions	3.14A £	3.15A £
• Capital allowances at 6% on equipment, including cars with higher CO2 emissions	3.16 £	3.17 £
• Zero-emission car allowance	3.16A £	
• Electric charge-point allowance	3.18 £	3.19 £
• The Structures and Buildings Allowance	3.18A £	
• Freeports and Investment Zones Structures and Buildings Allowance	3.18B £	
• 100% and other enhanced capital allowances claimed (you must make separate calculations)	3.20 £	3.21 £
Total capital allowances/balancing charges	total of column above 3.22 £	total of column above 3.23 £

Income and expenses for this accounting period

Read the Partnership Tax Return Guide before completing this section.

If your annual turnover was (or would have been if you had traded for the whole year):

- below £85,000, fill in boxes 3.24 to 3.26 instead of page 4
- between £85,000 and £15 million, ignore boxes 3.24 to 3.26 – now fill in page 4
- more than £15 million (combined annualised turnover from all of your activities), fill in boxes 3.24 to 3.26 and also send partnership accounts and computations

In all cases, complete box 3.83 or box 3.84 on page 5, and the other boxes on page 5 if applicable.

• Turnover including other business receipts, and goods taken for personal use (and balancing charges from box 3.23)	3.24 £
• Expenses allowable for tax (including capital allowances from box 3.22)	3.25 £
Net profit for this accounting period (put figure in brackets if a loss)	box 3.24 minus box 3.25 3.26 £

3.116 **Additional information**

SA800 2024 PARTNERSHIP TAX RETURN: PAGE 3

Trading and professional income for the year ended 5 April 2024 – continued

Income and expenses for this accounting period

You must fill in this page if your annual turnover was between £85,000 and £15 million. If the combined annualised turnover from all your activities was more than £15 million, fill in boxes 3.24 to 3.26 on page 3 and send in the partnership accounts and computations as well. In all cases, complete box 3.83 or box 3.84 on page 5, and the other boxes on page 5 if applicable. Read the Partnership Tax Return Guide, go to **www.gov.uk/taxreturnforms**

If you were registered for VAT, do the figures in boxes 3.29 to 3.64 include VAT? 3.27 [ ] or exclude VAT? 3.28 [ ]

	Disallowable expenses included in boxes 3.46 to 3.63	Total expenses	Sales/business income (turnover)
			3.29 £
• Cost of sales	3.30 £	3.46 £	
• Construction industry subcontractor costs	3.31 £	3.47 £	
• Other direct costs	3.32 £	3.48 £	
		Gross profit/(loss)	box 3.29 minus (boxes 3.46 + 3.47 + 3.48) 3.49 £
		Other income/profits	3.50 £
• Employee costs	3.33 £	3.51 £	
• Premises costs	3.34 £	3.52 £	
• Repairs	3.35 £	3.53 £	
• General administrative expenses	3.36 £	3.54 £	
• Motor expenses	3.37 £	3.55 £	
• Travel and subsistence	3.38 £	3.56 £	
• Advertising, promotion and entertainment	3.39 £	3.57 £	
• Legal and professional costs	3.40 £	3.58 £	
• Bad debts	3.41 £	3.59 £	
• Interest and alternative finance payments	3.42 £	3.60 £	
• Other finance charges	3.43 £	3.61 £	
• Depreciation and loss/(profit) on sale	3.44 £	3.62 £	
• Other expenses including partnership charges	3.45 £	3.63 £	
	Put the total of boxes 3.30 to 3.45 in box 3.66 below	Total expenses	boxes 3.51 to 3.63 3.64 £
		Net profit/(loss)	boxes 3.49 + 3.50 minus 3.64 3.65 £

Tax adjustments to net profit or loss for this accounting period

• Disallowable expenses	boxes 3.30 to 3.45 3.66 £	
• Goods taken for personal use and other adjustments (apart from disallowable expenses) that increase profits	3.67 £	
• Balancing charges (from box 3.23)	3.68 £	
Total additions to net profit (deduct from net loss)		boxes 3.66 + 3.67 + 3.68 3.69 £
• Capital allowances (from box 3.22)	3.70 £	
• Deductions from net profit (add to net loss)	3.71 £	boxes 3.70 + 3.71 3.72 £
Net business profit for tax purposes for this accounting period (put figure in brackets if a loss)		boxes 3.65 + 3.69 minus box 3.72 3.73 £

SA800 2024 PARTNERSHIP TAX RETURN: PAGE 4

Partnership business and investment income for the year ended 5 April 2024

Taxable profit or loss for this accounting period

- Adjustment on change of basis — 3.82 £ — Copy this figure to box 11A in the Partnership Statement

Net profit for this accounting period (if loss, enter '0' here) from box 3.26 or box 3.73 — 3.83 £ — Copy this figure to box 11 in the Partnership Statement

Allowable loss for this accounting period (if profit, enter '0' here) from box 3.26 or box 3.73 — 3.84 £ — Copy this figure to box 12 in the Partnership Statement

Tick box 3.93 if the figure in box 3.83 or box 3.84 is provisional — 3.93

Subcontractors in the construction industry

- Deductions on payment and deduction statements from contractors – construction industry subcontractors only — 3.97 £ — Copy this figure to box 24 in the Partnership Statement

Tax taken off trading income

- Tax taken off trading income (excluding deductions made by contractors on account of tax) — 3.98 £ — Copy this figure to box 24A in the Partnership Statement

Read the Partnership Tax Return Guide if you're a 'CT Partnership', go to **www.gov.uk/taxreturnforms**

Summary of balance sheet for this accounting period

Leave these boxes blank if you do not have a balance sheet or your annual turnover was more than £15 million.

Assets

- Plant, machinery and motor vehicles — 3.99 £
- Other fixed assets for example, premises or goodwill investments — 3.100 £
- Stock and work in progress — 3.101 £
- Debtors/prepayments/other current assets — 3.102 £
- Bank/building society balances — 3.103 £
- Cash in hand — 3.104 £ — boxes 3.99 to 3.104: 3.105 £

Liabilities

- Trade creditors/accruals — 3.106 £
- Loans and overdrawn bank accounts — 3.107 £
- Other liabilities — 3.108 £ — boxes 3.106 to 3.108: 3.109 £

Net business assets (put the figure in brackets if you had net business liabilities) — box 3.105 minus box 3.109: 3.110 £

Represented by partners' current and capital accounts

- Balance at start of period* — 3.111 £
- Net profit/(loss)* — 3.112 £
- Capital introduced — 3.113 £
- Drawings — 3.114 £
- Balance at end of period* — boxes 3.111 to 3.113 minus box 3.114: 3.115 £

* If the capital account is overdrawn, or the business made a net loss, show the figure in brackets.

Box 3.116 'Additional information' is on page 3.

Partnership trade charges

- Net partnership charges paid in the period 6 April 2023 to 5 April 2024 (not the accounting period) — 3.117 £

SA800 2024 PARTNERSHIP TAX RETURN: PAGE 5

Partnership Statement (short) for the year ended 5 April 2024

Please read these instructions before completing the Statement

Use these pages to allocate partnership income if the only income for the relevant return period was trading and professional income or untaxed interest and alternative finance receipts from UK banks and building societies. Otherwise you must download the 'Partnership Statement (Full)' pages to record details of the allocation of all the partnership income. Go to www.gov.uk/taxreturnforms

Step 1 Fill in boxes 1 to 29 and boxes A and B as appropriate. Get the figures you need from the relevant boxes in the Partnership Tax Return. Complete a separate Statement for each accounting period covered by this Partnership Tax Return and for each trade or profession carried on by the partnership.

Step 2 Then allocate the amounts in boxes 11 to 29 attributable to each partner using the allocation columns on this page and page 7, read the Partnership Tax Return Guide, go to www.gov.uk/taxreturnforms
If the partnership has more than 3 partners, please photocopy page 7.

Step 3 Each partner will need a copy of their allocation of income to fill in their personal tax return.

Partnership information

If the partnership business includes a trade or profession, enter here the accounting period for which appropriate items in this statement are returned.

Start **1** / /

End **2** / /

Nature of trade **3**

Mixed partnerships

Tick here if this Statement is drawn up using Corporation Tax rules **4**

Tick here if this Statement is drawn up using tax rules for non-residents **5**

Individual partner details

6 Name of partner

Address

Postcode

Date appointed as a partner (if during 2022–23 or 2023–24) **7** / /

Partner's Unique Taxpayer Reference (UTR) **8**

Date ceased to be a partner (if during 2022–23 or 2023–24) **9** / /

Partner's National Insurance number **10**

Partnership's profits, losses, income and tax credits

Tick this box if the items entered in the box had foreign tax taken off

Partner's share of profits, losses, income and tax credits

Copy figures in boxes 11 to 29 to boxes in the individual's Partnership (short) pages or as shown below

- for an accounting period ended in 2023–24

Source	Item	Tick box	Partnership box		Partner's box	Instruction
from box 3.83	Profit from a trade or profession	A	11 £	Profit	11 £	Copy this figure to box 8
from box 3.82	Adjustment on change of basis		11A £		11A £	Copy this figure to box 10
from box 3.84	Loss from a trade or profession	B	12 £	Loss	12 £	Copy this figure to box 8

- for the period 6 April 2023 to 5 April 2024*

Source	Item	Partnership box	Partner's box	Instruction
from box 7.9A	Income from untaxed UK savings	13 £	13 £	Copy this figure to box 28
from box 3.97	CIS deductions made by contractors on account of tax	24 £	24 £	Copy this figure to box 30
from box 3.98	Other tax taken off trading income	24A £	24A £	Copy this figure to box 31
from box 3.117	Partnership charges	29 £	29 £	Copy this figure to box 4, 'Other tax reliefs' section on page Ai 2 in your personal tax return

* If you're a 'CT Partnership' see the Partnership Tax Return Guide

SA800 2024 PARTNERSHIP TAX RETURN: PAGE 6

Partnership Statement (short) for the year ended 5 April 2024 – continued

Individual partner details

6 Name of partner

Address

Postcode

Date appointed as a partner (if during 2022–23 or 2023–24)

7 / /

Partner's Unique Taxpayer Reference (UTR)

8

Date ceased to be a partner (if during 2022–23 or 2023–24)

9 / /

Partner's National Insurance number

10

Partner's share of profits, losses, income and tax credits

Copy figures in boxes 11 to 29 to boxes in the individual's Partnership (short) pages or as shown below

	Box	£	
Profit	11	£	Copy this figure to box 8
	11A	£	Copy this figure to box 10
Loss	12	£	Copy this figure to box 8
	13	£	Copy this figure to box 28
	24	£	Copy this figure to box 30
	24A	£	Copy this figure to box 31
	29	£	Copy this figure to box 4, 'Other tax reliefs' section on page Ai 2 in your personal tax return

Individual partner details

6 Name of partner

Address

Postcode

Date appointed as a partner (if during 2022–23 or 2023–24)

7 / /

Partner's Unique Taxpayer Reference (UTR)

8

Date ceased to be a partner (if during 2022–23 or 2023–24)

9 / /

Partner's National Insurance number

10

Partner's share of profits, losses, income and tax credits

Copy figures in boxes 11 to 29 to boxes in the individual's Partnership (short) pages or as shown below

	Box	£	
Profit	11	£	Copy this figure to box 8
	11A	£	Copy this figure to box 10
Loss	12	£	Copy this figure to box 8
	13	£	Copy this figure to box 28
	24	£	Copy this figure to box 30
	24A	£	Copy this figure to box 31
	29	£	Copy this figure to box 4, 'Other tax reliefs' section on page Ai 2 in your personal tax return

SA800 2024 PARTNERSHIP TAX RETURN: PAGE 7

Other information for the year ended 5 April 2024

Q7 Did the partnership receive any other income which you've not already included elsewhere in the Partnership Tax Return?
Make sure that you fill in the pages for Questions 1 to 4 before answering Question 7

Yes ☐ If yes, read the guidance below

If you ticked the 'Yes' box and the only income was untaxed interest, or alternative finance receipts, from UK banks and building societies, fill in box 7.9A below. Otherwise download the Partnership Savings pages, go to www.gov.uk/taxreturnforms and leave box 7.9A blank. If you've more than one account, enter totals in the box.

Untaxed interest and alternative finance receipts from UK banks and building societies — Taxable amount **7.9A** £ — Copy this figure to box 13 in the Partnership Statement (short)

Q8 Are the details on the front of the Partnership Tax Return wrong? Yes ☐ If yes, make any corrections on the front of the form

Q9 Please give a daytime phone number (including the area code) in boxes 9.1 and 9.2
It's often simpler to phone if we need to ask you about your tax return.

Your phone number **9.1**

or, if you prefer, your adviser's phone number **9.2**

Your adviser's name and address **9.3**

Postcode

Q10 Other information

Please tick box 10.1 if this Partnership Tax Return contains figures that are provisional because you do not yet have final figures. The Partnership Tax Return Guide explains the circumstances in which provisional figures may be used and asks you to provide some additional information in box 3.116 on page 3. **10.1** ☐

Disclosure of tax avoidance schemes – read the notes about boxes 10.2 and 10.3 in the Partnership Tax Return Guide.

Scheme reference number or promoter reference number **10.2**

Tax year in which the expected advantage to the partners arises – year ended 5 April **10.3**

Q11 Declaration – I have filled in and am sending back to you the following:

- 1 TO 5 OF THIS FORM ☐
- 6 AND 7 PARTNERSHIP STATEMENT (SHORT) ☐
- 6 AND 7 PARTNERSHIP STATEMENT (FULL) ☐
- PARTNERSHIP UK PROPERTY ☐
- PARTNERSHIP FOREIGN ☐
- PARTNERSHIP TRADING ☐
- PARTNERSHIP DISPOSAL OF CHARGEABLE ASSETS ☐
- PARTNERSHIP SAVINGS ☐

I attach **11.1** additional copies of page 7. There were **11.2** partners in this partnership for that period.

Before you send the completed tax return back to your current HM Revenue and Customs office, you must sign the statement below.
If you give false information or conceal any part of the partnership's income or details of the disposal of chargeable assets, you may be liable to financial penalties and/or we may prosecute you.

11.3 **I the nominated partner,** declare that the information I have given on this Partnership Tax Return is correct and complete to the best of my knowledge and belief.

Nominated partner signature — Date

Print name in full here

If you have signed for someone else, please also:

- state the capacity in which you are signing (for example, as executor or receiver) **11.4**
- give the name of the person you are signing for and your name and address in the 'Additional information' box, box 3.116, on page 3.

SA800 2024 PARTNERSHIP TAX RETURN: PAGE 8

Example 6.7

Rio Bauer, Murray Anderson and Kaiya Reid have been trading in partnership for several years. The partnership produces accounts each year up to 30 June. Their partnership agreement states that the following salaries, rates of interest on capital, and share of remaining profits or losses apply.

	Salary (pa)	Interest on Capital	Share of Profit/Loss
Rio Bauer	£22,000	3%	40%
Murray Anderson	-	3%	40%
Kaiya Reid	£15,800	3%	20%

The partnership accounts for the twelve-month accounting period to 30 June 2024 show tax-adjusted profits of £165,000 (after deducting capital allowances).

The capital account balances for the partners are:

Rio Bauer	£ 80,000
Murray Anderson	£100,000
Kaiya Reid	£180,000

Calculate the trading income assessments for each of the three partners based on the adjusted profits for this period.

Appropriation Account	Total £	Rio	Murray	Kaiya
Profit/ (loss) for the year	**165,000**			
Less appropriation of profits				
Partner's salaries	37,800	22,000	0	15,800
Interest on capital	10,800	2,400	3,000	5,400
Profit available for distribution	**116,400**			
Profit Share				
Rio Bauer	46,560			
Murray Anderson	46,560			
Kaiya Reid	23,280			
Total profit distributed	**116,400**			

Profit for tax purposes 24/25	Rio £	Murray £	Kaiya £
Salary	22,000		15,800
Capital interest	2,400	3,000	5,400
Profit share	46,560	46,560	23,280
Totals	**70,960**	**49,560**	**44,480**

Activity 6.2

Morris and Valerie have been trading for several years and have net profits after adjustments of £118,500; profit is to be shared 3: 2 respectively.

Morris withdrew £17,500 from the business and Valerie withdrew £15,000 from the business.

Morris Invested £35,000 as his capital and Valerie invested £25,000 into the partnership.

The partnership agreement states:

- Interest on capital is to be received at a rate of 7%.
- Interest on drawings is to be charged at a rate of 5%.
- A salary of £20,000 is to be paid to Valerie.

Using the templates provided, calculate the trading income assessments for each of the partners that will be based on the adjusted profits for this period.

Appropriation Account	Total £	Morris £	Valerie £
Profit/ (loss) for the year			
Add			
Interest on drawings			
Less appropriation of profits			
Partner's salaries			
Interest on capital			
Profit available for distribution			
Profit Share			
Morris			
Valerie			
Total profit distributed			

Profit for tax purposes 24/25	Morris £	Valerie £
Salary		
Capital interest		
Profit share		
Less drawings interest		
Totals		

Activity 6.3

James and Jonathan set up in partnership to run a small printing company on the 6 April 2024. They have no partnership agreement in place.

James has agreed to deal with the partnership tax return and has completed a draft Trading Profit and Loss Account for the tax year to 5 April 2025.

	£	£
Gross Profit		84,500
Less - Expenses		
Rent	6,750	
Electricity	1,659	
General expenses	1,726	
Staff wages	15,500	
Irrecoverable debts	921	
Depreciation	5,130	
Total expenses		31,686
Net Profit for the year per the accounts		**52,814**

Additional Information;

- The bad debt charge consists of an irrecoverable debt write-off of £330 and a general allowance for doubtful receivables provision of £591.
- Capital allowances amounted to the value of £35,000 for printing presses.
- The figure for general expenses contains £500 for petrol used for private use, and £150 to entertain a customer.
- During the year James withdrew £6,000 for personal use and Jonathan withdrew £7,500

Adjust the net profit for tax purposes and complete a profit appropriation showing each partner's share of profits for tax purposes.

Adjustment of Profits	£
Net Profit before tax as per accounts	
Add	
Depreciation Doubtful receivables provision Entertaining customer Private fuel	
Deduct	
Adjusted trading profit before deduction of capital expenses	
Capital allowances	
Adjusted trading profit (trading income)	

State the adjusted trading profit. ______________

State the share of profit after appropriation. ______________

State the value of profit for tax purposes for James. ______________

State the value of profit for tax purposes for Jonathan. ______________

Activity 6.4

Priyanka and Jen have been trading as a partnership for many years sharing profits as follows:

- Priyanka is paid £1,500 per month and Jen £1,600 per month
- Remaining profits are shared equally

On 1 December 2024, Grace joined the partnership. The partners agreed to share profits as follows:

	Priyanka	Jen	Grace
Salary per month	£1,600	£1,750	£1,250
Profit share	40%	30%	30%

The partnership's taxable profits for the year ended 31 January 2025 were £244,884.

Calculate the trading profits for each partner by completing the missing entries in the appropriation of profits below. All entries should be stated to the nearest £.

	Priyanka £	Jen £	Grace £	Total £
Period to 31/11/24				
Salary			0	
Profit share			0	
Total			0	
Period to 31/01/25				
Salary				
Profit share				
Total				
Total for year				

NICs

National Insurance Contributions (NICs) are paid by employees, employers and the self-employed. The contributions collected are used to provide social security benefits such as the State Pension, Jobseekers Allowance and Maternity Allowance.

To be eligible to pay National Insurance, an individual must be over the age of 16 and earn at least £123 per week. There are different classes of NIC, depending upon the taxpayer's employment status and the amount they earn.

Classes of NI

Class 1 NICs are paid by employees and are referred to as Primary NICs.

Employees do not pay NICs on all of their earnings; there is a Lower Earnings Level (LEL) of £6,396 for Class 1 NICS.

Earnings between the LEL of £6,396 and the Primary Threshold of £12,570 will pay NIC at 0%. This effectively means that an employee earning less than £12,570 will not need to pay National Insurance Contributions.

Earnings between the Primary Threshold of £12,570 and the Upper Earnings Limit (UEL) of £50,270 are subject to NICs of 8%, whilst any earnings above £50,270 are subject to 2% NICs.

These rates apply to NIC Category A employees (which is most employees) – different rates apply for those employees in a different NIC category.

Class 1 NI is paid by employers on behalf of employees and is referred to as Secondary NICs.

In addition to the National Insurance contributions made by employees, employers must also pay National Insurance on behalf of their employees. This is calculated as 13.8% for all employees who earn between the Secondary Threshold (£9,100) and the Upper Earnings limit. The 13.8% contribution is also applied to benefits and expenses **(Class 1A NICs)**, although this is paid annually whilst Class 1 NICS are paid monthly.

The employer's Class 1A NICs are an additional cost to the employer over and above the employee's gross wage.

An employment allowance of up to £5,000 is available to employers if their Class 1 NICs were less than £100,000 in the previous tax year.

Class 4 NI contributions are paid by the self-employed.

It is the Class 4 calculations that are covered by the Business Tax unit. The other classes will be covered in the Personal Tax unit. However, you may need to know all of the relevant rates for the other classes for any tax planning questions.

Self-employed individuals pay their national insurance via Self-Assessment, similar to how they pay their taxes. The national insurance contributions (NICs) for the self-employed are divided into two types: Class 2 and Class 4.

Class 2 NICs will no longer be due for most self-employed individuals from 6 April 2024. They will exist to allow self-employed individuals with profits below the small profits threshold of £6,725 to make voluntary contributions. There will be no testing of Class 2 NICs within the AAT assessment for 2024/25.

Class 4 NIC

The majority of a self-employed person's NIC liability is likely to be class 4 NIC. This is charged at the rate of 6% on all trading profits between **£12,570 and £50,270** (24/25).

The lower profits limit from when self-employed people start paying Class 4 National Insurance is £12,570, meaning self-employed people can earn £12,570 before paying the 6% rate. All earnings above £50,270 are charged class 4 NIC at 2%.

Example 6.8

Bill has self-employed earnings of £100,000 in 2024-25.

Bill's Class 4 NICs for 2024-25 will be:

Bill will pay class 4 NIC at the following rates:

(£50,270 - £12,570) = £37,700 x 6% =	**£2,262.00**
(£100,000 - £50,270) = £49,730 x 2% =	**£994.60**

He therefore has a total NIC liability of;

Class 4 NIC of £2,262.00 + £994.60 = £3,256.60.

The following people do not have to pay class 4 NIC on any self-employed earnings:

- People under 16
- People not resident in the UK for tax purposes
- People over the state pension age.

Activity 6.5

Joshua is a self-employed artist and in 2024/25 his adjusted profits were £60,000. Joshua is aged 45 and lives in the UK for tax purposes.

Calculate Joshua's total NIC liability for 2024-25.

NICs and partnerships

As with income tax, each partner will be treated as a separate sole trader and class 4 contributions will be payable by each individual partner on their assessed profits.

Activity 6.6

Dom, Dick and Dell have been in partnership for several years, their accounts are prepared at the end of June each year.

The partners each received the following profit from the partnership **after** the appropriation of profits:

- Dom £66,324
- Dick £44,218
- Dell £59,867

Calculate the class 4 NICs each partner will be charged in respect of their taxable profits.

Profits applicable to class 4 NICs

Profits that will be applicable to Class 4 NIC liability would be taxable trade profits less any trading losses brought forward. Trading losses will be covered in Chapter 10.

Taxable trade profits	XXXX
Less trading losses b/f	(XXX)
Profits for Class 4 NICs	X

Dividends received are not subject to National Insurance.

Summary of Chapter 6

- Tax-adjusted profits for partnerships are calculated the same as those of a sole trader.
- Partners will share tax-adjusted profits between them according to profit-sharing arrangements.
- Any changes to partnership agreements and/or profit-sharing arrangements during a period of account will require profits to be time-apportioned to the relevant split periods.
- A partner's individual profit will be taxed according to the tax year the profit falls in.
- The majority of a self-employed person's NIC liability is likely to be class 4 NIC. This is charged at the rate of 6% on all trading profits between **£12,570 and £50,270** (24/25).
- All earnings above **£50,270** are charged class 4 NIC at 2%.

Assessment 6

You are now required to log in to your ROGO account to complete your online assessment before progressing to the next chapter.

This page is left intentionally blank

Chapter 7: Chargeable gains and allowable losses for incorporated Businesses

By the end of this chapter, you should:

- Be able to understand and calculate chargeable gains and allowable losses.
- Be able to understand and calculate rollover relief.
- Be able to understand and calculate indexation allowance.
- Be able to apply matching rules for companies on disposals of shares.
- Be able to account for bonus issues, rights issues and indexation on disposal of shares for limited companies.

Introduction

Capital Gains Tax (CGT) is payable and calculated separately for Income Tax purposes for individuals (sole traders and partnerships). However, for an incorporated Limited Company, chargeable gains and allowable losses are calculated as part of the Corporation Tax computation, see the highlighted area below in the CT computation template.

Corporation Tax computation for 12 months ended 20XX	
	£
Trading income	**X**
Add:	
Non-trade Interest	X
Property Income	X
Chargeable gains	**X**
Total profits	X
Less:	
Qualifying charitable donations	(X)
Taxable total profits (TTP)	X

A Limited Company will pay Corporation Tax on the profit (chargeable gain) from the sale or disposal of an asset. The gain or profit is normally the difference between the purchase price and the selling price.

Assets that can give rise to a gain are:

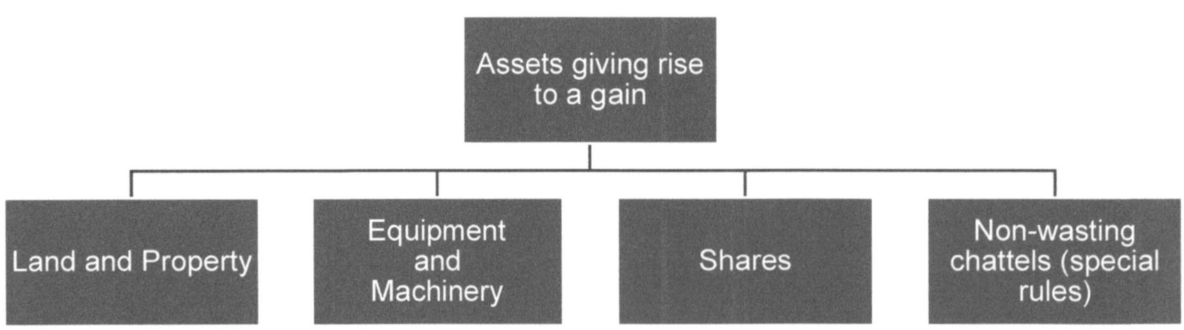

Disposals cover:

- Assets that are fully or partly sold
- Assets that are given away for no value received (gifts)
- Assets that may have been lost or destroyed

The most common situation in which a chargeable gain will occur is clearly when an asset is sold; however, where the disposal occurs on loss or destruction of the asset a chargeable event still arises, although the disposal proceeds (the value of the asset) will usually be nil unless there are proceeds from an insurance claim, in which case the disposal proceeds will be the value of the insurance claim.

There are some items that are exempt from disposal for chargeable gains and these are:

a) Motor vehicles including vintage and classic cars, but not single-seat sports cars, racing cars, taxis, vans and lorries.

b) Inventory (trading).

c) Some wasting chattels like racehorses, greyhounds and boats. A **chattel** is a tangible, movable thing – they are things that you can see, touch and move; most personal property would be classed as chattels. A **wasting chattel** is one with an estimated remaining life of less than 50 years when it was first acquired. Calculations on wasting chattels will not be tested in an AAT assessment.

d) Non-wasting chattels with sale proceeds and cost of £6,000 or less like antiques or works of art. Again, calculations on non-wasting chattels will not be tested in an AAT assessment.

e) Government securities or gilts.

The main differences between CGT for individuals and Corporation Tax for companies are:

- There is no annual exemption amount applicable to limited companies.
- Companies include chargeable gains in the taxable total profits and apply the CT rate applicable.
- Matching rules for shares are different for companies than individuals.
- Indexation allowance is only available to companies and not individuals.

Example 7.1

Identify which of the following disposals would give rise to a chargeable gain:

- Trytun Ltd is a construction business that builds houses. It has built a development of 3 houses of which 2 have now been sold.

  This would be **exempt** as the proceeds from the 2 houses are **trading** income.

- Thaitania Ltd, a small builder of oriental buildings sold a work of art for £8,500. The painting had been purchased to decorate the reception area of the show home.

  This would be **chargeable** as the painting is a non-wasting chattel sold for **more than** the value of £6,000.

- Hoberon Ltd has sold a motor vehicle used for business purposes for a gain of £2,500.

  This would be **exempt** as motor vehicles are part of the exemptions list and dealt with under capital allowances/disposals.

- Moonshine Ltd has sold a production machine for a gain of £75,000.

  This would be a **chargeable** asset.

Activity 7.1

Identify whether the following disposals give rise to a chargeable gain or are exempt.

Disposal	Chargeable or Exempt?
A painting which cost £750 and sold for £9,000	
An antique ornament costing £3,000 which sold for £5,500	
A classic car sold for £40,000	
Inventory that has become obsolete sold for £6,000	
Land sold for £5,900 purchased for £2,900	

Indexation allowance

Indexation Allowance (IA) is a relief for companies from inflationary gains when an asset is disposed of. The Indexation allowance relief is applied when computing chargeable gains or allowable losses.

In the Autumn 2017 Budget, it was announced that the Indexation allowance was going to be frozen as of **31 December 2017**. Indexation allowance is referenced to movements in the retail price index (RPI) for the period the asset is owned.

The Retail Price Index (RPI) / Consumer Price Index (CPI)

The most common measures of general price inflation in the UK are calculated each month using a representative 'basket' of goods. The goods in the basket represent 'typical' expenditure by a 'typical' household. They are updated periodically by the government to reflect current tastes and technology.

When the first Retail Price Index was developed in 1947, it included items such as:

- Lard
- Unskinned rabbits
- Back-laced ladies' corsets
- A gallon of lamp oil
- Brussels sprouts (only removed in 2007)

In 2008, smoothies and muffins were added; frozen vegetarian ready meals, microwave ovens, 35mm film and CD singles were removed. In 2024 air fryers, gluten-free bread and edible sunflower seeds have been added, and hand hygiene gel, hot rotisserie-cooked chicken and bakeware have been removed.

When a company makes a chargeable gain on or after 1 January 2018, the IA that is applied in order to calculate the amount of the chargeable gain will be calculated up to the **end of December 2017. Therefore, this would apply to the 2024/25 tax year.**

When a company acquires an asset **on or after** 1 January 2018, **no IA will be available** to offset against any gain on disposal. This is to bring it in line with an individual's taxation (income tax).

The following template can be used for the chargeable gains computation:

Chargeable gains computation	**£**
Disposal proceeds	X
Less: incidental cost of disposal	(X)
Net sale proceeds	**X**
Less original costs for acquisition	(X)
Less cost of enhancements	(X)
Less incidental cost of acquisition	(X)
Unindexed gain/loss	**X/(X)**
Indexation allowance on original costs	(x)
Indexation allowance on enhancement	(x)
Indexed chargeable gain	**X**

Indexation factors

As the Indexation Allowance was frozen in December 2017, indexation can only be applied for ownership of the asset up to December 2017, the RPI figure at that time being 278.10.

Example 7.2

Iyo Limited purchased an asset in July 2012 for £20,000. The asset was then sold for £40,000 in March 2019.

By locating the IA allowance table for December 2017 at the following link:
https://www.gov.uk/government/publications/corporation-tax-on-chargeable-gains-indexation-allowance-2017/indexation-allowance-december-2017.

Guidance

Indexation Allowance - December 2017

Updated 16 March 2018

Contents

The value of the Retail Price Index, as published by the Office for National Statistics, for December 2017 is 278.1 (January 1987 = 100).

The indexed rise to be used in calculating the Indexation Allowance in respect of assets disposed of in December 2017 is as follows:

	2010	2011	2012	2013	2014	2015	2016
January	0.276	0.214	0.168	0.131	0.101	0.089	0.075
February	0.269	0.202	0.159	0.123	0.094	0.083	0.070
March	0.260	0.196	0.155	0.118	0.091	0.082	0.065
April	0.248	0.186	0.147	0.115	0.088	0.078	0.064
May	0.244	0.182	0.147	0.112	0.087	0.076	0.061
June	0.241	0.182	0.150	0.114	0.085	0.074	0.057
July	0.244	0.185	0.149	0.114	0.086	0.075	0.056
August	0.239	0.178	0.144	0.108	0.082	0.070	0.052
September	0.234	0.169	0.139	0.104	0.080	0.071	0.050
October	0.232	0.168	0.132	0.104	0.079	0.072	0.050
November	0.226	0.166	0.132	0.103	0.082	0.070	0.047
December	0.218	0.162	0.127	0.101	0.080	0.067	0.041

It can be seen that the Indexation factor for July 2012, the date of purchase is **0.149.** The computation is cost £20,000 x 0.149 factor = £2,980 allowance.

The gain is therefore £40,000 selling price less (£20,000 + £2,980) = **£17,020** gain chargeable to corporation tax.

The indexation factor calculated using the RPI tables is:

$$\text{Indexation factor} = \frac{\text{RPI at month of disposal} - \text{RPI at month of purchase}}{\text{RPI at month of purchase}}$$

December 2017 = 278.10 RPI
July 2012 = 242.10 RPI

$$\frac{278.10 - 242.10}{242.10} = \mathbf{0.149}$$

The RPI figure for December 2017 is used even though the asset disposal date was March 2022 as the IA has been frozen since December 2017.

The chargeable gains computation template is completed as follows:

Chargeable gains computation		£
Disposal proceeds		40,000
Less: incidental cost of disposal		0
Net sale proceeds		**40,000**
Less original costs for acquisition		(20,000)
Less cost of enhancements		0
Less incidental cost of acquisition		0
Unindexed gain/loss		**20,000**
Indexation allowance on original costs	**0.149**	(2,980)
Indexation allowance on enhancement		0
Indexed chargeable gain		**17,020**

Indexation should be applied to the original costs of purchase and not to the unindexed gain, **this is an easy error to make**.

The indexation factor for the period concerned will be given to you in an assessment, you will not be expected to look it up.

Activity 7.2

Kallistow Limited purchased an asset on 15 August 2010 for £35,000. The asset was sold for £53,000 on 30 April 2024.

Calculate the chargeable gain arising on the sale of the asset and complete the computation table. Indexation factors: August 2010 to December 2017 = **0.239**.

Chargeable gains computation	£
Disposal proceeds	
Less: incidental cost of disposal	
Net sale proceeds	
Less original costs for acquisition	
Less cost of enhancements	
Less incidental cost of acquisition	
Unindexed gain/loss	
Indexation allowance on original costs	
Indexation allowance on enhancement	
Indexed chargeable gain	

Incidental costs of disposal and acquisition

Disposal incidental costs could include marketing costs, transportation costs, legal fees, advertising, etc. applicable to the disposal and sale of the asset.

Acquisition incidental costs are the expenses incurred for professional and legal fees like surveyors and auctioneer's costs and costs for conveyancing for the original purchase of the asset.

These incidental costs **are allowable** and are part of the chargeable gain calculations.

Example 7.3

Humbriele Limited purchased a chargeable asset in January 2011 for £33,700. Legal fees incurred on the purchase were £600 extra. In June 2024 they advertised the chargeable asset for sale and advertising costs were £120. Disposal costs were for transportation of the chargeable asset to the buyer at a cost of £750 and sale proceeds were £45,000. The indexation factor from January 2011 to December 2017 is **0.214**.

Complete the chargeable gains computation rounding up where required and not giving any decimal places (e.g. 7340.2 becomes 7,340 but 7340.6 would be 7,341):

Chargeable gains computation	£
Disposal proceeds	45,000
Less: incidental cost of disposal (750+120)	(870)
Net sale proceeds	**44,130**
Less original costs for acquisition	(33,700)
Less cost of enhancements	0
Less incidental cost of acquisition	(600)
Unindexed gain/loss	**9,830**
Indexation allowance on original costs 33,700+600 = 34,300 x **0.214**	(7,340)
Indexation allowance on enhancement	0
Indexed chargeable gain	**2,490**

Enhancement expenditure

Any enhancement expenditure must be 'capital' in nature and lead to an improvement in the asset, such as an extension to an existing building. This is a **further allowable cost** to the initial purchase price and causes a change to the calculation of the Indexation Allowance.

In these circumstances there is a requirement for two separate IA calculations:

1) Indexation arising from original acquisition date and value.
2) Indexation arising from enhancement changes date and value.

Example 7.4

Pheebee Limited purchased a shop in February 2005 for £70,000. Legal costs for the purchase amounted to £2,750. In June 2012 the company spent £4,800 on improvements to the shop.

1) The indexed rise from February 2005 to December 2017 is: 0.467
2) The indexed rise from June 2012 to December 2017 is: 0.150

In May 2024 they had outgrown the shop premises and sold it for £184,500 which *included* legal costs of £4,000. Round answers to the nearest whole number and do not use decimal places within the calculations.

Chargeable gains computation	£
Disposal proceeds	188,500
Less: incidental cost of disposal	(4,000)
Net sale proceeds	**184,500**
Less original costs for acquisition	(70,000)
Less cost of enhancements	(4,800)
Less incidental cost of acquisition	(2,750)
Unindexed gain/loss	**106,950**
1) Indexation allowance on original costs 70,000+2,750 = 72,750 x 0.467	(33,974)
2) Indexation allowance on enhancement 4,800 x 0.150	(720)
Indexed chargeable gain	**72,256**

Activity 7.3

Neireid Limited purchased a chargeable asset in August 1999 for £22,000 incurring legal fees on the purchase of £550.

The company enhanced the asset with an allowable amount of £4,000 in December 2006.

The asset was sold on disposal in July 2024 for £52,000 incurring legal fees on the sale of £1,600.

IA August 1999 – December 2017: 0.680
IA December 2006 December 2017: 0.372

Complete the chargeable gains table showing the gain on disposal:

Chargeable gains computation	£
Disposal proceeds	
Less: incidental cost of disposal	
Net sale proceeds	
Less original costs for acquisition	
Less cost of enhancements	
Less incidental cost of acquisition	
Unindexed gain/loss	
Indexation allowance on original costs	
Indexation allowance on enhancement	
Indexed chargeable gain	

Indexation cannot be used to turn a gain into a loss and is not available where there is an unindexed loss.

Example 7.5

CAF Ltd is selling a manufacturing machine in July 2024. The machine was purchased in July 1996 for £20,000 and the following are possible proceeds of sale:

a) £50,000
b) £23,000
c) £15,000

Calculate the possible gain or loss for each of these proceeds.

The indexation factor from July 1996 to December 2017 is **0.825**

a) 50,000

Chargeable gains computation		£
Disposal proceeds		50,000
Net sale proceeds		**50,000**
Less original costs for acquisition		(20,000)
Unindexed gain/loss		**30,000**
Indexation allowance on original costs	20,000 x 0.825	(16,500)
Indexed chargeable gain		**13,500**

b) £23,000

Chargeable gains computation		£
Disposal proceeds		23,000
Net sale proceeds		**23,000**
Less original costs for acquisition		(20,000)
Unindexed gain/loss		**3,000**
Indexation allowance on original costs	20,000 x 0.825	(3,000)
Indexed chargeable gain		**0**

The indexation allowance on original costs of £16,500 is restricted to £3,000 because the indexation cannot create a loss.

c) £15,000

Chargeable gains computation	£
Disposal proceeds	15,000
Net sale proceeds	**15,000**
Less original costs for acquisition	(20,000)
Unindexed gain/loss	**(5,000)**
Indexation allowance on original costs	0
Indexed chargeable gain	**(5,000)**

There is no indexation allowance applicable because indexation cannot increase a loss.

Net chargeable gains

When all of the individual gains and losses have been calculated they should be summarised and then the total of the chargeable gain summary will be entered into the corporation tax computation template. An annual exemption does not apply to companies.

Summary of net chargeable gains	£
1) Chargeable gain	X
2) Chargeable gain	X
3) Chargeable gain	X
Gross chargeable gains current CAP period	**X**
4) Allowable loss	(X)
Net chargeable gains/(losses) current CAP period	**X**
Less: Capital losses b/f previous period	(X)
Net chargeable gains	**X**

Example 7.6

Chargeable accounting period (CAP) ending 31 March 2025. The business had four asset disposals during the accounting period up to the end of March 2025. Three chargeable gains, one for £35,200, one for £17,020 and one for £2,490 and an allowable loss of £5,000. The business also had capital losses b/f of £14,500.

To calculate the net chargeable gain:

Chargeable accounting period ending 31 March 2025	£
1) Chargeable gain	35,200
2) Chargeable gain	17,020
3) Chargeable gain	2,490
Gross chargeable gains current CAP period	54,710
4) Allowable loss	(5,000)
Net chargeable gains/(losses) current CAP period	**49,710**
Less: Capital losses b/f previous period	(14,500)
Net chargeable gains	**35,210**

The net chargeable gain will be entered into the CT computation.

Corporation Tax computation	
	£
Trading profit (trading income)	
Add:	
Non-trade Interest	
Property Income	
Chargeable gains	**35,210**
Total profits	
Less:	
Qualifying charitable donations	
Taxable total profits (TTP)	

The corporation tax liability is then calculated in the normal way at the relevant rate.

Any losses would be carried forward to be offset against future **chargeable gains.**

On the CT600 tax return, the chargeable gains section is covered in Boxes **210 – 220**.

Box 210 will give the gross chargeable gains.

Box 215 will give the allowable losses including losses brought forward

Box 220 will show the net chargeable gains being box 210 less box 215

Using the above figures in Example 5.9 the boxes would be completed as follows:

Chargeable gains	
210 **Gross chargeable gains**	£ 54710.00
215 **Allowable losses including losses brought forward**	£ 19500.00
220 **Net chargeable gains** - box 210 minus box 215	£ 35210.00

Activity 7.4

Kayle Limited had three asset disposals during the accounting period up to the end of March 2025. Two chargeable gains, one for £15,000 and one for £11,600 and an allowable loss of £3,000.

Kayle Limited had allowable capital losses brought forward of £2,300.

a) How much net chargeable gain/(loss) will be included in the CT calculation for the year ending 31 March 2025?

Chargeable accounting period ending 31 March 2025	£
1) Chargeable gain	
2) Chargeable gain	
Gross chargeable gains current CAP period	
3) Allowable loss	
Net chargeable gains/(losses) current CAP period	
Less: Capital losses b/f previous period	
Net chargeable gains	

b) Complete the relevant boxes in the CT600 return.

Chargeable gains	
210 **Gross chargeable gains**	£ .00
215 **Allowable losses including losses brought forward**	£ .00
220 **Net chargeable gains** - box 210 minus box 215	£ .00

Replacement of business assets (Rollover) relief

Individuals and companies may be able to delay paying tax on gains if they sell certain business assets, and then use all or part of the proceeds from that sale to buy other **qualifying** new assets. This is referred to as **Rollover Relief** and it is available to assist individuals and companies to defer a chargeable gain. Rollover relief will only be examined for a **limited company** in AAT assessments for Business Tax FY2024.

The replacement new asset does not necessarily have to be the same as the original old asset type. For instance, initially selling a fixed piece of production plant to then using the proceeds for the purchase of a building.

Relief can also be claimed where the business is **planning** to buy new assets with the proceeds but hasn't yet done so, or where the proceeds are used to improve assets which are already owned by the business.

The new assets must be bought **within 3 years** of selling or disposing of the old ones, or up to **one year before**. The business must actually be trading at the time when the old assets are sold and the new ones bought, and both the old and new assets must be used in the trade of the business (but can be different types of trade).

Relief can be claimed on qualifying assets such as:

- Land and buildings.
- **Fixed** plant and machinery.
- Goodwill (individuals only).

Shares in a company and buildings rented out to tenants are **not** classified as qualifying assets.

If "Business Asset (Rollover) Relief" is claimed, any tax owing on the gain from the disposal of the original asset is 'rolled over' (i.e. deferred) until the replacement asset is sold at some point in the future.

You must claim rollover relief within 4 years of the end of the tax year that the new asset was acquired.

There are **different rules** if only part of the proceeds from selling the old assets are reinvested (partial reinvestment) if the old assets were only partly used in the business or if the proceeds are used to buy 'depreciating assets' (fixed plant or machinery, or assets expected to last for less than 60 years).

In the case of a short leasehold property with a lease of less than 60 years, this would be classified as a depreciating asset (predictable life of less than 60 years) and the base cost of the property would not be adjusted.

The chargeable gain would then be held over for **10 years from the date of acquisition**, the date the property is sold, or the date that it is no longer used in the business.

Example 7.7

Niphe Limited purchased a building in March 2008 for £130,000 which was used for trading purposes. They decided to sell this building in October 2024 for £375,000, as they did not efficiently use it for the business any more. They required the proceeds from the sale to be used to purchase a production machine in January 2025. The indexation factor from March 2008 to December 2017 is 0.311.

a) Calculate the gain on disposal of the original building purchased in March 2008.

From this calculation, the chargeable gain before any available reliefs for reinvestment is £204,570. In normal circumstances, corporation tax would be applied to this gain at the relevant rate.

Chargeable gains computation on old asset	£
Net sale proceeds	**375,000**
Less original costs for acquisition	(130,000)
Unindexed gain/loss	**245,000**
Indexation allowance on original costs 130,000 x 0.311	(40,430)
Indexed chargeable gain before reliefs	**204,570**

b) Calculate the revised base cost of the **new** production machine where the new machine costs **£400,000**.

In this instance all of the sale proceeds from the original asset (£375,000) are being reinvested so there is a **full** "rollover relief" applied and the chargeable gain of £204,570 is not immediately taxable. The revised base cost of £195,430 will be used to calculate any gains if the new asset is sold in the future and indexation will be calculated on the base cost and not the actual cost.

Revision of base cost of new production machine	£
Original cost	400,000
Less rollover relief from a) above	(204,570)
Revised base cost	**195,430**

The full rollover of £204,570 is claimed from the original asset and the **old** asset computation now gives a **NIL** balance.

Chargeable gains computation on old asset	£
Disposal proceeds	375,000
Net sale proceeds	**375,000**
Less original costs for acquisition	(130,000)
Unindexed gain/loss	**245,000**
Indexation allowance on original costs 130,000 x 0.311	(40,430)
Indexed chargeable gain before reliefs	**204,570**
Less: Rollover relief	(204,570)
Chargeable gain	**NIL**

c) Calculate the base cost of the new production machine where the **new** machine only costs **£350,000**.

In this instance, not all of the proceeds from the sale of the old asset are used to purchase the new asset. As the proceeds that are not invested (£25,000) are lower than the whole of the chargeable gain (£204,570), there will be less rollover relief to be claimed.

Disposal proceeds are £375,000 and the new asset is now £350,000, therefore £25,000 will be the value of the proceeds not invested on the sale of the old asset and the rollover relief will be £204,570 less £25,000 = **£179,570.**

Revision of base cost of new production machine	£
Original cost	350,000
Less partial rollover relief £204,570 - £25,000	(179,570)
Revised base cost	**170,430**

In this instance, the original computation for the disposal of the original asset shows a chargeable gain to be taxed of **£25,000**.

Chargeable gains computation on old asset	£
Net sale proceeds	**375,000**
Less original costs for acquisition	(130,000)
Unindexed gain/loss	**245,000**
Indexation allowance on original costs 130,000 x 0.311	(40,430)
Indexed chargeable gain before reliefs	**204,570**
Less: Partial Rollover Relief	(179,570)
Chargeable gain	**25,000**

d) Calculate the base cost of the new production machine where the new machine now costs **£165,000**.

In this instance, not all of the proceeds from the sale are used to purchase the new asset, which gives rise to an immediate gain. As the proceeds that are not invested are more than the whole of the chargeable gain, there will **not** be any rollover relief applied.

Proceeds that are not invested £375,000 - £165,000 = £210,000
Whole of the chargeable gain = £204,570

The gain that is chargeable is now the lower of the two being **£204,570.** The base cost of the new asset remains at £165,000 and the chargeable gain on the old asset remains at £204,570.

Revision of base cost of new production machine	£
Original cost	165,000
Rollover relief balance	NIL
Revised base cost	**165,000**

Chargeable gains computation on old asset	£
Net sale proceeds	**375,000**
Less original costs for acquisition	(130,000)
Unindexed gain/loss	**245,000**
Indexation allowance on original costs 130,000 x 0.311	(40,430)
Indexed chargeable gain before reliefs	**204,570**
Less: Rollover relief	NIL
Chargeable gain	**204,570**

Activity 7.5

Borred Limited purchased fixed plant (qualifying business asset) for £185,000 in September 1999 and sold it for £450,000 in May 2024 incurring incidental costs on disposal of £150 and generating a chargeable gain before reliefs of £140,345.

Chargeable gains computation	£
Disposal proceeds	450,000
Less: incidental cost of disposal	150
Net sale proceeds	**449,850**
Less original costs for acquisition	(185,000)
Unindexed gain/loss	**264,850**
Indexation allowance on original costs 185,000 x 0.673	(124,505)
Indexation allowance on enhancement	0
Indexed chargeable gain before reliefs	**140,345**

Borred Limited purchased a new building in April 2024 for £415,000 (qualifying business asset).

Calculate the value of the rollover relief available (if applicable) and complete the base cost of the new asset and any chargeable gains on the old asset.

Revision of base cost of new production machine	£
Original cost	
Less partial rollover relief	
Revised base cost	

Chargeable gains computation	£
Indexed chargeable gain before reliefs	
Less: Partial Rollover Relief	
Chargeable gain	

Share disposals

For calculating chargeable gains when it comes to the disposal of shares and securities there are **matching rules** to be followed for limited companies. Disposals are matched against purchases on the basis of:

1. Shares purchased on the **same day** as the disposal
2. Shares purchased within **nine days prior** to the disposal (referred to as the 9-day rule, first in, first out basis)
3. Shares in the 1985 (FA85) pool or 'share pool'

These rules exist so that it can be determined which actual shares have been sold and how allowable costs and indexation allowances can be calculated and deducted from the proceeds of the sale. This is to stop businesses selling and rebuying shares in short periods of time to reduce taxation.

When the disposals are matched with either rule number 1 (same day) or rule number 2 (nine days prior), then there is **no indexation allowance to be applied.**

Example 7.8

Codd Limited made 3 purchases of shares in Basse Limited over a period of 10 years.

Date purchased	Quantity of shares	Total Value £	Each £
1 October 1997	600	2,400	4.00
15 February 2000	400	1,800	4.50
5 July 2007	700	3,010	4.30

Within 2024, 200 of these shares are sold but the uncertainty is, it is not known which 200 shares have been disposed of. It could be any of the quantity of shares purchased over the 10 years, which all have various values.

This is where the matching rules apply and as none of the shares match purchases on the same day or against purchases made within nine days prior to the disposal, the 1985 share pool would apply.

The pool would consist of 600 + 400 + 700 = 1,700 shares in the pool and the 200 disposed of would be from this pool of 1,700.

Principles of operating the share pool

The pool holds shares purchased from 1 April 1982. (Shares purchased before this date will not be included in this material). Indexation is applied in the same way as when calculating other chargeable gains from the date of purchase until 31 December 2017 (when it was frozen). This indexation is referred to as an **"indexed rise"** rather than an allowance. Any new event like a purchase, or sale disposal is referred to as an **"operative event".**

The following template can be followed for the workings of the pool. More rows can be added depending on how many changes of purchases, sales and disposals of shares are required to be recorded and re-indexed. Whenever a new event happens a re-indexing rise value will be required to be calculated on the new totals.

Events	Number	Cost £	Indexed cost £
Purchase	X	X	X
Index to next event			X
Record event (purchase)	X	X	X
	X	X	X
Index to next event			X
	X	X	X
Record event (sale)	(X)	(X)	(X)
Pool c/f	X	X	X

Example 7.9

Playce Ltd has sold **6,000** shares in Turbut Limited for **£30,000** on 1 March 2025. These shares had previously been purchased as follows:

Date purchased	Quantity of shares	Total Value £
1 June 2001	2,000	4,000
1 October 2011	2,000	5,000
28 February 2025	1,000	2,400
1 March 2025	3,000	12,000
	8,000	**23,400**

Step 1. The first matching rule applies to the 3,000 shares purchased on 1 March 2025 for £12,000, the same day as the disposal of 6,000 shares.

To calculate the first chargeable gain, you take the quantity of shares purchased from 1 March 2025 being 3,000 and divide this by the total amount of shares being sold of 6,000 and multiply this by the total amount received for 6,000 sold being £30,000. This then gives the sale proceeds applicable to the 3,000 only. Then deduct the allowable cost which is the original cost of purchase of the 3,000 being sold being £12,000.

3,000/6,000 = 0.5 x £30,000 = £15,000 – £12,000 = **£3,000 chargeable gain.**

Chargeable gains computation	£
Total disposal proceeds £30,000 Sale proceeds for 3,000/6,000 x £30,000	15,000
Less original costs for acquisition of 3,000	(12,000)
Chargeable gain first matching rule 3,000 shares	**3,000**

Step 2. The second matching rule applies to the 1,000 shares purchased on 28 February 2025, as these were purchased within the **9 days prior** to the disposal on 1 March 2025.

To calculate the second chargeable gain, you take the quantity of shares purchased from 28 February 2025 being 1,000 and divide this by the total amount of shares sold being 6,000 and multiply this by the total amount received for 6,000 sold being £30,000. This then gives the sale proceeds applicable to the 1,000 only. Then deduct the allowable cost which is the original cost of purchase of the 1,000 being sold being £2,400.

1,000/6,000 = 0.16666666666 x £30,000 or 1/6 of £30,000 = £5,000.

Chargeable gains computation	£
Total disposal proceeds £30,000 Sale proceeds for 1,000/6,000 x £30,000	5,000
Less original costs for acquisition	(2,400)
Chargeable gain second matching rule 1,000 shares	**2,600**

Step 3. The last 2,000 shares will come from the **share pool** which consists of:

1 October 2011 2,000 @ £5,000
1 June 2001 2,000 @ £4,000
Total 4,000 shares in the share pool

The share pool disposals will have an Indexation rise to be applied and the indexation factors to be used are:

1. June 2001 – October 2011 - **0.304**
2. October 2011 – December 2017 - **0.168**

In an exam situation, you will be given the relevant indexation factors for calculations as these have now been archived in the National Archives.

Using the template provided enter the **first event** which is the initial purchase of 2,000 shares in June 2001 at a cost of £4,000 into the share pool.

Events	Number	Cost £	Indexed cost £
Purchase June 2001	**2,000**	**4,000**	**4,000**

The next step is to apply the indexation factor relevant to this purchase. £4,000 x 0.304 = £1,216.

Events	Number	Cost £	Indexed cost £
Purchase June 2001	2,000	4,000	4,000
Index to next event 1. 0.304			**1,216**

The next purchase made in October 2011 is then added to the table as the next event and all columns re-totalled.

Events	Number	Cost £	Indexed cost £
Purchase June 2001	2,000	4,000	4,000
Index to next event 1. 0.304			1,216
Purchase October 2011	**2,000**	**5,000**	**5,000**
	4,000	**9,000**	**10,216**

It is this new total that is then re-indexed to the next indexation rate of 0.168. **£10,216** x 0.168 = £1,716 and the columns re-totalled. Do not use the cost figure of £9,000 – it must be **the indexed cost figure** used for the indexation rise calculation.

Events	Number	Cost £	Indexed cost £
Purchase June 2001	2,000	4,000	4,000
Index to next event 1. 0.304			1,216
Purchase October 2011	2,000	5,000	5,000
	4,000	9,000	10,216
Index to next event 2. 0.168			**1,716**
	4,000	**9,000**	**11,932**

To record the sale from the share pool:

6,000 total shares sold on 1 March 2025 less 3,000 matched same day, less 1,000 matched under 9-day rule = **2,000 required from the share pool.** This is a straightforward half of the total shares in the share pool, but if required the calculation would be:

2,000/4,000 x cost £9,000 = **£4,500 cost**

2,000/4,000 x indexed cost £11,932 = **£5,966 indexed cost**

When these have been deducted the pool is totalled for a c/f balance.

This then leaves 2,000 shares in the share pool at an indexed cost of £5,966.

Events	Number	Cost £	Indexed cost £
Purchase June 2001	2,000	4,000	4,000
Index to next event 1. 0.304			1,216
Purchase October 2011	2,000	5,000	5,000
	4,000	9,000	10,216
Index to next event 2. 0.168			1,716
	4,000	9,000	11,932
Sale 01/3/25	**(2,000)**	**(4,500)**	**(5,966)**
Pool c/f	**2,000**	**4,500**	**5,966**

Step 4. To calculate the chargeable gain of the **2,000 shares** purchased **from the share pool**:

Chargeable gains computation	£
Total disposal proceeds £30,000 Sale proceeds for 2,000/6,000 x £30,000	10,000
Less allowable costs £4,500	(4,500)
Unindexed gain	**5,500**
****Less** Indexation allowance £5,966-£4,500 =	**(1,466)**
Chargeable gain	**4,034**

** The indexation allowance for the shares sold is the difference between the indexed cost of £5,966 and the actual cost (£4,500).

The indexation allowance cannot create a loss or increase a loss.

Step 5. Once all of the calculations have been done for matching rules 1, 2 and 3 the total chargeable gains on disposal of the 6,000 shares on 1 March 2025 can be added up.

£3,000 + £2,600 + £4,034 = £9,634 total chargeable gains on sale of 6,000 shares.

Example 7.10

Pyke Ltd sold 6,000 shares in Karp Ltd for £40,000 on 2 February 2025. The shares in Karp Ltd were purchased as follows:

Date purchased	Quantity of shares	Total Value £
01/07/1999	2,000	4,500
01/09/2009	2,000	5,000
27/01/2025	1,000	2,500
02/02/2025	3,000	11,000

The first matching rule applies to the 3,000 purchased on 2 February 2025 for £11,000.

Chargeable gains computation	£
Total disposal proceeds £40,000 Sale proceeds for 3,000/6,000 x £40,000	20,000
Less original costs for acquisition of 3,000	(11,000)
Chargeable gain first matching rule 3,000 shares	**9,000**

The second matching rule applies to the 1,000 purchased on 27 January 2025 for £2,500.

Chargeable gains computation	£
Total disposal proceeds £40,000 Sale proceeds for 1,000/6,000 x £40,000	6,667
Less original costs for acquisition of 1,000	(2,500)
Chargeable gain second matching rule 1,000 shares	**4,167**

The last 2,000 sold will be taken from the share pool. Indexation allowance factors are:

- July 1999 to Sept 2009 **0.304**
- Sept 2009 to Dec 2017 **0.292**

Events	Number	Cost £	Indexed cost £
Purchase July 1999	2,000	4,500	4,500
Index to next event 1. 0.304			1,368
Purchase Sept 2009	2,000	5,000	5,000
	4,000	9,500	10,868
Index to next event 2. 0.292			3,173
	4,000	9,500	14,041
Sale 02/2/25	**(2,000)**	**(4,750)**	**(7,021)**
Pool c/f	**2,000**	**4,750**	**7,020**

Chargeable gains computation	£
Total disposal proceeds £40,000 Sale proceeds for 2,000/6,000 x £40,000	13,333
Less allowable costs £4,750	(4,750)
Unindexed gain	**8,583**
Less Indexation allowance £7,021-£4,750 =	**(2,271)**
Chargeable gain	**6,312**

Total chargeable gains on the 6,000 share disposals are £9,000 + £4,167 + £6,312 = **£19,479.**

Activity 7.6

Bhril Limited sold 5,000 shares in Macheril Limited for £30,000 on 15 February 2025.

Share purchases have been made from July 2000 until February 2025.

Date purchased	Quantity of shares	Total Value £
01/07/00	3,000	6,000
01/12/15	3,000	7,000
08/02/25	1,500	5,000
15/02/25	2,000	6,000

a) Complete the chargeable gain for any first matching rules:

Chargeable gains computation	£
Total disposal proceeds £30,000	
Less original costs for acquisition	
Chargeable gain	

b) Complete the chargeable gain for any second matching rules:

Chargeable gains computation	£
Total disposal proceeds £30,000	
Less original costs for acquisition	
Chargeable gain	

c) Complete the share pool calculations showing the purchases and sales including re-indexing.

Index rate from July 2000 – December 2015 **0.528**

Index rate from December 2015 – December 2017 **0.067**

Events	Number	Cost £	Indexed cost £
Purchase			
Index to next event			
Purchase			
Index to next event			
Sale			
Pool c/f			

d) Complete the chargeable gains computation for the shares from the share pool

Chargeable gains computation	£
Total disposal proceeds £30,000	
Less original costs for acquisition	
Chargeable gain	
Indexation allowance	
Chargeable gain	

e) What are the total chargeable gains on the complete 5,000 shares disposal?

Other types of acquisition – rights issues and bonus issues

A **Rights Issue** is an issue of new shares by a company which are initially made available to existing shareholders in proportion to their existing shareholding. Rights Issues are first offered to existing shareholders at a discounted rate, and the shareholders have the option to take up the issue or decline it. Any shares which are declined are subsequently sold to the general public at an undiscounted price.

A **Rights Issue** is therefore a way of raising finance for a company by offering new shares to existing shareholders at a reduced price. There is a maximum number of Rights Issue shares which any investor can buy based on the number of shares they already owned at the time of the Issue. This is expressed in the form **"an X for Y Rights Issue"** - for example, a **1 for 5 Rights Issue** means each shareholder is entitled to buy a maximum of **1** new share for every **5** shares they own at the time of the Issue being made.

A **Bonus Issue** is similar to a Rights Issue, in that it is an issue of new shares by a company which are initially made available to existing shareholders in a designated ratio to their existing shareholding. However, bonus issues are **free issues of shares** - there is no cost attached to the shares for the shareholder – they are effectively given free shares. Companies may do this for a number of reasons, but the most common one is to enable them to restructure the equity section of their balance sheet.

With rights and bonus issues, there is always a new acquisition of shares. However, when matching, the acquisitions apply to the original shareholdings.

Example 7.11

Westons Ltd acquired shares in Marcle Ltd as follows:

Date purchased	Quantity of shares	Total Value £
July 1994	3,000	17,250
November 1995	1 for 2 bonus issues	
January 2002	1 for 4 rights issue at £4 share	
January 2025	Sold 2,600 shares	£32,000

Matching would be applied as follows:

Events	Number of shares
Purchase July 1994	3,000
November 1995 bonus issue 1 for 2. 1 / 2 x 3,000	1,500
January 2002 rights issue 1 for 4	**4,500**
1 / 4 x 4,500	1,125
	5,625
Sale January 2025	(2,600)
Pool c/f	**3,025**

With the issue of bonus shares, there **will not** be an operative event as there is no cost involved. The bonus shares are added to the shares already in the pool. When the next event happens, indexation would be done from the operative event prior to the bonus issue (being July 1994).

Events	Number	Cost £	Indexed cost £
Purchase July 1994	3,000	17,250	17,250
Nov 1995 bonus issue1 / 2 x £3,000	**1,500**	**NIL**	**NIL**
	4,500	17,250	17,250

As the rights issue **does** involve cost, there **will** be an operative event and the rights issue should be recorded as a normal purchase in the share pool. The indexed rise from July 1994 to January 2002 is 0.199 and from January 2002 to December 2017 is 0.605.

Events	Number	Cost £	Indexed cost £
Purchase July 1994	3,000	17,250	17,250
November 1995 bonus issue 1 / 2 x £3,000	1,500	NIL	NIL
	4,500	17,250	17,250
Indexed rise to Jan 2002 £17,250 x 0.199			3,433
	4,500	17,250	20,683
Rights issue 1 for 4 @ £4 share	**1,125**	**4,500**	**4,500**
	5,625	**21,750**	**25,183**
Indexed rise to Dec 2017 £25,183 x 0.605			15,236
	5,625	**21,750**	**40,419**

Workings for the sale of shares allocation of costs would be:

2,600 / 5,625 x £21,750 = £10,053

2,600 / 5,625 x £40,419 = £18,683

Events	Number	Cost £	Indexed cost £
Purchase July 1994	3,000	17,250	17,250
November 1995 bonus issue 1 / 2 x £3,000	1,500	NIL	NIL
	4,500	17,250	17,250
Indexed rise to Jan 2002 £17,250 x 0.199			3,433
	4,500	17,250	20,683
Rights issue 1 for 4 @ £4 share	1,125	4,500	4,500
	5,625	21,750	25,183
Indexed rise to Dec 2017 £25,183 x 0.605			15,236
	5,625	21,750	40,419
Sale January 2025	**(2,600)**	**(10,053)**	**(18,683)**
Pool c/f	**3,025**	**11,697**	**21,736**

Chargeable gains computation	£
Total disposal proceeds	32,000
Less allowable costs	(10,053)
Unindexed gain	**21,947**
Less Indexation allowance £18,683 - £10,053 =	**(8,630)**
Chargeable gain	**13,317**

Activity 7.7

On 21 September 2024, Ross Ltd sold 2,000 shares in Yat Ltd for £6,000. The previous share transactions were:

Date purchased	Quantity of shares	Total Value £
June 2004 pool b/f	2,000 shares, £4,000 qualifying costs	5,250 Indexed costs
5 May 2005	1 for 2 bonus issue	
20 Feb 2006	1 for 5 rights issue at £2.50 share	
21 Sept 2024	Sold 2,000 shares	£6,000

The indexed rise from June 2004 to Feb 2006 is 0.038, and from February 2006 to December 2017 is 0.432. What is the chargeable gain on the disposal of the 2,000 shares sold on 21 September 2024?

Events	Number	Cost £	Indexed cost £
Pool b/f June 2004			
May 2005 bonus issue			
Indexed rise to Feb 2006			
Rights issue 1 for 5			
Indexed rise to Dec 2017			
Sale September 2024			
Pool c/f			

Chargeable gains computation	£
Total disposal proceeds	
Less allowable costs	
Unindexed gain	
Less Indexation allowance	
Chargeable gain	

Summary of Chapter 7

- There is no indexation allowance for individuals, just for companies.
- A chargeable gain arises on the disposal of a chargeable asset.
- The indexation allowance was frozen in December 2017.
- Enhancement costs can be utilised and indexed individually from the month the cost is incurred (or to Dec 2017).
- Rollover relief is available to companies.
- Incidental costs are allowable and are part of the chargeable gains computation.
- The share matching rules for companies are same day acquisitions, previous 9 days acquisitions and shares in the 1985 share pool.
- A rights issue is an operative event, but a bonus issue is not.

Assessment 7

You are now required to log in to your ROGO account to complete your online assessment before progressing to the next chapter.

Chapter 8: Business disposals and capital gains for sole traders/partnerships

By the end of this chapter, you should:

- Understand the income tax and capital gains tax implications of disposing of an unincorporated business.

- Understand the capital gains tax reliefs on 'gift relief' and 'business asset disposal relief' on the disposal of:

    - An unincorporated business.
    - Shares in a personal company.

- Calculate capital gains on the disposal of:

    - Trade and assets.
    - Shares in a personal company.
    - Capital gains tax reliefs available on disposal of trade and assets.
    - Capital gains tax reliefs available on shares in a personal company.

- Calculate post-tax proceeds following a business disposal.

Introduction

This chapter considers the tax which can affect individuals trading as unincorporated businesses like sole traders and partnerships – **Capital Gains Tax**. Whereas income tax is a tax on income streams of the individual (i.e. regular incomes such as earnings from self-employment, employment or profits from property), Capital Gains Tax (CGT) is applied to one-off gains made on the disposal of an asset. In theory, the disposal of **any** asset potentially gives rise to a chargeable event.

DISPOSAL – a disposal arises when an asset is either:

- sold
- given away
- lost
- destroyed.

The most common situation in which a chargeable gain will occur is clearly when an asset is sold; however, where the disposal occurs on loss or destruction of the asset a chargeable event still arises, although the disposal proceeds (the value of the asset) will usually be nil unless there are proceeds from an insurance claim, in which case the disposal proceeds will be the value of the insurance claim.

Example 8.1

Mike Evans, a sole trader, sold a statue for £280,000 and an antique watch for £45,000 during 2024-25. He also lost a collection of postage stamps which were insured for £4,300, and accidentally destroyed a table worth £10,000 which was not insured.

What would be the disposal proceeds of each event?

Statue:	£280,000
Watch:	£45,000
Stamps:	£4,300
Table:	£NIL

Exempt from CGT items

Not all disposals will give rise to a chargeable event. The following disposals are exempt from CGT for sole traders and partnerships.

Transfers between spouses or civil partners
Husbands and wives, or civil partners, may transfer the ownership of assets between each other **without incurring** a CGT liability.

Principal Private Residences (PPR)
The main residential house of a taxpayer is generally **exempt from CGT** when it has been sold. This allows people to sell their main home for a gain without being taxed under CGT. There are some exceptions to these rules.

Cars
Almost all cars **are exempt** from CGT – this includes vintage and classic cars, but not single-seat sports cars, racing cars, taxis, vans and lorries.

Disposals after death
Disposals of assets which arise on the death of an individual **are exempt** from Capital Gains Tax (although they may be chargeable under Inheritance Tax which is not covered in this Business Tax unit).

Wasting Chattels
A **chattel** is a tangible, movable thing – they are things that you can see, touch and move; most personal property would be classed as chattels. A **wasting chattel** is one with an estimated remaining life of less than 50 years when it was first acquired by the individual. Certain chattels are always treated as wasting assets, for example, plant and machinery which are always treated as having a predictable life of less than 50 years. Wasting chattels **are exempt** from Capital Gains Tax and any losses on it will not be allowable. One reason for this is that HMRC do not want an individual to have masses of usable capital losses and they have offset this by saying that any capital gain (unlikely to arise) is exempt from CGT.

Chattels Bought and Sold for less than £6,000
Non-wasting Chattels (i.e. tangible, movable objects with a useful life of more than 50 years) are chargeable. Typically, this includes items such as antiques, works of art and jewellery. However, where the asset was both acquired for and sold for **less than £6,000**, the disposal **is exempt** from CGT.

Government Securities ('Gilts')
The disposal of these is specifically exempt from Capital Gains Tax.

Shares held in Individual Savings Accounts (ISAs)
We saw earlier that income from ISAs is exempt from Income Tax; in addition, any gains made on the disposal of shares which have been held in an ISA are also exempt from Capital Gains Tax.

Gifts to Charity
Gifts of assets to a registered charity are exempt from Capital Gains Tax

The disposal of any asset which is not included in the list above would potentially give rise to a chargeable event under Capital Gains Tax.

Example 8.2

Veronica made the following disposals in 2024-25.

- A racehorse for £48,000
- A hot tub for £3,800
- A necklace for £4,900 which originally cost £2,150
- A vintage car for £38,000

- Her only house, where she had lived for ten years
- A painting for £12,800 which had cost £20 at a car boot sale.

Which of these disposals give rise to a chargeable gain?

Only the disposal of the painting is chargeable to CGT. The first two disposals are both of wasting chattels; the necklace is a non-wasting chattel but was bought and sold for less than £6,000. Cars are specifically exempt from CGT, as are principal private residences. The painting is a non-wasting chattel with a disposal value of more than £6,000, and so is chargeable to CGT.

Calculating total gains/losses for CGT

The chargeable gain (i.e. the amount on which the taxpayer is taxed) for the disposal of an asset is calculated on the difference between the **disposal proceeds** (net of any disposal costs) and the **acquisition costs** (including any incidental costs of acquisition, and any subsequent enhancement expenditure).

Like the computation for a limited company for corporation tax, a separate computation must be carried out for **each** chargeable disposal which takes place during the tax year for an individual. Unlike an incorporated company calculation, individuals **are not entitled to an indexation allowance,** this was eliminated in 2008 for individuals and taper relief was introduced (covered in a later chapter under inheritance tax).

STEP 1: Identify the original acquisition cost.

STEP 2: Add any incidental costs of acquisition – including costs such as valuation fees, legal fees, transportation costs etc.

STEP 3: Identify the disposal proceeds.

STEP 4: Deduct any incidental costs of disposal – such as marketing costs, transportation costs, legal fees etc.

STEP 5: Calculate the chargeable gain.

The pro forma computation would therefore appear as follows:

Chargeable gains computation	£
Disposal proceeds	X
Less: incidental cost of disposal	(X)
Net sale proceeds	**X**
Less original costs for acquisition	(X)
Less cost of enhancements	(X)
Less incidental cost of acquisition	(X)
Gain/loss	**X/(X)**

Any enhancement expenditure must be 'capital' in nature and lead to an improvement in the asset, such as the professional restoration of an antique or an extension to a building.

Example 8.3

Violet sold an antique sideboard used in her sole trader business in 2024-25 for £47,000. She incurred auction fees of £5,600 in making the sale. She had originally bought the sideboard in 2010 for £8,700 and paid an additional £380 to have it delivered to her house. In 2013, she paid £6,100 having it professionally restored.

What would be Violet's chargeable gain on the disposal of the sideboard?

Chargeable gains computation	£
Disposal proceeds	47,000
Less: incidental cost of disposal	5,600
Net sale proceeds	**41,400**
Less original costs for acquisition	8,700
Less cost of enhancements	6,100
Less incidental cost of acquisition	380
Gain/loss	**26,220**

The disposal proceeds are usually taken to be the amount for which the asset was sold. However, there are some exceptions to this basic rule:

- If the asset has been **lost or destroyed** the disposal proceeds will be **nil.** The exception to this is where there is a successful insurance claim, in which case the proceeds of the claim will indicate the disposal proceeds for any CGT calculation.
- If the asset is **given away (gifted)** (to anyone except a spouse or civil partner, or a registered charity), or is sold at below the market value for the asset to a **connected person** (see information below), the **MARKET VALUE** of the asset must be used in the computation instead of the actual disposal proceeds.

All gains and losses in the tax year must be calculated separately. The gains are added together, and any losses made on individual disposals in the year are then deducted. Assuming the value of all gains is greater than the value of any losses, the net figure (i.e. total gains - total losses) is the net gain for the year.

Connected person

Special rules exist for disposals between **connected persons.** In any disposal between connected persons for less than the market value, the market value (rather than the actual proceeds) **must be** used in any CGT computation.

A taxpayer's "connected persons" include:

- **Ancestors** – parents, grandparents, great-grandparents
- **Spouse's Ancestors** – spouse's parents, grandparents, great-grandparents
- **Siblings** – brothers and sisters, as well as their spouses
- **Spouse's siblings** – spouse's brothers and sisters, as well as their spouses
- **Lineal descendants** – sons and daughters, grandchildren, great-grandchildren
- **Spouse's lineal descendants** – spouse's children, grandchildren etc

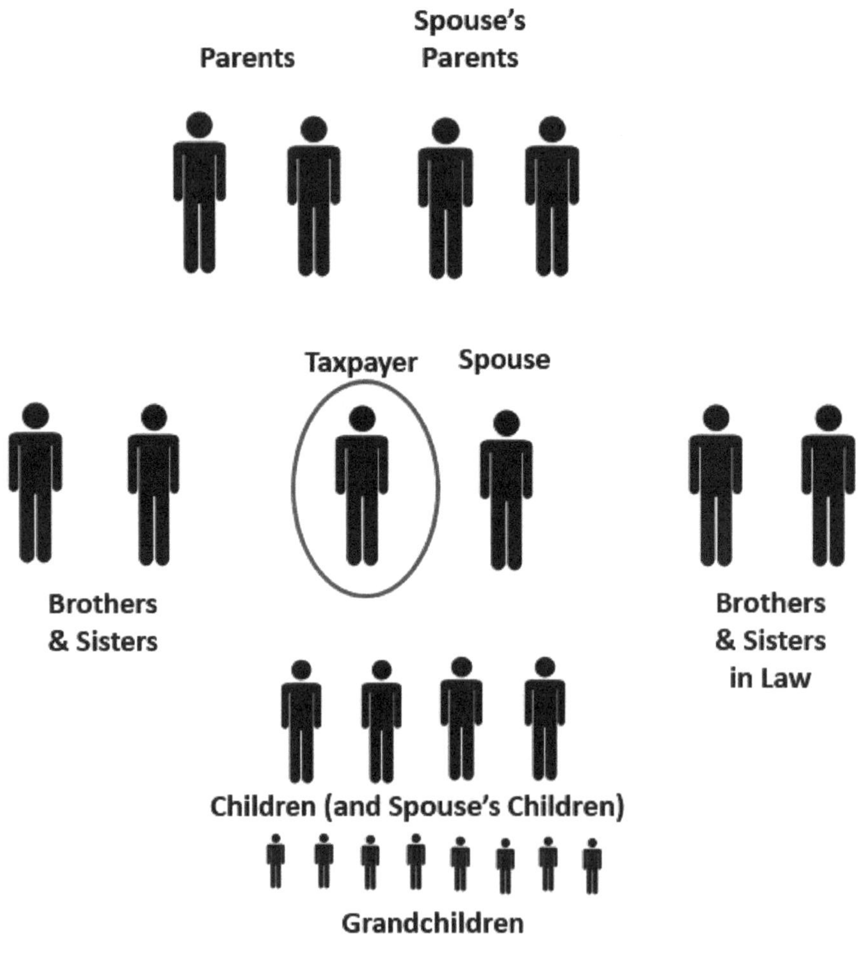

Any spouses of any of the above are also classed as a "connected person".

Business partners (and their spouses, partners and relatives) are also treated as connected persons.

The term "spouse" above means legal husband or wife; the same regulations apply to civil partners in all cases.

Example 8.4

Alfie sold the following items to members of his family in 2024-25 for amounts which were significantly **below market value**.

a. A picture to his nephew for £8,000 which was worth £12,800.
b. A signed 1966 World Cup winner's shirt for £300 to his brother-in-law. Similar shirts have sold for £7,000 at auction
c. An antique table to his wife's daughter (from a previous relationship) for £6,500 when it was worth £8,000.
d. A car to his cousin for £300 when it was worth £6,800.

What would be the correct value which would be included in CGT calculations for Alfie?

a. The nephew is not a connected person, so the proceeds of £8,000 would be used.
b. His brother-in-law is a connected person, so the market value (£7,000) would be used.
c. His wife's daughter is a connected person, so the market value of £8,000 would be used.
d. The car is an exempt asset for CGT purposes, so it is irrelevant whether the buyer is a connected person or not.

Spouses / Civil Partners

Any disposal between a husband and wife, or between civil partners, does not give rise to a chargeable disposal at that time. Instead, the transfer of assets is treated as a **no-gain, no-loss** transaction. The disposal proceeds are calculated as being just enough to create a zero gain on the disposal – meaning that the acquisition cost used for any subsequent disposal of the asset will remain the original acquisition cost.

Example 8.5

Margot transferred an asset to her civil partner Jane in 2024-25, she had originally bought it for £28,000 in 2015.

Disposal proceeds = £28,000. This creates a no-gain/no-loss situation.

If Jane subsequently sold the asset for £50,000, she will be able to claim the original cost of the asset to be £28,000 (even though she didn't actually pay anything for it herself). Her gain would therefore be (£50,000 - £28,000) = **£22,000.**

Annual exempt amount

Every individual taxpayer is allowed to make net gains up to the **Annual Exempt Amount (AEA)** each year without paying capital gains tax on those gains. In 2024-25 the AEA is **£3,000.**

Where the net gain is greater than the AEA of £3,000, only the difference will be taxed under CGT. Most Capital Gains are taxed at **10%** (basic) or **20%** (higher), depending on the individual's taxable income for that year.

Capital Gains are taxed **after** income has been taxed (covered in Chapter 1), so if the taxpayer has any basic rate band (normally up to £37,700 for 24/25) left then any gains up to this threshold are taxed at 10%. Once the threshold has been passed, however, any gains are taxed at 20%. If the taxpayer is already a higher rate (or additional rate) taxpayer then all gains will be taxed at 20%.

However, any gains on **property** (such as on the sale of a second home) are taxed at 18% in the basic rate and 28% in the higher rate bands.

Summary of net chargeable gains	**£**
Current year chargeable gains	X
Less current year allowable losses	(X)
Net chargeable gains/(losses)	**X**
Less: Annual exempt amount (AEA)	(X)
	X
Losses b/f from previous years	(X)
Taxable gains	**X**

Example 8.6

Vicky Regaisse made four gains in 2024-25, as follows:

Sale of a bronze statuette	£10,400
Sale of a coin collection	£ 8,250
Sale of shares	£ 1,890
Sale of a car	£ 1,800

She also made a loss of £4,880 on the sale of a diamond brooch.

The following calculations are required:

a) Calculate Vicky's net gain for 2024-25

b) Calculate Vicky's taxable gain for 2024-25

c) Calculate Vicky's CGT liability if her other taxable income for the year is:

i. £17,500
ii. £31,000
iii. £65,900

a)

Total Gains	£20,540	*(The gain on the sale of the car is exempt.)*
Total Losses	(£ 4,880)	
NET GAIN	**£15,660**	

b)

Net Gains	£15,660
AEA	(£ 3,000)
TAXABLE GAIN	**£12,660**

c)

i. £12,660 x 10% = **£1,266** *(All income and gains will be taxed at the basic rate.)*

ii.

£37,700 – £31,000 = £6,700 x 10% =	£ 670
£12,660 – £6,700 = 5,960 x 20% =	£1,192
	£1,862

iii. £12,660 x 20% = **£2,532**

In C ii, the chargeable gains take the taxpayer from the basic rate into the higher rate. There is £6,700 of unused basic rate band available after the income tax has been calculated – thus the first £6,700 of capital gains is taxed at 10%, with the remainder being taxed at the higher rate of 20%.

In C iii the whole gain will be taxed at 20% as Vicky would be a higher rate taxpayer.

CGT losses

Not all disposals of capital items will lead to a gain – some disposals will create a loss for the taxpayer.

We have already seen that individual losses are simply set off against other gains from the year – thereby reducing the overall gains for that tax year. Where the total losses for the year **exceed** the total gains, a net loss is made for the year. When this is the case, the treatment is as follows:

STEP 1: Set all losses in the current year against all gains in the current year, until the gains are reduced to £NIL. In this case, the Annual Exempt Allowance for the year in question **could be lost.**

STEP 2: Any excess loss after this is known as the **allowable loss**; it cannot be used to reduce other taxable income in the year (e.g. income from employment) but must be **carried forward** to be offset against chargeable gains in the future.

STEP 3: In future years, the allowable loss brought forward is used to reduce chargeable gains - **but only to the extent that chargeable gains are reduced to the Annual Exempt Amount for that year.** Brought forward capital losses are set off against gains after deducting the AEA, so the AEA is not wasted.

STEP 4: In future years, once the loss brought forward has been used to reduce gains to the AEA, if there is still some unused loss brought forward this is carried forward to future gains in future periods.

Example 8.7

Mercy Me, a sole trader business, made a net loss in the 2023-24 tax year of £8,700, and a chargeable gain in the 2024-25 tax year of £8,900.

The loss in 2023-24 is used as follows:

2023-24 Assessment = £NIL, Loss c/f = £8,700

2024-25 Gain = £8,900 – AEA £3,000 = gain of £5,900 less the loss c/f 8,700 = a loss to be c/f to 2025-26 of £2,800 (gain £5,900 – loss £8,700).

2025-26 Capital loss c/f £2,800

Summary of net chargeable gains	**£**
Current year chargeable gains	8,900
Less current year allowable losses	0
Net chargeable gains/(losses)	8,900
Less AEA	**(3,000)**
	5,900
Capital losses b/f	(5,900)
Taxable gains	**0**
Capital losses c/f to 2025/26 (£8,700 - £5,900)	£2,800

After deducting the AEA, only part of the capital losses b/f is being used to bring the gain for the year down. The remainder will be carried forward.

Example 8.8

Louisa made the following gains and losses in 2024-25.

Gain on sale of necklace	£ 5,500
Gain on sale of shares	£11,150
Gain on sale of car	£ 3,000
Loss on sale of picture	(£15,100)

She has a loss brought forward from 2023-24 of £9,250.

Louisa's CGT computation for 2024-25 is:

Summary of net chargeable gains	£
Current year chargeable gains	16,650
Less current year allowable losses	(15,100
Net chargeable gains/(losses)	1,550
Less AEA	**(3,000)**
	0
Capital losses b/f	0
Taxable gains	**0**
Capital losses c/f to 2025/26	**9,250**

Loss c/f to 2025-26 is £9,250 (i.e. the loss b/f from 2023-24).

Disposal of cars is exempt. Louisa must utilise any losses made in the year against any gains in the same year, leaving her with a net gain of £1,550. The AEA more than covers this amount of gain for the year, she will not have to pay any CGT for 2024-25. The remaining £1,450 (£3,000 – £1,550) of the AEA **will be lost** as HMRC does **not permit** any unused AEA to be carried forward to the following year.

Activity 8.1

Lawrence made the following gains and losses in 2024-25:

Gain on sale of antique rifle	£ 3,200
Gain on sale of shares	£13,270
Gain on sale of watch	£ 2,500
Loss on sale of diamond ring	(£14,180)

He has a loss brought forward from 2023-24 of £13,900.

Using the template provided, show Lawrence's CGT computation for 2024-25 and calculate any loss carried forward to 2025-26.

Summary of net chargeable gains	£
Current year chargeable gains	
Less current year allowable losses	
Net chargeable gains/(losses)	
Less AEA	
Capital losses b/f	
Taxable gains	
Capital losses c/f to 2025/26	

Chargeable Gains – reliefs for individuals

As well as rollover relief that applies to both companies and individuals, there are two other reliefs available to **individuals only** who run businesses (sole traders and partnerships).

Business Asset Disposal Relief

Business Asset Disposal Relief (BADR) can be claimed by an individual who is selling their business and is either a sole trader or a partner in a business partnership, who has owned the business for at least 2 years (24 months) before the date it is sold.

As well as selling a business you can claim business asset disposal relief if you are closing your business and then you must sell assets from it within three years of closing it down.

If an individual sells shares in a company in which they owned at least 5% of the shares and have owned them for at least 2 years prior to selling, they may be eligible to pay a reduced rate of Capital Gains Tax on any gains they make.

The Company must be a "personal trading company" and the individual must have voting rights as well as 5% of either:

- Profits that are available for distribution and assets on winding up the company
- Disposal proceeds if the company is sold.

If **all** of an individual's gains in a tax year qualify for BADR, then **all gains** are taxed at the lower rate of **10%**. For disposals on or after 11 March 2020, this will be limited to the **first £1million** of lifetime gains. The limit diminishes each time a claim for the relief has been made.

Where the taxpayer has other gains (i.e. which do not qualify for Business Assets Disposal Relief) then these would be taxed as normal – at 10% for basic rate taxpayers (18% for property gains) and 20% for higher rate taxpayers (28% for property gains).

The relief must be claimed by 31 January 2027 for a 2024/25 tax year and applied to the disposal of:

- The whole or part of a business carried on by an individual
- Assets of an individual in a trading business that has ceased
- Shares as long as the shares are in the individual's personal trading company and the individual is an employee of the company.

Taxing specific assets:

- Goodwill: Goodwill is an intangible asset and in the case of a sole trader or partnership, the sale of goodwill is a disposal of a capital asset. BADR may apply if conditions are met.
- Property: Gains on the sale of business premises are subject to CGT. Rollover relief may be available if reinvested.
- Plant & Machinery: Usually, these assets don't trigger CGT, as they are subject to capital allowances. However, if sold for more than their tax written down value, a balancing charge may arise, which is treated as income and will affect trading profit.

- Net current assets: Not chargeable for CGT. However, an adjustment is made to trading profit using market value. Where the MV exceeds cost, an increase will be made to trading profit and if the MV is less than cost, a reduction will be made to trading profit.

Example 8.9

Paulus is selling his sole trader business at which time his assets are valued below:

Asset	Market value £	Original cost £	TWDV £	Impact
Factory	180,000	120,000		Capital gain
Warehouse	110,000	120,000		Capital loss
Machinery	50,000	80,000	10,000	Increase trading profit
Goodwill	28,000	0		Capital gain
Inventory	8,000	10,000		Decrease trading profit

As the factory could be sold for £180,000, there will be a chargeable gain of £60,000.

As the warehouse could be sold for £110,000, there will be a capital loss of £10,000.

The machinery will have had capital allowances claimed against it. As the MV is greater than the TWDV by £40,000, there is a balancing charge adjustment which will increase trading profit.

As goodwill has been valued at £28,000, this will create a capital gain of £28,000.

As inventory is not a chargeable asset and the MV is less than cost, there will be a £2,000 decrease in trading profit.

Example 8.10

Grant King sells his manufacturing and retail business which he had owned for the last 8 years. The purchaser is a company in which Grant and his family have no interest. The following gains and losses are made on the business assets:

Factory premises	£1.45 million
Goodwill	£1.1 million
Retail shop loss	(£700,000)

The gains and losses on the factory premises, the goodwill and the shop are aggregated and will together qualify for Business Asset Disposal Relief but only on the first £1 million of gains, the remaining £850,000 will be subject to tax at the higher rate.

Example 8.11

Melania set up her unincorporated trading business in 1998 and in September 2024, she sold her business realising the following gains on the disposal of the business:

Factory	£225,000
Goodwill	£280,000
Warehouse	£175,000

In November 2024, Melania also sold a painting for a gain of £12,450.

Melania needs to calculate the capital gains tax payable for tax year 2024/25.

The factory, goodwill and warehouse are eligible for business asset disposal relief.

Total qualifying for BADR = £680,000 @ 10% CGT = **£68,000.**

The painting is eligible for AEA. £12,450 - £3,000 = £9,450 gain @ 20% CGT = **£1,890.** (This is taxed at 20% because the basic rate tax band would have been completely utilised by the gains for BADR).

Activity 8.2

Agnes sold her unincorporated business in the 2024/25 tax year and made a total gain on the assets of the business of £500,000. Capital losses brought forward from 2023/24 are £19,000.

How much of the gain on the sale of the business is taxed at 10%? Complete the workings template given below.

a) £500,000

b) £481,000

c) £478,000

d) £497,000

Summary of net chargeable gains	£
Chargeable gains	
Less: Annual exempt amount	
Chargeable gain after the AEA deduction	
Less capital losses b/f	
Taxable gains	

Example 8.12

Charles has calculated gains eligible for BADR of £30,000 and gains not eligible for BADR of £80,000. He has a taxable income of £25,000 and b/f capital losses of £7,400.

	Qualifying for BADR £	Not qualifying for BADR £	CGT due
Eligible gains	30,000		
Ineligible gains		80,000	
AEA		(3,000)	
Capital losses b/f		(7,400)	
Gains to be taxed	30,000	69,600	
BADR relief 10%	3,000		3,000
Higher rate band tax 20%		13,920	13,920
Total CGT due			**16,920**

There would be no lower basic rate band left after taxing income and the gain eligible for BADR being £25,000 and £30,000 = £55,000.

Activity 8.3

Carloz Saint disposed of his business on 21 September 2024, with a gain of £10,000 which qualifies for BADR. Other gains in the year that are not eligible for BADR are £42,750. Carloz also has a taxable income of £25,450.

Complete the template showing the total CGT payable by Carloz:

	Qualifying for BADR £	Not qualifying for BADR £	CGT due
Eligible gains			
Ineligible gains			
AEA			
Gains to be taxed			
BADR relief 10%			
Basic rate band 10%			
Higher rate band tax 20%			
Total CGT due			

Gift Relief (Holdover)

As mentioned previously when an asset is 'gifted' by an individual, the CGT rules require the gain to be calculated on the **market value** of the asset. However, hold-over relief may be claimed for gifts. This means that the individual person making the gift (donor) does not pay any tax on disposing of the asset, but instead passes on the gain to the person receiving the gift (receiver) and this gain is deducted from their base cost. The person receiving the gift will be responsible for paying CGT (if any is due) when they sell or dispose of the asset. The claim for gift relief must be made by both the donor and receiver. The asset must have been used for the purpose of the trade.

Example 8.13

	Donor £		Receiver £
Market value	60,000	Market value	60,000
Less: cost	(20,000)		
	40,000		
Less: gift relief	(40,000)	Less: held over gain	(40,000)
Chargeable gain	**NIL**	CGT base cost	**20,000**

To qualify for gift relief, the qualifying business assets would be:

- Used in a **trading** situation by the donor or their personal trading company (where the donor has at least 5% of the voting shares). There is no requirement for the donor to work for the company.
- Shares and securities in an unquoted trading company. There is no minimum shareholding requirement.
- Shares and securities in the donor's personal trading company.

Criteria would be:

- Gift relief requires both donor and receiver to make a joint claim
- Claim must be made by 5 April 2029 for tax year 24/25 (four years)

Example 8.14

A father has gifted the building that was used for his manufacturing business to his son on 21 June 2024, the market value of the building is £585.00. The building originally cost the father £175,000 when he purchased it in September 2005. As the building was used in the trade of the father and therefore the building is a qualifying asset, gift relief can be claimed.

If gift relief is claimed, the chargeable gain for the father and base cost for the son would be:

	Father £		Son £
Market value	585,000	Market value	585,000
Less: cost	(175,000)		
	410,000		
Less: gift relief	(410,000)	Less: held over gain	(410,000)
Chargeable gain	**NIL**	CGT base cost	**175,000**

Activity 8.4

Frances gave a shop that she used for her trade in cake making to her daughter Assisi when its market value was £215,000.

Frances purchased the shop for £122,000, ten years ago.

A valid qualifying gift relief claim is made.

1) Who must the gift relief claim be claimed by?

    a) Frances only

    b) Assisi only

    c) Both Frances and Assisi

2) What is the chargeable gain on disposal for Frances?

3) What is the base cost for Assisi?

	Frances £		Assisi £
Market value		Market value	
Less: cost			
Less: gift relief		Less: held over gain	
Chargeable gain		CGT base cost	

Example 8.15

River has run her sole trader business for over 12 years. At the end of December 2024, she decided to retire and gift her business to her daughter Phoenix.

River pays income tax at the higher rate and has not made any earlier capital disposals.

At 31 December 2024, the business assets were valued as:

	Market Value £	Original cost £	TWDV £	Capital Gain/loss £
Warehouse	150,000	50,000		100,000
Plant	25,000	35,000	1,500	0
Goodwill	50,000	0		50,000

What are the capital gains or losses that may arise on the disposal of each individual asset if no reliefs are claimed?

There has been a capital gain on the warehouse of £100,000. Market value £150,000 less original cost £50,000.

The plant is subject to capital allowances; therefore the £23,500 difference would increase trading profit and would not be a capital gain or loss.

There has been a capital gain on the goodwill of £50,000.

Shares in a personal company – gift relief

As mentioned earlier a personal company is one in which the donor holds at least 5% of the voting rights. For gift relief, there is no requirement for the taxpayer to be an employee of the company as in the case of BADR.

Gift relief **does require** a joint claim by both the donor and receiver.

Example 8.16

On 5 May 2024, Sebastian gave his 75% shareholding in his personal company (market value £2 million) to his son Teval.

The resulting gain for the purposes of CGT was £360,000.

If gift relief is claimed Sebastian's assessable gain would be NIL. Teval's base cost for the gifted shares would be £1,640,000.

	Sebastian £		Teval £
Market value	2,000,000	Market value	2,000,000
Less: cost	(1,640,000)		
Less: gift relief	(360,000)	Less: held over gain	(360,000)
Chargeable gain	**NIL**	CGT base cost	**1,640,000**

It is not a rule that gift relief must be claimed, but if it is it has to be claimed by both the donor and receiver.

Activity 8.5

Calculate the following CGTs where a) a claim for gift relief has been made and b) where a claim for gift relief has not been made.

Valerie Botts purchased 10,000 shares in an unquoted company for £40,000 in May 2011. Valerie gave these shares to Alison Fernandez in August 2024, when they were worth £75,000 at market value. Alison sold these shares in February 2025 for £88,000.

a) If gift relief is not claimed Valerie's chargeable gain would be **£** ....

Chargeable gains computation Valerie	£
Deemed sale proceeds at market value	
Less original costs for acquisition	
Gain/loss	

Alison's chargeable gain would be **£** ....

Chargeable gains computation Alison	£
Net sale proceeds	
Less original costs for acquisition (Market value)	
Gain/loss	

b) If gift relief is claimed Valerie's chargeable gain would be **£** ....

Alison's chargeable gain would be **£** ....

	Valerie £		Alison £
Market value		Market value	
Less: cost			
Less: gift relief		Less: held over gain	
Chargeable gain		CGT base cost	

Chargeable gains computation Alison	£
Net sale proceeds	
Less original costs for acquisition (Market value)	
Held over gift relief	
Gain/loss	

Summary of Chapter 8

- Wasting chattels are exempt assets.
- Disposals to connected persons are at market value.
- An annual exempt amount is allowable.
- Disposals between spouses or civil partners take place on a no-gain/no-loss basis.
- Business asset disposal relief is available to qualifying individuals.
- Gift relief is available to qualifying individuals.
- A personal company is one in which the donor holds at least 5% of the voting rights.

Assessment 8

You are now required to log in to your ROGO account to complete your online assessment before progressing to the next chapter.

This page is left intentionally blank.

Chapter 9: Trading losses

By the end of this chapter, you should:

- Be able to understand the options available to sole traders, partnerships and companies to utilise trading losses:
    - Opening years.
    - Carry back.
    - Current year.
    - Carry forward.
    - Terminal.

- Be able to calculate available loss relief using:
    - Carry back.
    - Current year.
    - Carry forward.

- Be able to understand the best use of a trading loss for sole traders, partnerships and limited companies.

Introduction

In previous chapters, adjustable trading profits have been calculated and dealt with.

Within this Chapter, adjusted trading losses and tax reliefs for those losses will be dealt with.

If a business **does** make an adjusted trading loss after capital allowances have been deducted, then the trading profit assessment for the period becomes **NIL** and not a negative profit (loss) figure.

Trading losses limited companies

The following template for adjustment of trading Profit shows an example of a **Nil** assessment.

Adjustment of Profit/(Loss)	£
Profit before tax as per financial accounts	20,000
Add Disallowable expenses e.g. depreciation	5,000
	25,000
Less Items in the accounts not taxable as trading, e.g. rental income	(2,000)
Adjusted trading profit before deduction of capital allowances	**23,000**
Less Expenditure deductible from trading profits e.g. capital allowances	(25,000)
Adjusted trading loss	**(2,000)**
Trading profit assessment	**NIL**

The negative profit (loss) figure then becomes the trading loss of £2,000 and there are several loss-relieving options that can be applied depending on the circumstances of the business and any other profits requiring relief:

Limited companies are able to consider utilising loss relief by:

a) current year claim followed by carry back claim then carry forward any remaining loss.
b) current year claim followed by carrying forward any remaining loss.
c) carry forward all loss.

Within all of the options, it is important to be aware of the impact that losses can have on qualifying charitable donations (QCDs), as these can be wasted in some circumstances which may not be the best option for the business.

Current year relief

This is when a trading loss can be relieved against **total profits** (including other gains or profits in the business) before deducting qualifying charitable donations in the period that the loss arose (current year). This is also referred to as using the loss "*as early as possible*". A claim for current year relief must be made within two years of the end of the loss-making accounting period.

Example 9.1

The current results for Presse Limited are for the year ending 31 March 2025. The adjusted trading loss has been calculated as a £20,000 loss.

Adjusted trading loss	**(20,000)**
Trading profit assessment	**NIL**

The next step is to complete the CT computation using the following information:

- Trading profit is NIL
- Property Income is £5,000
- Chargeable gains are £25,000
- Qualifying charitable donations (QCDs) are £5,000

Therefore, **total profits** before any loss relief are £30,000.

The current year's loss relief can now be applied in the CT computation.

Corporation Tax computation for 12 months ended 31 March 2025	
	£
Trading profit	**NIL**
Add: Property Income	5,000
Chargeable gains	25,000
Total profits	30,000
Less: Loss relief – current year	**(20,000)**
	10,000
Less: Qualifying charitable donations	(5,000)
Taxable total profits (TTP)	**5,000**

It is recommended to set up a *Loss Memorandum workings sheet* to ensure losses that have been identified in the period are recorded in it and details of how the loss is utilised as a relief are also recorded. This will be maintained to ensure correct loss relief claims are made going forward.

Loss Memorandum workings	£
Year ending 31 March 2025	
Current period loss	20,000
Loss relieved in current period	(20,000)
Loss c/f	**NIL**

The £5,000 TTP will then have the relevant CT rate applied to calculate the liability.

The CT600 will be completed with a £0.00 for Trading profits in Box 155 which will then carry forward to Box 165 showing the NIL trading profit assessment. Box 160 will not show the current loss as this box is to show a b/f loss from a previous period.

Income

Box	Description	£
155	Trading profits	0 · 00
160	Trading losses brought forward set against trading profits	· 00
165	Net trading profits – box 155 minus box 160	0 · 00
170	Bank, building society or other interest, and profits from non-trading loan relationships	· 00
172	Put an 'X' in box 172 if the figure in box 170 is net of carrying back a deficit from a later accounting period	

Box 190 will show the property income as normal of £5,000 followed by chargeable gains in boxes 210 and 220.

Box 235 will then show the total of the profits before other deductions and reliefs.

Income - continued

Box	Description	£
175	Annual payments not otherwise charged to Corporation Tax and from which Income Tax has not been deducted	
180	Non-exempt dividends or distributions from non-UK resident companies	
185	Income from which Income Tax has been deducted	
190	Income from a property business	5000
195	Non-trading gains on intangible fixed assets	
200	Tonnage Tax profits	
205	Income not falling under any other heading	

Chargeable gains

Box	Description	£
210	Gross chargeable gains	25000
215	Allowable losses including losses brought forward	
220	Net chargeable gains - box 210 minus box 215	25000

Profits before deductions and reliefs

Box	Description	£
225	Losses brought forward against certain investment income	
230	Non-trade deficits on loan relationships (including interest) and derivative contracts (financial instruments) brought forward set against non-trading profits	
235	Profits before other deductions and reliefs - net sum of boxes 165 to 205 and 220 minus sum of boxes 225 and 230	30000

The loss of £20,000 will be entered in Box 275, 295 and Box 300 will then show the profits before qualifying donations.

Box 305 shows the £5,000 qualifying donations to be deducted which then leaves the £5,000 profit shown in Box 315.

Deductions and Reliefs - continued

Box	Description	£
263	Carried forward non-trade deficits from loan relationships and derivative contracts (financial instruments)	·00
265	Non-trading losses on intangible fixed assets	·00
275	Total trading losses of this or a later accounting period	20000·00
280	Put an 'X' in box 280 if amounts carried back from later accounting periods are included in box 275	
285	Trading losses carried forward and claimed against total profits	·00
290	Non-trade capital allowances	·00
295	Total of deductions and reliefs - total of boxes 240 to 275, 285 and 290	20000·00
300	Profits before qualifying donations and group relief - box 235 minus box 295	10000·00
305	Qualifying donations	5000·00
310	Group relief	·00
312	Group relief for carried forward losses	·00
315	Profits chargeable to Corporation Tax - box 300 minus boxes 305, 310 and 312	5000·00
320	Ring fence profits included	·00
325	Northern Ireland profits included	·00

All of the loss relief claim must be utilised and applied **prior to QCDs**. However, this may mean that the QCDs may not be relieved and any excess will be lost **as QCDs cannot be carried forward or back.**

If, in the above example, total profits had been £30,000 as before but the loss relief had also been £30,000, then the QCD would be unrelieved and lost or wasted, as in the following example. The most you can deduct is the amount that reduces your company's profits to zero.

If you donate more QCDs than your total profits you can't:

- Declare trading losses on your tax return
- Carry over any remaining amount to your next tax return

Total profits	30,000
Less: Loss relief – current year	**(30,000)**
	0
Less: Qualifying charitable donations	Wasted
Taxable total profits (TTP)	**0**

The loss that has been utilised is also then recorded in Box 780 on Page 9 of the CT600.

Losses, deficits and excess amounts

Amount arising

	Amount	Maximum available for surrender as group relief
Losses of trades carried on wholly or partly in the UK	780 £ 20000	785 £

Carry back relief

A carry back claim can only be made when the current year's claims have been fully utilised.

After the current year claim has been made then the trading loss can be carried back and offset against total profits in the preceding 12-month period (not accounting period). Again, the loss is set off before QCDs.

For example, if your company has a total loss of £6,000 in the accounting period 1 January 2024 to 31 December 2024 and profits of £18,000 in the earlier 12 months, you can carry back the £6,000 loss to be offset against the profits for the previous accounting year which will then reduce them from £18,000 by £6,000 to £12,000.

Again, this is only if the business is carrying on the same trade in the current period or periods that fall in the previous 12 months. A claim must be made within 2 years of the end of the loss-making period.

Any loss left after the current period and the previous 12 months have been relieved can then be utilised by carrying forward any remaining loss.

If a company ceases to trade then the carry back relief can be applied for 36 months rather than just the 12 months.

Short previous accounting period

If a previous accounting period is less than 12 months then it is possible to carry the loss back further to the preceding period to cover a proportion of those profits.

If a previous accounting period straddles that 12-month period, the profit for that period would be apportioned with the loss being only applicable to that portion.

For example, a company has a loss of £6,000 in their new changed accounting period 1 January 2024 to 31 December 2024 and the previous periods and profits were:

- £2,000 for 1 July 2023 to 31 December 2023
- £4,000 for 1 July 2022 to 30 June 2023

In this instance you could carry back £2,000 of the £6,000 loss from 01/01/24 to 31/12/24 to cover the whole of the profit for the period ending 31 December 2023, being a 6-month period.

However, the balance of £4,000 cannot entirely be carried back as only 6 months of the profits of £4,000 fall into the earlier 12 months of the loss-making period.

Only £2,000 loss can be used and the balance of £2,000 would be available to be carried forward to the year ending 31 December 2025.

Example 9.2

Grayter Limited has the following results for years ending 31 March 2024 and 31 March 2025.

Use the loss "**as early as possible**" **to relieve trading profits**, complete the Corporation tax computation **revision** for 2024 and calculation for 2025, and complete the Loss Memorandum Workings Sheet.

• Adjusted trading profit/(loss)	2024 £70,000 2025 (£120,000)
• Non-trade Interest	2024 £2,000 2025 £3,000
• Qualifying charitable donation	2024 £1,000 2025 £500

Corporation Tax Computations	2024 revised	2025
	£	£
Trading profit/(loss)	**70,000**	**NIL**
Add: Non-trade Interest	2,000	3,000
Total profits	72,000	3,000
Less: Loss relief – current year		**(3,000)**
Loss relief – carry back	**(72,000)**	
	NIL	**NIL**
Less: Qualifying charitable donations	Wasted	Wasted
Taxable total profits (TTP)	**0**	**0**

The taxation for 2024 would have **originally** been calculated on £71,000 profits (£72,000 less the £1,000 QCDs which would have originally been applied in the 2024 calculation). The 2024 tax return would have been prepared and submitted to Companies House along with the relevant payment. The calculation above is revised for reference to show how the loss is carried back against the previous year's profit. Note that in this revised working the QCD for 2024 would be wasted and not utilised as profits have already been reduced to zero.

This is then entered into the Loss Memorandum workings sheet.

Loss Memorandum workings	£
Year ending 31 March 2025	
Current period loss 31 March 2025	120,000
Loss relieved in current period 31 March 2025	(3,000)
Loss relieved in previous period 31 March 2024	(72,000)
Loss c/f 2026	**45,000**

£45,000 loss balance can then be carried forward to 2026.

You can make a claim to carry back a trading loss when you submit your Company Tax Return for the period when you made the loss.

You can do this if your company was carrying on the same "trade" within the earlier 12-month period.

You can make your claim in your return or in an amendment to the return, as long as you're within the time limit to amend it.

A claim should be made within 2 years of the end of the accounting period when you made the loss. If you are offsetting a loss against a previous period where you have already paid the tax due, you will then receive a repayment from HMRC.

You can also make your claim in a letter.

If you're making a claim in your return that reduces your Corporation Tax liability for an earlier period, you must make sure you have put an 'X' in the appropriate **box 45** on the CT600 form showing that you have a claim or relief affecting an earlier period.

About this return

This is the above company's return for the period

30 from DD MM YYYY

35 to DD MM YYYY

Put an 'X' in the appropriate box(es) below

40 A repayment is due for this return period

45 Claim or relief affecting an earlier period X

No carry back claim can be made until the return for the period of the loss has been delivered. Identify in the computations (loss memorandum working sheet) the accounting period or periods from which the losses are carried back.

Your claim should include:

- the name of your company or organisation
- the period when the loss is made
- the amount of the loss
- how the loss is to be used

Activity 9.1

Rhod Limited has produced the following business results for three accounting periods to 31 March 2025.

Year ended 31 March	**2023**	**2024**	**2025**
	£	£	£
Trading profits/(loss)	15,000	11,000	(38,000)
Building Society Interest	400	500	600
Chargeable gains	0	0	3,500
Qualifying charitable donations	300	300	300

Use the loss "as soon as possible" to relieve trading profits and complete the Corporation Tax computations and Loss Memorandum working sheet.

Corporation Tax Computations	2023	2024	2025
Trading profit/(loss)			
Add: Non-trade Interest			
Chargeable Gains			
Total profits			
Less: Loss relief – current year			
Loss relief – carry back			
Less: Qualifying charitable donations			
Taxable total profits (TTP)			

Loss Memorandum workings	£
Year ending 31 March 2025	
Current period loss 31 March 2025	
Loss relieved in current period 31 March 2025	
Loss relieved in previous period 31 March 2024	
Loss c/f	

Non-trading Loan relationship Deficits can be carried back 12 months, but can only be relieved against *non-trading loan relationship* ***credits*** of the previous 12 months and **not against total profits** of the previous 12 months.

Carry forward relief

Since 1 April 2017, when trading losses are carried forward the losses do not have to be offset against the first available profits. The new flexible rules mean that carried forward losses can be offset against **any type of profits** in the same company and a choice can be made to offset in the current period or carry forward to future periods.

Carried forward post-April 2017 trading losses	(£40,000)
Current year non-trading loan relationship profits	£15,000
Current year trading profits	£ 8,000

Under the April 2017 rules, the carried forward loss can be applied to both the £15,000 current year non-trading loan relationship profits and the £8,000 current year trading profits. No tax would be due in the period and a trading loss of £17,000 would be carried forward.

Example 9.3

Choping Limited has the following results for the 3 years to 31 March 2025.

- (£10,000) loss 2023
- £5,000 profit 2024
- £8,000 profit 2025
- £3,000 Non trade interest 2024
- £2,000 Non trade interest 2025

Corporation Tax Computations	2023 £	2024 £	2025 £
Trading profit/(loss)	**NIL**	**5,000**	**8,000**
Add: Non-trade Interest	0	3,000	2,000
Total profits	NIL	8,000	10,000
Less: Loss relief – carry forward		**(8,000)**	**(2,000)**
		0	8,000
Less: Qualifying charitable donations	0	0	0
Taxable total profits (TTP)	**0**	**0**	**8,000**

Loss Memorandum workings	£
Year ending 31 March 2025	
Loss year ended 31 March 2023	10,000
Less: used in year ended 31 March 2024	(8,000)
Less: used in year ended 31 March 2025	(2,000)
Loss c/f	**NIL**

In 2023 the loss of £10,000 is carried forward.

In 2024 the total profits of £8,000 are relieved by using £8,000 of the £10,000 loss c/f.

In 2025 the profits of £10,000 are partially relieved by the remaining £2,000 loss c/f and the remaining £8,000 TTP would be taxable.

Example 9.4

Greensleeves Limited commenced trading on **1 April 2023.** The company incurred a loss in its first accounting period which it wants to relieve as soon as possible.

The company's results for the first two accounting periods are:

Year ended 31 March

	2024	2025
	£	£
Trading profit/(loss)	(180,000)	90,000
Property Income	9,000	9,000
Chargeable Gain	20,000	15,000
QCDs	(1,000)	(1,000)

1) How much loss can Greensleeves relieve in the year ended 31/3/24?

As Greensleeves has made an adjusted trading loss in 2024, the trading profit assessment for the period becomes **NIL**. The profit from property income and chargeable gains is £29,000. For current year relief, the loss relief claim must be utilised and applied prior to QCDs, so the QCD is unrelieved and lost in this period.

Corporation Tax computation for 12 months ended 31 March 2024	
	£
Trading profit	**NIL**
Add Property Income	9,000
Chargeable gains	20,000
Total profits	29,000
Less: Loss relief – current year	**(29,000)**
Less: Qualifying charitable donations	wasted
Taxable total profits (TTP)	**0**

The loss memorandum workings account can be started:

Loss Memorandum workings	£
Year ending 31 March 2024	180,000
Loss relieved in current year 2024	(29,000)
Loss c/f	151,000

2) How much loss can Greensleeves Limited claim in the year ended 31 March 2025?

The total profits consist of the trading profit plus the property income and chargeable gains for the period = £114,000.

The carried forward loss can be applied against **total profits** and there is no reason to lose the QCDs. Greensleeves Ltd can specify the amount it wants to claim and should therefore specify £113,000 as this amount avoids wasting its qualifying charitable donations. Therefore, the loss relief claim in the year ended 31 March 2025 would be £113,000.

Corporation Tax computation for 12 months ended 31 March 2025	
	£
Trading profit	**90,000**
Add: Property Income	9,000
Chargeable gains	15,000
Total profits	114,000
Less: Loss relief – future year	**(113,000)**
Less: Qualifying charitable donations	(1,000)
Taxable total profits (TTP)	**0**

Loss Memorandum workings	£
Year ending 31 March 2024	180,000
Loss relieved in current year 2024	(29,000)
Loss c/f	151,000
Loss relieved in future year 2025	(113,000)
Loss c/f	38,000

Activity 9.2

Jooser Limited commenced trading on 1 April 2023. In the first accounting period, it incurred a loss which it wants to relieve as soon as possible.

Jooser Limited has the following results for the first two accounting periods:

- £180,000 loss year ending 31/3/2024
- £12,000 property income 31/3/2024
- £20,000 chargeable gain 31/3/2024
- £1,000 QCDs 31/3/2024
- £90,000 profit year ending 31/3/2025
- £12,000 property income 31/3/2025
- £15,000 chargeable gain 31/3/2025
- £1,000 QCDs 31/3/2025

a) How much loss can Jooser Limited relieve in the first year ending 31/3/2024?

1) nil
2) £12,000
3) £32,000
4) £31,000

b) How much loss can Jooser Limited relieve in the year ending 31/3/2025?

1) £117,000
2) £102,000
3) £148,000
4) £116,000

Corporation Tax Computation	2024	2025
	£	£
Trading profit/(loss)		
Add: Property Income		
Chargeable Gains		
Total profits		
Less: Loss relief – current year		
Loss relief – carry forward		
Less: Qualifying charitable donations		
Taxable total profits (TTP)		

Activity 9.3

Panza Limited expect to incur a non-trading loan relationship deficit in the year ending 31 March 2025 and needs to make a decision on its options for claiming any available relief. Which of the following is **not** an acceptable way of claiming relief for the non-trading loan deficit?

a) The deficit can be relieved against non-trading loan relationship credits within the previous 12 months.

b) The deficit can be relieved against total profits in the future.

c) **The deficit can be relieved against the previous 12 months' total profits.**

d) The deficit can be relieved against total profits from the same accounting period.

Due to the flexibility of choice when it comes down to utilising loss relief there are certain considerations that a business should make:

- Cashflow benefits to the business. If a business is suffering losses, then it may be beneficial to them not to incur the taxation cost too early. The advantages of a current and carry back claim would benefit them.
- Rates of relief. To achieve the benefits of tax savings a company would prefer to claim relief in periods where it is paying the highest rates of tax. For example, a CT year tax rate may be 25% one year but 19% in another, so it would be more beneficial to utilise the loss in the higher 25% tax year. (Note: current year relief must be claimed first before carrying forward a trading loss).
- QCDs. To try to avoid wasting QCDs where possible as they are unable to be carried back or forward and could be lost completely.

Terminal loss relief

If your company stops trading, you may be eligible to claim Terminal Loss Relief. This relief can be applied to a loss in the final 12 months of trading (a terminal loss) and can be carried back against **total profits** of the preceding **three years** where tax has already been paid and a refund can be claimed from HMRC.

For each of the three years, you can only offset the loss against the profits in that year if your company was carrying on the same "trade" at some point in the accounting period. Any loss must be offset against the profits of the most recent years first before it can be carried back to earlier years. Losses must be used in the order they're made starting with the earliest, also referred to as LIFO (last in first out).

If any of the earlier accounting periods in the 3-year period are less than 12 months, then you will have to apportion the profit relevant to that accounting period.

Example 9.5

Mickser Ltd ceased trading on 31 August 2024. The company's results for the last five periods of trading are:

	Period ending 31/12/20	**Period ending 31/12/21**	**Period ending 31/12/22**	**Period ending 31/12/23**	**Year ending 31/8/2024**
Trading profit/(loss)	50,000	80,000	65,000	50,000	(230,000)
Property profit	8,500	6,500	6,500	-	-
Chargeable gains	5,100	-	-	-	-
QCDs	(800)	(1,000)	-	(1,200)	-

How can Mickser Ltd relieve its terminal loss of £230,000 for the year ending 31/8/2024?

Mickser Ltd is able to relieve the terminal loss against total profits of the preceding 3 years on a LIFO basis. Therefore, in the period ending 31/12/20, they are able to allocate 4 months of the loss carried back as this would be in the preceding 3-year period being September, October, November and December 2019.

Losses would be relieved before the deduction of qualifying charitable donations; therefore, these would be wasted within 2023 and 2021.

The claim to relieve the terminal loss for the year ending 31 August 2024 would need to be done by 31 August 2026. (Within 2 years of the end of the loss-making period).

	Period ending 31/12/20	Period ending 31/12/21	Period ending 31/12/22	Period ending 31/12/23	Year ending 31/8/2024
Trading profit/(loss)	50,000	80,000	65,000	50,000	(230,000)
Property profit	8,500	6,500	6,500	-	-
Chargeable gains	5,100	-	-	-	-
	63,600	**86,500**	**71,500**	**50,000**	**(230,000)**
Loss relief	(21,200)	(86,500)	(71,500)	(50,000)	
	42,400	0	0	0	
QCDs	(800)	wasted	-	wasted	-
Taxable total profits	41,600	-	-	-	-

Loss Memorandum workings	£
Year ending 31 August 2024 loss	230,000
Loss relieved in 2023	(50,000)
Loss relieved in 2022	(71,500)
Loss relieved in 2021	(86,500)
Loss relieved in 2020 max £63,600 / 12 x 4	(21,200)
Trading loss unrelieved	800

Capital losses

As a reminder, a capital loss when it occurs within the current period can be relieved against **current period** capital gains. Any unused capital loss can then be carried forward to relieve against any **capital gains** in future accounting periods.

A capital loss can only be used against a capital gain (no other profits like trade profits) and there is *no facility for a carry back* to earlier periods. Earlier in this textbook, the following summary template was given for the calculation of capital gains and losses.

	£
1) Chargeable gain	X
2) Chargeable gain	X
3) Allowable loss	(X)
Net chargeable gains/(losses) current CAP period	**X**
Less: Capital losses b/f previous period	(X)
Net chargeable gains	**X**

Within a business scenario, there will be many calculations to be made so it is important to be able to calculate capital gains and losses separately and understand that capital losses cannot be applied to trading losses.

You will need to know the difference between capital and trade losses so it may be beneficial if necessary to revisit Chapter 7 to fully understand chargeable gains and losses.

Trading losses for individuals (sole traders and partnerships)

Where a sole trader (or a partnership) makes a trading loss, like with a limited business, the trading income assessment for that year will be **NIL (not the negative 'loss' figure).**

There are several options for relieving these losses and these may be different from the loss-relieving options of a limited company.

The principal reliefs for individuals (sole traders and partners) that are available are as follows:

Opening year loss relief – loss in first four years of trade

Trading losses arising in the first four years of **an individual's** business can be carried back and set against **any** income of the previous three tax years – the earliest years first. Claims should be made by 31 January 2027 for the 2024/25 tax year.

Example 9.6

May left her employed job as a florist and opened a business as a sole trader in 2024-25, making a loss in her first year of £10,000. She can carry this loss back and relieve it against **any** income e.g. her employment income from the florists, a 2024/25 loss can be carried back and relieved against any income for the tax years 2021-22, 2022-23 and then 2023-24.

This is clearly done retrospectively, and so May should be able to claim a rebate from HMRC in respect of this.

Current year/carry back relief

An established trader (who has been trading for a number of years) can make a claim to set off their trading loss against **any** income for the tax year in which the loss arises and/or any income for the previous year (if the loss is large enough). This includes all types of income (e.g. from employment, property, interest or trading profits), and can also be utilised against capital gains if the taxpayer wishes. This loss relief is **optional** and the taxpayer can choose whether or not to claim it and cannot be restricted to preserve the personal allowance. This means that the personal allowance would be wasted if the loss is applied to the current year's losses and carried back to the previous year's losses and any total income is less than the personal allowance.

Example 9.7

Keith has been a sole trader plumber for many years. In 2024-25 his business made a loss of £5,000. Keith also had a property income of £3,000 in 2023-24 and 2024-25.

Keith can obtain relief for his 2024-25 trading loss by offsetting £3,000 of the £5,000 loss against his property income for 2024-25, and also carry back the remaining £2,000 against his 2023-24 property income. However, this is not recommended as both the current year's and the prior year's total income are already covered by the personal allowance.

Carry forward relief

The loss can be carried forward to reduce **any** profits for later tax years from the same trade only. Any losses brought forward must be utilised as quickly as possible and applied automatically to the first available profits – saving any to be used against future profits is not an option. This is the most straightforward way of obtaining relief though not necessarily the most tax beneficial. It applies after any other elections or if no elections are made.

Example 9.8

Maurice made a loss from his sole trader business in 2023-24 of £4,000. He elects to carry this loss forward to use against future profits in the same trade. In 2024-25 he made a profit of £22,000, which would be reduced to £18,000 by using the loss brought forward.

Terminal loss relief

If a loss arises on cessation of trade, relief can be claimed against the **same trade** profits for the final tax year and then carried back against trading profits of the **previous three** tax years, the latest first (LIFO basis). Claim within 4 years from the end of the last tax year of trade. In the event that a sole trader or partner leaves the business to go into paid employment, losses cannot be carried forward against that employment income as the losses can only be set against profits of the same trade. This is when a terminal loss relief claim can be available and beneficial.

Example 9.9

Barry ceases trading in 2024-25, making a loss in his final period of trade of £8,000. His profit in 2023-24 was £5,000, and in 2022-23 it was £10,900.

Barry can obtain relief for the loss in 2024-25 by carrying back the loss, using £5,000 against 2023-24 profits and £3,000 against the 2022-23 profits.

Achieving the best use of a trading loss for sole traders and partnerships

From a tax perspective, the principal objective of utilising losses is to obtain the maximum tax relief at the earliest opportunity.

Example 9.10

Zach is a sole trader artist who sells his art on the internet. He has the following adjusted trading results for the periods ending 31 March 2023, 2024, and 2025, and other taxable income for the corresponding tax years.

Accounting Period	Accounting Year ended 31 March 2023	Accounting Year ended 31 March 2024	Accounting Year ended 31 March 2025
Trading Profit / (Loss)	£20,800	-£17,200	£19,500
Tax Year	2022-23	2023-24	2024-25
Income from Property	£7,200	£6,000	£4,500

How can Zach relieve his £17,200 trading loss from the year ended 31 March 2024?

The tax year for the loss is 2023-24 (1 April 2023 to 31 March 2024)

There are four different ways in which the loss can be relieved:

1. Set against total income of 2023-2024 (the year of the loss), and then carry back any excess loss against total income in the previous year.

The first £6,000 of the loss will be offset against the £6,000 property income for 2023-24. The remaining £11,200 is carried back to be used against the 2022-23 total income of £28,000, reducing this to £16,800. The personal allowance of £12,750 for the 2023-24 tax year is wasted using this approach, although there should be an immediate tax rebate in relation to the overpaid tax for 2022-23.

2. Set against total income of 2022-23 (the previous year).

All £17,200 will be offset against the total income of 2022-23 (£28,000), meaning total taxable income in 2022-23 will be £10,800. There will be no loss to set against the 2023-24 property income in this approach.

3. Set against total income of 2023-24 (the year of loss), but carry any excess loss forward to be used against future trading profits.

The first £6,000 of the loss is offset against the £6,000 property income, with the remaining £11,200 being carried forward to be used against the 2024-25 trading profits only – these will be reduced to £8,300 (£19,500 – £11,200).

4. Carry forward losses of 2023-24 to future profits from the same trade – using them as soon as possible.

The whole loss of £17,200 is carried forward to 2024-25, where it is offset against the trading profit of £19,500, making the trading profit for 2024-25 £2,300.

Summary of Chapter 9

- If a business **does** make an adjusted trading loss after capital allowances have been deducted, then the trading profit assessment for the period becomes **NIL** and not a negative profit (loss) figure.
- There are several loss-relief options that can be applied depending on the circumstances of the business and any other profits requiring relief:
    1) Current year relief
    2) Carry back relief
    3) Carry forward relief
    4) Terminal loss relief
- If your company stops trading, you may be eligible to claim Terminal Loss Relief.
- A capital loss when it occurs within the current period can be relieved against **current period** capital gains.

Assessment 9

You are now required to log in to your ROGO account to complete your online assessment before progressing to the next chapter.

This page is left intentionally blank.

Chapter 10: Administrative requirements of the UK's tax regime

By the end of this chapter, you should be able to:

- Understand tax return filing deadlines for sole traders, partnerships and companies.
- Understand tax payment dates for sole traders, partnerships and companies.
- Understand the time limits for notifying chargeability to tax.
- Understand the enquiry time window.
- Understand the time period within which amendments to a tax return can be made.
- Understand what records need to be maintained and for what time period.
- Understand the penalties and interest for non-compliance.
- Calculated penalties and interest for non-compliance.

Introduction for limited company administrative requirements

Corporation Tax Self-Assessment (CTSA) expects an incorporated business to submit a completed tax return for every chargeable accounting period. The tax due is then expected to be paid by the due date.

It is now a requirement of HMRC that all companies submit their Company Tax return online (with very few exceptions). The tax return which includes the financial statements and all relevant working calculations must be submitted in 'Inline eXtensible Business Reporting Language' (iXBRL) format.

Small companies with simple accounts that do not use accounting software are able to apply to use the HMRC Corporation Tax Online Service. This can only be used by companies that have straightforward financial affairs. It includes specially formatted accounts and computations templates which if used will ensure the data is submitted in the right format (iXBRL).

HMRC and Companies House also provide an optional joint filing service that enables small companies to enter their accounts data only once. This service enables small or micro-entity accounts to be submitted over the Internet to HMRC as part of the Company Tax return and also to send these – or an abridged version – to Companies House. If the template does not include items that a business has in its own accounts data and returns then they will not be able to use the online service template from HMRC.

The process for Corporation Tax Self-Assessment is:

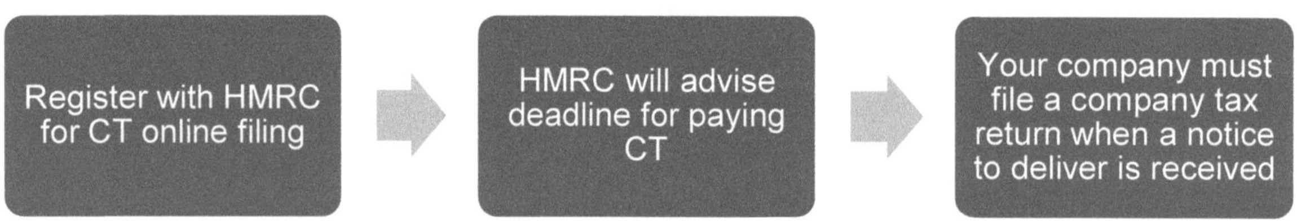

Corporation Tax Self-Assessment is where the company uses an Agent or they themselves do the calculations of the CT payable for the accounting period covered by the return and then do the requirements to file by the deadlines to avoid penalties.

Filing the return – limited companies

The CT Return also includes the accounts and computations working sheets and is due on or before the filing due date.

The filing due date is the **later** of:

- 12 months after the end of the period of account
- 3 months from the date of the notice requiring the return.

If a notice to file a return is not received then the company ***must inform*** HMRC within 12 months of the end of the accounting period to avoid incurring a penalty.

A business that is liable to pay tax for the first time must notify HMRC within 3 months of the start of its first chargeable accounting period.

A tax return for a limited company can be amended within 12 months of the filing date.

Example 10.1

Spune Limited has prepared its accounts for 12 months ending 31 August 2024.

They have received a notice to file a return from HMRC which was issued on 1 May 2025. The date that Spune Limited must file their CT Return for the year ending 31 August 2024 is 31 August 2025 being the later of 31 August 2025 (12 months from the end of the period of account) and 1 August 2025 (3 months after notice to deliver).

Example 10.2

Mashur Limited has prepared accounts for the 16 months to 30 June 2024.

2023									**2024**						
M	**A**	**M**	**J**	**J**	**A**	**S**	**O**	**N**	**D**	**J**	**F**	M	A	M	J
12 months												4 months			

The period of account is the period for which the accounts are prepared being 16 months ending June 2024. What would be the filing dates for the two accounting periods?

- First 12 months ending February 2024 has a filing date of 30 June 2025
- Balance of 4 months ending June 2024 has a filing date of 30 June 2025

Both accounting periods are filed 12 months after the end of the period of account.

Late filing and penalties – limited companies

If a company fails to submit a tax return by the due date, it will be subject to a penalty.

Penalties are applied according to how long the return becomes overdue. HMRC penalty guidelines are as follows:

Overdue By	Penalty
Less than 3 months	£100
More than 3 months	£100 + another £100 = £200
More than 6 months	£200 plus 10% of tax due
More than 12 months	£200 plus 20% of tax due

If the tax return is late 3 times in a row, the £100 penalties **are increased to £500 each**.

If the tax return is more than 6 months late, HMRC will write to the business giving an estimate of how much Corporation Tax they think they must pay – called a 'tax determination' and add a penalty of 10% of the unpaid tax.

This 'tax determination' must be paid and no appeals can be made against it.

Example 10.3

Sheeres Limited received a notice to deliver a CT return on 31 July 2023 for the year ending 31 May 2023.

The completed return was submitted by the company on 31 January 2025 at which time they also paid the corporation tax liability of £40,000.

- What date should the return have been submitted and how overdue was it?

The return was due to be filed on 31 May 2024, 12 months after the end of the period of account. The return was physically filed 8 months late.

- What would be the maximum penalties that can be charged for the late filing?

A fixed penalty of £200 plus 10% of tax due. This would be an additional penalty of £40,000 x 10% = £4,000 making a total of £4,200 penalty due.

Activity 10.1

The filing due date of a CT Return is the later of:

a) 6 months from notice to deliver and 12 months from the end of the period of account.

b) 12 months from notice to deliver and 6 months from the end of the period of account.

c) 12 months from the end of the period of account and 3 months from notice to deliver.

When filing two returns because there is a long period of account (more than 12 months long) the returns will have the same filing date being 12 months after the end of the period of account.

Each CT return – one for 12 months and one for the balance will have a filing date of 12 months from the end of the period of account (accounting period date).

Activity 10.2

Wiske Limited has prepared accounts for the 18 month period to the end of December 2024.

What is the filing date of the first CT return covering the first 12-month period?

a) 30 June 2025

b) 31 December 2025

c) 31 March 2025

d) 30 June 2024

Activity 10.3

Read the following and decide whether the statements are true or false.

Statement	True or False?
A CT return that is filed 7 months late with a liability of £27,000 would incur a penalty of £200 and £5,400	
A company whose period of account ends on 30 June 2024 should file their return by 30 June 2025.	
The maximum HMRC can charge as a penalty for a late filing of a CT return is £200.	
If a tax return is filed on 15 July 2025 for the year ending 30 July 2024 a penalty of £100 will be incurred.	

Amending the return and dealing with errors – limited companies

Changes or amendments to a CT return must be made within 12 months of the filing deadline.

Any obvious errors can be amended by HMRC within 9 months of the date the CT return was filed or 9 months of the filing of any amendments by the company.

If the company feels that they disagree with HMRC amendments then they can reject it as long as the rejection is made within the normal time limit for amendments, or if that has expired, within three months of the date of correction.

Incorrect returns and penalties – limited companies

As an agent for taxation or as the client, there are responsibilities to ensure returns are carefully checked and are accurate to avoid incurring penalties.

Penalties for late filing were covered earlier in the chapter. This section deals with the penalty system for **errors** in tax returns that was introduced on 1 April 2009. Your client may be charged a penalty if their return or calculations for **corporation tax** were inaccurate and tax has been unpaid, understated, over-claimed or under-assessed as a result.

The penalty system for errors is based on the type of error involved and the level of the penalty is linked to the reason why the error incurred. The percentage is based on the under-declared tax.

Type of error	Penalty
Lack of reasonable care	Between 0% and 30% of the extra tax due
Deliberate	Between 20% and 70% of the extra tax due
Deliberate and concealed	Between 30% and 100% of the extra tax due

Lack of reasonable care is an inaccuracy that occurs through carelessness. However, HMRC does take into account the level of knowledge and size of the company. While expecting each person or company to make and preserve sufficient records for making a complete and accurate return they do realise that a small company will only keep a simple regime that is followed carefully but a larger company with more complex tax affairs will need to ensure more sophisticated systems are followed as carefully as if it was a small company. If a company is seen to take care and attempt to understand a transaction and then if any doubt ensues, highlight this in the return. By doing this reasonable care is being followed. However, not understanding and just "guessing" or omitting that transaction will prove a lack of reasonable care.

These penalties can be reduced to a minimum depending on HMRC discretion based on the timing of disclosure of information and whether prompted or unprompted. The following table shows the typical minimum penalties:

Error	Minimum penalties	
	Unprompted disclosure % tax due	Prompted disclosure % tax due
Lack of reasonable care	0-14%	15-30%
Deliberate	20-34%	35-70%
Deliberate and concealed	30-49%	50-100%

Activity 10.4

Decide whether the following companies would incur penalties from HMRC and what type of penalty, where applicable.

a) Skales Limited, a micro entity has unknowingly entered an incorrect figure in their CT return ending 31 March 2025 even though the return was thoroughly checked. After realising their mistake, they inform HMRC on 5 April 2025.

b) Jugg Limited, a small entity struggled to meet the deadline for filing and therefore sent in the CT return without it being checked carefully. Within the month following filing, a number of substantial errors were identified at which time the details were sent to HMRC.

c) Boule Limited, a small entity had deliberately concealed information which resulted in an understatement of tax. HMRC have realised and has requested disclosure and Boule Limited has assisted them with the request.

Late payments and interest charges – limited companies

Corporation tax is due for payment nine months and one day after the end of the accounting period for non-large companies like micro and small entities as long as taxable total profits plus dividends are less than £1,500,000 for a 12-month accounting period. The payment due date is before the requirement to file the CT return (12 months).

Large companies with annual profits greater than £1.5 million must estimate the year's tax liability and pay 25% of the estimate on the 14th day of each of the 7th, 10th, 13th and 16th month from the start of the accounting period.

Example 10.4

A large company with annual profits greater than £1.5 million who submits accounts to 31 December 2024 would need to pay by instalments on the following dates:

- 14 July 2024 (7th month)
- 14 October 2024 (10th month)
- 14 January 2025 (13th month)
- 14 April 2025 (16th month)

Interest will be charged by HMRC if corporation tax payments are late, underpaid or not paid at all. This is referred to by HMRC as 'late payment interest' and is automatically applied until the date the tax payment is paid.

Corporation Tax payments can no longer be paid by post and can now be paid by:

- Faster payment through online or telephone banking (same day or next day)
- CHAPS (same day)
- BACS (3 working days)
- Direct debit (3 working days if a previous debit has been set up)
- Direct debit (5 working days when a debit has not been set up previously)
- Debit or credit card online (3 working days)
- Bank or Building Society (3 working days)

You need to take into account the time it takes for the payment to get to HMRC to avoid late payment and interest charges.

Any late payment interest paid to HMRC is tax deductible for CT purposes and can be included as an expense in your company accounts for the accounting period when the interest was incurred.

The current late payment interest rate applied to Corporation Tax is 7.5% (from Aug 2024).

Interest on tax overpaid to HMRC – limited companies

If corporation tax is overpaid to HMRC then interest will be paid by them from the date that the overpaid tax was paid until the date it is refunded. The current rate of interest from HMRC is 4.0% (Aug 2024).

The refund would normally be based on a monthly basis covering the period from when the overpayment was made until it was refunded by HMRC.

For example, if an overpayment of £6,000 was made on 1 April 2025 and was refunded on 1 September 2025 this would equate to 5 months.

£6,000 x 4.0% = £240/12 months = £20 x 5 months = £100 applicable to the 5- month period.

Any interest received from HMRC for overpaid corporation tax can be included as non-trade interest income in the company accounts. The interest is taxable and will be included as Income in the tax return. It will therefore be deducted from adjustable trading profits and added back in the CT computation.

You will not be required to prepare a detailed computation in an assessment but you must be aware of the details on overpaid tax to HMRC.

Record keeping – limited companies

Incorporated companies must keep records for **6 years** from the end of the last company financial year they relate to, or longer if:

- They show a transaction that covers more than one of the company's accounting periods
- The company has bought something that it expects to last more than 6 years, like equipment or machinery
- You sent your company tax return late
- HMRC has started a compliance check into your company tax return.

Failure to keep records can lead to a penalty of up to **£3,000** for each accounting period affected and you may be disqualified as a company director.

Introduction for sole traders and partnerships administrative requirements

For most employees, tax is collected **at source** through the Pay As You Earn (PAYE) scheme, where tax is deducted directly from an employee's pay by the employer on a weekly or monthly basis, and then paid over directly to HMRC. National Insurance is collected in an identical way.

However, for many other taxpayers, the process is a little more complex, and they must complete an annual self-assessment tax return. Around 10 million people must complete self-assessment returns each year in the UK. This includes the self-employed including partnerships, company directors, employees earning more than £100,000, anybody with capital gains after selling assets, and any individual with income from overseas.

The deadline for submitting the (online) tax return is 31 January after the end of the tax year (so for 2024-25 the deadline is 31 January 2026). This date is also the deadline for ensuring that any tax owing for the tax year has been paid to HMRC. If the taxpayer has been given the choice to file a paper return, then this must be completed, signed and returned by 31 October following the end of the tax year.

Any amendments can be made within 12 months of filing.

Notification of chargeability is required by 5 October following the end of the tax year.

Payments on account for individuals

HMRC require some taxpayers to pay their tax liability for a year in instalments, known as **Payments on Account**. This is simply to improve cash flow for the receipt of tax for the Government. If your last self-assessment tax bill was less than £1,000, you are not required to make payments on account.

- **First Payment on Account**
  The first payment on account must be paid by 31 January **within the tax year that it relates to**.

- **Second Payment on Account**
  The second payment on account is then paid by 31 July approximately three months **after** the end of the tax year.

- **Final Payment (the Balancing Payment)**
  This must be paid by 31 January after the end of the tax year - in other words, the normal self-assessment filing and payment date.

The amount which must be paid on each of the first two payments on account is based on the amount of Tax & Class 4 NIC payable (i.e. not including tax suffered at source such as PAYE) in the **PREVIOUS** tax year. This is because at the time the first POA is due, the tax year hasn't actually come to an end and so the taxpayer will not know what their tax & NIC class 4 liability is for the year at that point. The taxpayer therefore makes the first two payments on account as follows:

- POA 1 (31 January in the tax year) = 50% of the previous year's liability payable
- POA 2 (31 July just after the tax year) = 50% of the previous year's liability payable

By the time the third (and final) Payment on Account is due, on 31 January after the tax year, the taxpayer will have completed their tax return for the year and will know exactly how much tax is payable. If this figure is more than the total of the two payments on account already made, the taxpayer must make a **balancing payment** to HMRC for the difference.

On the other hand, if they have already paid too much for this year through the first two payments on account, a **balancing refund** can be claimed from HMRC.

The three dates for tax year 2024-25 for payments on account are 31 January 2025, 31 July 2025 and the final balancing payment or refund on 31 January 2026.

Of course, in addition to the final balancing payment or refund for 2024-25, the taxpayer must also make their first payment on account for 2025-26 on that date, which will be 50% of the tax payable for 2024-25.

Example 10.5

Michael received £25,000 profit from his self-employment business in 23/24 and the income tax payable was £5,000. Income tax payable for 24/25 based on taxable trade profits for the year ending 31 July 2024 is £7,200. Ignoring NICs, Michael's payments in respect of the income tax liability for 24/25 would be:

Previous year's tax = £5,000 / 2 = £2,500 payment on account 1 31 January 2025

£2,500 payment on account 2 31 July 2025

Third balancing payment £7,200 - £5,000 = £2,200 payment on account 3 31 January 2026.

He would then be required to pay the first payment on account for the new tax year:

First payment on account based on 24/25 tax payable £7,200 / 2 = £3,600 payment on account 1 31 January 2026.

Therefore, on 31 January 2026, he would be paying £2,200 and £3,600 = £5,800.

Example 10.6

Virendar had a total tax liability in 2023-24 of £8,750. In 2024-25 his total tax liability is £11,340.

Identify Virendar's payments on account in relation to his **2024-25** tax, and state the dates these must be paid by.

For 2024-25

Payment on Account 1	(31 Jan 2025)	**£4,375** *(£8,750 / 2)*
Payment on Account 2	(31 July 2025)	**£4,375** *(£8,750 / 2)*
Balancing Payment	(31 Jan 2026)	**£2,590** *(£11,340 - £8,750) (£4,375 x 2)*

In addition to the balancing payment of £8,260 on 31 January 2026, Virendar will also need to make his first POA for 25-26 of £5,670 (£11,340 / 2) = **£8,260 in total.**

National Insurance

Much in the same way as income tax due, class 4 National Insurance contributions are paid and payments on account and balancing payments are calculated the same.

Capital Gains

NI's payments on account are not required for capital gains.

Example 10.7

Michele has income from employment of £15,750 during the year 24/25 of which £636 was deducted under PAYE, she also receives £25,000 profit from her self-employment business.

- Calculate what the total tax liability for the year would be.
- State what Michele's payments on account would be and on what dates they would be paid.

Taxable Income – employment income £15,750 + self-employment income £25,000 = £40,750 less the personal allowance £12,570 = £28,180.

£28,180 x 20% = **£5,636** tax due.

We now need to calculate the NIC class 4 on the self-employment (NIC class 1 will be deducted from the employment income by the employer).

Self-employment income £25,000 – NIC threshold £12,570 = £12,430
£12,430 x 6% = class 4 NIC **£745.80**
This gives a total tax and NIC class 4 liability for 24/25 of £6,381.80 (£5,636 + £745.80) - £636.00 tax deducted at source = £5,745.80;

Payment on Account 1 (31 Jan 2026)	£2,872.90 (£5,745.80 / 2)
Payment on Account 2 (31 July 2026)	£2,872.90 (£5,745.80 / 2)

Michele would therefore pay £5,745.80 owing for the 24/25 tax year plus the first payment on account of £3,190.90 (£6,381.80 / 2) on 31 January 2026.

Previous year tax less than £1,000

Payments on account do not have to be made in the following situations:

a. The amount of tax payable in the **previous year** was less than **£1,000**

   or

b. More than **80%** of the total tax due in the previous year had been collected at source (PAYE).

In addition, a taxpayer can claim not to make payments on account if they genuinely believe their tax payable for the coming year will be lower than in the previous year.

Example 10.8

Graham had a total income tax liability in 2023-24 of £8,100, of which £6,700 was collected at source through PAYE. He expects his income and tax payable to be broadly similar in 2024-25.

Will Graham need to make payments on account for 2024-25?

Graham had tax payable of £1,400 (£8,100 - £6,700) in 2023-24, which is higher than the £1,000 threshold.

However, £6,700 is more than 80% of the total tax liability for 2023-24 (£8,100 x 80% = £6,480), meaning more than 80% of the tax liability was collected at source. Therefore, payments on account **do not** need to be made for 2024-25.

Penalties and interest

Tax returns and tax payments must be submitted by the 31 January following the end of the tax year – for 2024-25 this means 31 January 2026.

We also saw how some taxpayers may have to make payments on account on 31 January in the tax year and 31 July following the tax year, with the balancing payment or rebate on 31 January after the year-end.

If a taxpayer fails to meet their obligations under Self-Assessment, HMRC will apply penalties and interest. This could arise where:

1) The taxpayer fails to submit their tax return by the filing date of 31 January after the year-end.
2) The taxpayer fails to make payments by the correct dates.
3) The taxpayer submits a tax return, but it contains errors.
4) Failure to keep records.

1) Failure to submit the tax return on time - late filing

In most situations, the tax return must be submitted by 31 January following the end of the tax year – from April 2021 only a very small minority of taxpayers who HMRC have Identified cannot file online will be allowed to submit paper returns, in which case these must be filed by midnight on 31 October following the end of the tax year. A taxpayer who misses the deadline for submitting the paper return would still be able to file their return online, and so there would be no penalty applied for missing the October deadline so long as the 31 January deadline was met with an online return.

A taxpayer who fails to submit their online tax return by midnight on 31 January following the end of the tax year will face an automatic penalty of £100. This penalty is applied in all cases, although the taxpayer may appeal to HMRC in certain situations which have made timely submission of the return impossible. 'Reasonable excuses' include serious health issues or catastrophic events such as fire or flood.

In addition to the automatic £100 penalty, there are then further penalties applied when the return is significantly late.

More than three months late: Once the return is more than three months late (i.e. after 30 April) the taxpayer is fined an additional penalty of ***£10 per day*** for the following 90 days – to a maximum of £900.

More than six months late: There is an additional penalty of **£300**, or **5%** of the tax due if this is greater (this will apply where the tax due is more than £6,000)

More than twelve months late: A further **£300** is charged or, if greater, **5%** of the tax due for not deliberate late filing.

If deliberate and not concealed after 12 months, **70%** of the tax due (or **£300** if greater).
In serious cases where the late filing is deliberate and concealed, this penalty could be **100%** of the tax due (or **£300** if greater).

Example 10.9

Boris forgets to submit his 2024-25 tax return until 28 June 2026. The tax owed by Boris for 2024-25 is £8,350.

What late submission penalty will Boris face?

Automatic late submission penalty	£100
Additional penalty (more than 3 months after 30 April) (1 May – 28 June = 59 days x £10 per day)	£590
Total late submission penalty	**£690**

Example 10.10

Nell forgets to submit her 2024-25 tax return until 25 November 2026. The tax owed by Nell for 2024-25 is £10,160.

What late submission penalty will Nell face?

Automatic late submission penalty	£100
Additional penalty (90 days)	£900 *(90 days x £10)*
6-month penalty	£508 *(£10,160 x 5%)*
Total late submission penalty	**£1,508**

2) Failure to pay the tax due on time

Failure to pay the tax due by the payment date of 31 January following the year-end attracts the following **penalties:**

Delay	**Penalty imposed**
30 days late	5% of the tax you owe at that date
6 months late	5% of the tax you owe at that date; this is as well as the 5% above
12 months late	5% of the tax unpaid at that date; this as well as the two 5% penalties above

There are no penalties applied to late payments of payments on account.

In addition to the penalties for late payment, **interest** is also charged on any tax which is paid late. This could be where the taxpayer fails to make payment at all or makes an underpayment of tax.

Although **no** penalties apply to late payments on account, **Interest** will be applied to late Payment on Account that are paid late.

Interest as of August 2024 is charged at 7.5% and calculated on a daily basis to the day before the payment is eventually made. HMRC charges interest at a daily rate using the following formula; "Tax amount owing x 7.75% times by the amount of days the payment is late divided by 365".

Example 10.11

Nell (from example 10.10 doesn't pay her 2024-25 tax owing of £10,160) until 25 November 2026.

What would be the total penalties and interest Nell will be charged in relation to 2024-25?

The penalty for late payment is £10,160 x 10% (2 x 5%) = **£1,016.00**. This is because the payment is more than 6 months, but less than 12 months late.

Interest is applied from 1 February 2026 to 24 November 2026. This is a period of 297 days.

Interest charged = £10,160 x 7.5% x 297/365 = **£620.04**

The total cost is therefore:

Late submission penalty	£1,508.00
Late payment penalty	£1,016.00
Interest applied to late payment	£ 620.04
Total Penalties and Interest	**£3,144.04**

3) The Tax Return Contains Errors

HMRC expect that the tax return which is submitted should be free from material errors. Where this is not the case, it is important that the taxpayer notifies HMRC as soon as they become aware of the error or omission.

If the taxpayer has paid too much tax as a result of the error, HMRC will issue a refund, and will also pay interest to the taxpayer at a rate of 4.0% on the amount of the refund.

If it results in a situation where not enough tax has been paid, the outstanding balance of tax owing must be paid, and interest is applied on it retrospectively from the day it was originally due to the day before it was paid. Interest is charged at 7.50% in exactly the same way as for late payment of tax (Example 10.11).

In addition to the interest charged, HMRC will also review the circumstances leading to the incorrect tax return and may apply penalties to the taxpayer. Where there is a 'genuine' error which led to the mistake on the tax return, and where the taxpayer has notified HMRC of the issue and co-operated with them, there will be no penalty. However, there is a sliding scale of penalties which can be applied in other situations.

The objective of the HMRC system of penalties is to 'modify' taxpayer behaviour – in other words, to encourage taxpayers to be honest and organised and to prepare their returns with integrity. HMRC acknowledge that tax is a complex issue and that genuine errors will occur, and they do not wish to be unduly harsh in penalising these.

They focus therefore on penalising errors which were careless, deliberate, and deliberate **and** concealed. The penalty is also increased where it is HMRC who discovers the error and brings it to the attention of the taxpayer (a "prompted" disclosure), rather than the taxpayer identifying the error themselves and bringing it to the attention of HMRC (an "unprompted" disclosure").

If the taxpayer notifies HMRC as soon as they discover the error, assists the HMRC in any investigation and provides HMRC with access to relevant documentation and records they will be able to minimise any penalties which HMRC may choose to apply.

A 'sliding scale' of penalties is applied, based on taxpayer behaviour. The percentage figures refer to the minimum and maximum percentage of the taxpayer's tax owing that will be charged in each set of circumstances. This applies to individual's tax returns and not to limited companies.

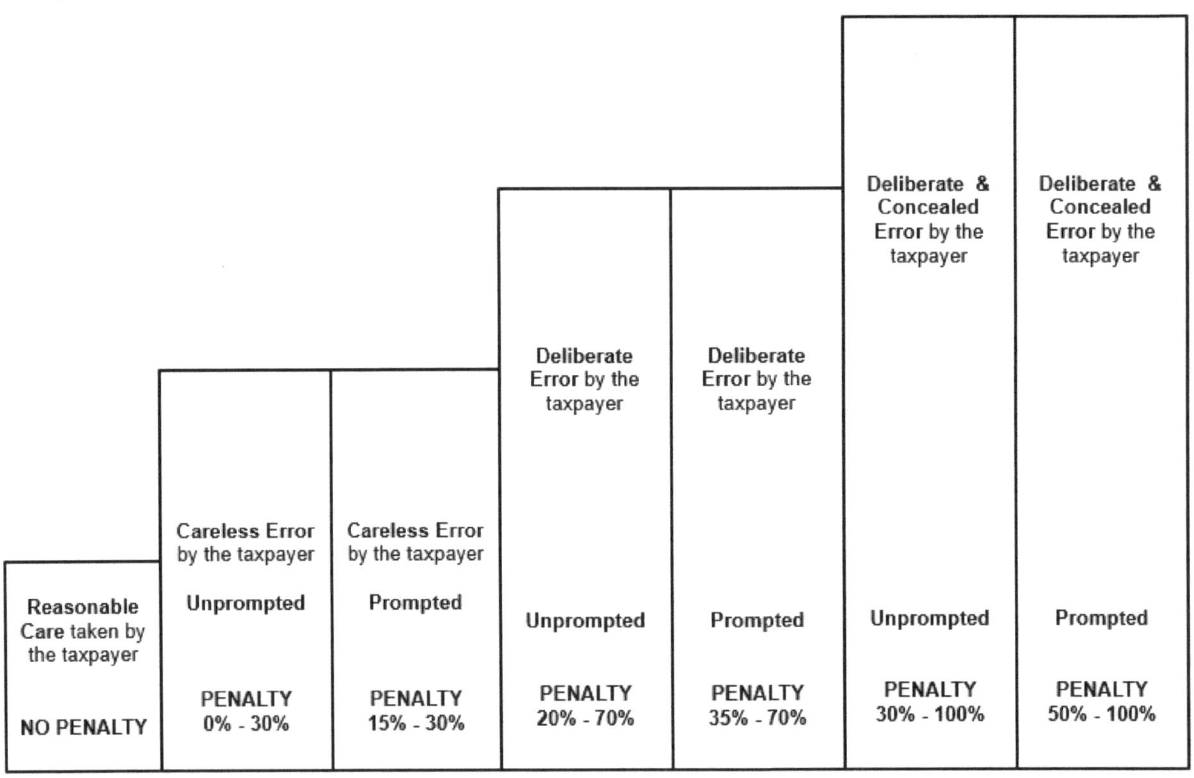

Example 10.12

Dennis completed his tax return for 2024-25 and submitted it on 20 January 2026. He has now realised there are some errors of interpretation of some recently introduced changes to legislation in the return and so contacts HMRC to advise them.

What are the likely penalties which will be faced by Dennis?

Dennis would appear to have taken **reasonable care** and has notified HMRC himself so is unlikely to face a penalty.

Example 10.13

Joe deliberately understated his income in his tax return for 2024-25 by not including his income from a second job. He later realised that this was both unethical and illegal, and so notified HMRC of his error.

What are the likely penalties which will be faced by Joe?

Joe deliberately included false information but made an **unprompted disclosure** to HMRC. He is likely to receive a penalty of between 20% and 70% of the tax owed.

Example 10.14

Hazel completed her tax return on time. She deliberately overstated her expenses on her return, meaning she made very little taxable profit for the year. HMRC are investigating this, and Hazel has destroyed all records and documentation and is refusing to help the HMRC with their investigation.

What are the likely penalties which will be faced by Hazel?

Hazel has deliberately included false information and did not disclose this until HMRC began to investigate. She appears to be **deliberately obstructive**, and so potentially faces a penalty of 100% of the tax owing.

Time limits for making amendments to a tax return

A taxpayer can notify HMRC of an error in a previous tax return. However, they only have twelve months from the filing date (31 January following the tax year) to 'repair' the return by submitting an amended return (either online or in paper format according to how the original was submitted). After this, any amendments must be made to HMRC in writing. The deadline for doing this is within four years after the end of the tax year – so the deadline for 2024-25 is 5 April 2029.

If HMRC spot an 'obvious error or omission' in a taxpayer's return they can correct it without necessarily contacting the taxpayer. This could include errors of arithmetic or errors of principle (such as applying the wrong tax rate). HMRC must make any 'amendments within nine months of the date the return was filed with them (not necessarily 31 January if the taxpayer submitted their return earlier than the deadline).

If it is a genuine error this amendment must be made within four years; however, if the errors are careless this is extended to six years and if the error was a result of deliberate taxpayer action HMRC has a window of twenty years in which to investigate.

Timescales for HMRC Amendments to Tax Returns	
HMRC can 'amend' obvious errors and omissions themselves	9 months after submission
HMRC can investigate and amend a Return after a genuine error by a taxpayer	4 years after submission
HMRC can investigate and amend a Return after a careless error by a taxpayer	6 years after submission
HMRC can investigate and amend a Return after a deliberate error by a taxpayer	20 years after submission

4) Failure to keep records

HMRC can apply a maximum penalty of £3,000 per tax year for each failure to keep adequate records. If you are self-employed you need to keep your records for five years from 31 January following the tax year for which the tax return is made.

HMRC enquiries

HMRC have powers to inspect premises, assets and records (e.g. financial information) belonging to a business, and to ask taxpayers and other third parties (such as tax practitioners) for further information or additional documentation.

HMRC is required to 'act reasonably' in relation to any inspections they carry out; this means, for example, they would provide written notice of an intention to commence an investigation. It is usual for at least seven days' notice to be provided in this way.

One of the fundamental principles of self-assessment is **'process now, check later'**.

Processing involves submitting the tax return to HM Revenue & Customs as quickly as possible, so that liabilities, as calculated by the taxpayer, are recorded, whilst the enquiry procedure forms the 'check later' part of the equation.

HMRC have the right to issue an enquiry at any time during a fixed period after submission of the return, known as the enquiry window, and must give the taxpayer written notice when they intend to make an enquiry.

The enquiry window in respect of Income Tax, Partnership and Corporation Tax Returns closes **twelve months after the date the return was delivered**. This is designed to encourage an even flow of work for advisers and HMRC during the year, rather than the heavy workload of submissions towards the 31 January filing deadline.

Such enquiries may relate to specific aspects of the return or may result from random selection. Taxpayers must by law keep all documents relating to the preparation and completion of the Tax Return for **5 years** after 31 January following the end of the tax year, in order that they are available to deal with any enquiries. If any enquiries are raised, the records should be kept until the conclusion of those enquiries and penalties of up to £3,000 may be imposed for failing to keep records for the required period.

Taxpayers and tax practitioners must keep sufficient records to enable HMRC to verify and substantiate any tax return which has been submitted.

If the return is sent on or before the deadline then records should be kept for at least **22 months** from the end of the tax year to which they relate- this is one year after the normal 31 January filing and payment date.

However, for clients with their own business (e.g. sole traders), or who let property, the records must be retained for a **further 4 years** - a total of five years and ten months from the end of the tax year. For the tax year 2024-25, therefore, records should be kept until at least 31 January 2030.

If there is an ongoing HMRC enquiry then records must be retained until at least the conclusion of the investigation.

Failure to produce enquiry documents has a penalty of £300 + £60 per day, the same as unlimited businesses.

Summary of Chapter 10

- Corporation Tax Self-Assessment is where the company uses an Agent or they themselves do the calculations of the CT payable for the accounting period covered by the return and then do the requirements to file by the deadlines to avoid penalties.
- The filing due date for a limited company is the **later** of:
  12 months after the end of the period of account
  3 months from the date of the notice requiring the return.
- If a company fails to submit a tax return by the due date, it will be subject to a penalty.
- Changes or amendments to a CT return must be made within 12 months of the filing deadline.
- Corporation tax is due for payment nine months and one day after the end of the accounting period for a small company.
- Large companies with annual profits greater than £1,5 million must estimate the year's tax liability and pay 25% of the estimate on the 14th day of each of the 7th, 10th, 13th and 16th month from the start of the accounting period.
- If corporation tax is overpaid to HMRC then interest will be paid by them from the date that the overpaid tax was paid until the date it is refunded.

- The deadline for submitting the (online) tax return for an individual is 31 January after the end of the tax year.
- HMRC require some taxpayers to pay their tax liability for a year in three instalments, known as **Payments on Account**.

Assessment 10

You are now required to log in to your ROGO account to complete your online assessment before progressing to the mock exam.

Mock Exam

You will have **2 hours and 30 minutes** to complete this **Business Tax** practice assessment.

- This assessment contains **10 tasks** and you should attempt to complete **every** task.
- Each task is independent. You will not need to refer to your answers to previous tasks.
- The total number of marks for this assessment is **100.**
- Read every task carefully to make sure you understand what is required.
- Where the date is relevant, it is given in the task data.
- Both minus signs and brackets can be used to indicate negative numbers **unless** task instructions state otherwise.
- You must use a full stop to indicate a decimal point. For example, write 100.57 NOT 100,57 or 100 57.
- You may use a comma to indicate a number in the thousands, but you don't have to. For example, 10000 and 10,000 are both acceptable.
- If your answer requires rounding, apply normal mathematical rules **unless** the task instructions say otherwise.

Task 1 (8 marks)

This task is about adjusting accounting profits and losses for tax purposes.

The profit or loss account of Herron Ltd is as follows:

	£
Sales	195,148
Cost of sales	(89,663)
Gross profit	105,485
Other income	9,000
Interest received	690
	115,175
Expenses:	
Depreciation	12,444
Repairs and maintenance	2,000
Sales and Marketing	2,500
Administration	40,000
Legal expenses	12,506
Interest payable	500
	(69,950)
Net profit	45,225

Additional information has been provided as follows:

1. Other income relates to property rental income.
2. Interest received is bank deposit interest for the year ending 31/12/2024.
3. Repairs and maintenance are the repair cost to the factory floor.
4. Sales and marketing include:
    - Entertaining customers £675
    - Donation to a local charity £200
    - Political donation £400
5. Administration includes:
    - Patent registration £15,000
    - Dividend received £2,000
    - Decrease in general bad debt provision £1,300
    - Profit on sale of machine £2,800
6. Interest payable refers to a trading loan

Calculate the taxable trading profit for Herron Ltd by entering adjustments to the accounting profit below. If no adjustment is required, you should enter a zero. If any adjustments are deducted from accounting profits, these should be shown as a negative figure using minus signs (for example, a deduction of 1,000 should be shown as -1000 or -1,000.

	£
Accounting profit	
Depreciation	
Property rental income	
Interest received non-trading	
Repair to factory floor	
Entertaining customers	
Donation to local charity	
Political donation	
Patent registration	
Dividend received	
Decrease in general bad debt provision	
Profit on sale of machine	
Interest payable	
Taxable profit	

Task 2 (12 marks)

This task is about capital allowances.

1. James owns his own business and prepares his accounts to 31 December each year.

On 1 January 2024, his TWDV b/fwd on his main pool was £55,950.

During the year he purchased the following:

- 1 April 2024 he purchased a motor vehicle with emissions of 115g/km registered 1 May 2023 for £32,975, the car was used both for business and private use at a rate of 70% business and 30% private based on mileage figures agreed with HMRC.
- 15 September he purchased office furniture for £17,640.
- 5 November he disposed of his old computer for £250 and purchased a new one for £3,674.
- 2 December he purchased further office furniture for £10,240

Complete the capital allowance computation for the period ending 31 December 2024. The brought forward figures have already been entered. (9 marks)

Ensure that:

- Any additions are included in the correct column.
- All allowances are included in the total allowances column
- Carried forward balances are clearly shown.
- Figures are rounded up to whole numbers
- Any boxes with no required figures should have a 0 entered.
- Enter a minus sign when any amounts are being deducted.

Additions	AIA	General pool	Private use asset	Total allowances
£	£	£	£	£
TWDV b/f		55,950	0	
Plant & Machinery				
AIA allowance				
Transfer to general pool				
Other additions				
Disposals				
Balance				
WDA 18%				
WDA 6%				
Allowances for period				
c/f total				

2. Plowver Limited has a financial year end of 31 March. On 1 April 2024, the TWDV b/f in the main pool is £18,460. Plowver Ltd ceased to trade on 31 December 2024. Plowver will be required to calculate the final accounting period. Additions and disposals in the final period to 31 December 2024 are:

- 1 May 2024 purchased plant costing £6,000
- 30 September 2024 disposal of plant £33,500

Complete the capital allowances template showing either a negative or positive balancing charge. Enter a 0 in any boxes not requiring a figure and use a minus sign for any deductions. (3 marks)

	Additions/ Disposals	General pool	Total allowances
£		£	£
TWDV b/f		**18,460**	
Additions			
Disposals			
Transfer to general pool			
Balancing allowance			
Balancing charge			
Balance			
Allowances for period			

Task 3 (8 marks)

This task is about analysing the profits and losses of a partnership and calculating NICs.

Dave and Sue are in partnership, trading as consultants with an accounting year end of 31 July 2024. They share profits 3:1 respectively. From 1 May 2024, Tim joined the partnership. It was agreed that Tim would be paid a salary of £12,000 per annum and that the profits would now be shared 2:2:1 for Dave, Sue and Tim.

The taxable profit for the year ended 31 July 2024 was £108,000.

a) Calculate the trading profits for each partner by completing the missing entries in the appropriation of profits below. All entries should be stated to the nearest pound. Complete all boxes and any values that are nil, enter a 0. (6 marks)

	Dave £	Sue £	Tim £	Total £
Period to 30 April 2024				
Profit share				
Period to 31 July 2024				
Salary				
Profit share				
Total profit for the year				

b) Sarah is 35 years old and has taxable adjusted trading profits of £6,800 for the year ended 2024/2025. Her accounts show a net profit of £6,010 for the year ended 31 March 2024.

Calculate Sarah's Class 4 national insurance contributions for 2024/2025. Your answer should be to the nearest penny and if your answer is zero or nil, enter 0. (1 mark)

NIC	Amount payable (£)
Class 4	

c) Lauren is 48 years old and has a self-employed income of £30,000.

Calculate the amount of class 4 NICs that would be payable. Your answer should be to the nearest pound and if your answer is zero or nil, enter 0. (2 marks)

NIC	Amount payable (£)
Class 4	

Task 4 (8 marks)

This task is about chargeable gains and allowable losses of companies.

a) Greab Ltd sold a freehold office building on 1 June 2024 for £550,000. The building had cost £245,000 on 7 June 2005. Greab Ltd is using the funds to purchase a piece of manufacturing plant on 1 July 2024 costing £520,000. Both the building and plant have been used for the purposes of the trade of Greab Limited. Greab Ltd produces its financial accounts to the end of December each year.

Relevant indexation factor:

June 2005 – December 2017 is 0.447

Calculate the chargeable gain to be included in the corporation tax computation of Greab Ltd for the year ended 31 December 2024.

Any amounts to be deducted in calculating the gain should be shown as a negative figure using minus signs. All entries should be stated to the nearest £. (6 marks)

Chargeable gains computation	£
Proceeds	**550,000**
Cost including acquisition expenses	
Unindexed gain/loss	
Indexation allowance	
Indexed chargeable gain before reliefs	
Less relief	
Chargeable gain	

b) Identify whether the following statements are true or false. (2 marks)

Statement	True or False?
The new assets must be bought within 3 years of selling or disposing of the old ones, or up to one year before.	
As the Indexation Allowance was frozen in December 2018, indexation can only be applied for ownership of the asset up to December 2018.	

Task 5 (9 marks)

This task is about calculating chargeable gains and allowable losses in company disposal of shares.

Dimecross Ltd had the following transactions in the shares of Creative Products Ltd.

Date	Event	Number of Shares	£ per share
March 2010	Purchase	2,800	20
April 2011	Bonus Issue	1 for 4	-
Nov 2012	Rights issue	1 for 2	22
10 Oct 2024	Purchase	2,000	40
18 Oct 2024	Sale	3,000	42

Indexation factors that are relevant are:

Month	April 2011	November 2012	December 2017
March 2010	0.084	0.126	0.280
April 2011	-	0.068	0.188
Nov 2012	-	-	0.135

a) Complete the share pool for Dimecross Ltd. The purchase in March 2010 has already been included. Show the balance of shares carried forward and give your answers to the nearest £. You may have been given more spaces than you will need. (5 marks)

Events Description	Number of shares	Cost £	Indexed cost £
Purchase March 2010	2,800	56,000	56,000

b) Calculate the chargeable gain or allowable loss on the disposal of the shares in Creative Products Ltd by Dimecross Ltd in the year ended 31 October 2024. You may have been given more spaces than you will need. (4 marks)

Chargeable gains computation	£
Proceeds	

Task 6 (10 marks)

This task is about calculating taxable profits and corporation tax payable.

a) The accounts for D&C Engineers Ltd show the following information for the 16 months ended 31 March 2025.

Trading profits	£160,000
Rental income	£44,000
Chargeable gain 11 November 2024	£122,000
Capital loss on 15 December 2024	£106,000
Qualifying charitable donation on 1 July 2024	£6,000

Additional information:

The company is not entitled to any capital allowances during the period.

Calculate the total corporation tax liability of D&C Engineers Ltd for the 16-month trading period using the table below. Any items that should be deducted should be indicated with a minus sign (-). **Any boxes that are nil enter a '0'. (6 marks)**

	Year ended 30 November 2024	Four Months ended 31 March 2025
	£	£
Trading profit		
Rental income		
Chargeable gain		
Charitable donation		
Total taxable profits		
Corporation tax liability		
Total corporation tax liability		

b) Quartz Ltd has taxable total profits of £135,000 for the six-month period ended 31 December 2024. It has no associated companies.

Calculate the corporation tax payable for the period ending 31 December 2024. State your answer to the nearest pound (£). (2 marks)

£

c) Diamonte Ltd has taxable total profits of £140,000 for the year ended 31 March 2025. It has one associated company.

Calculate the corporation tax payable for the period ending 31 March 2025. State your answer to the nearest pound (£). (2 marks)

£

Task 7 (15 marks)

This task is about the administrative requirements for UK tax law.

1. Lycett Ltd is a small company and they have received a notice to file a return for the year ended 30 June 2024 on 20 July 2024.

Identify the correct deadline for the actions below from the following options. (4 marks)

- 30 June 2024
- 30 June 2025
- 20 July 2025
- 1 April 2025

The filing date of the company's corporation tax return for the year ended 30 June 2024 is:	
The payment date of the corporation tax for the year ended 30 June 2024 is:	

2. Solus Ltd is a large company with annual profits greater than 1.5 million and pays corporation tax in quarterly instalments for the year ended 31 March 2025.

Complete the following table to show when the instalments are due. Enter your dates in the format of XX/XX/20XX. (4 marks)

Instalment	Payment Date
First	
Final	

3. Identify whether the following statements are true or false. (6 marks)

	True or false
a) The maximum penalty for late filing of an income tax return if it is less than 3 months late is £100.	
b) The maximum penalty for submitting a corporation tax return more than 6 months but less than 12 months late is £200 + 10% of the tax due.	
c) The penalty for failure to keep records for 6 years is up to £3,000 in total.	
d) The maximum penalties for errors made by individuals in their tax returns can vary from 20% to 100%.	
e) An individual has up to one year from the date of the filing deadline to amend a return, not the date of submission.	
f) Late payment penalties are only payable for late payment of balancing payments, not payments on account.	

4. Jai made a sudden voluntary disclosure to HMRC, who then considered it to be a deliberate error concealed by Jai. HMRC has decided that a further £6,000 is payable. (1 mark)

	£
What is the minimum penalty he may incur?	
What is the maximum penalty he may incur?	

Task 8 (12 marks)

This task is about tax planning and the responsibilities of the business and agent.

1. HMRC has an area which has a source of tax guidance. Does this guidance have force of law? (1 mark)

2. Parhut Limited has decided not to include some income from renting out part of their business premises on their Corporation Tax return. Does this omission constitute? (1 mark)

   a) Tax evasion
   b) Tax avoidance
   c) Tax planning

3. Annie is a sole shareholder and director of a small limited company that has no employees. The profits of the limited company (for tax and accounting purposes) are expected to be £35,000 before corporation tax each year. Annie has other income from employment of £50,000 and dividend income of £4,000 which will make her a higher rate taxpayer.

   What would be the maximum dividends that Annie will be able to take each year? (1 mark)

   £

4. From 1 January 2025 the Annual investment allowance is £1,000,000. Is this true or false? (1 mark)

5. To operate as a tax practitioner, you must have an agent code before you can set up agent authorisation for tax, to be able to deal with your client's tax details. Is this true or false? (1 mark)

6. Henrietta is a sole director of Henny's Ltd and as well as dividends she also receives income from employment and is a higher rate taxpayer. Her husband Henry does not have any income as he is the full-time parent responsible for the children.

Which of the following would be advantageous to Henrietta and Henry for keeping their taxes low? There may be more than one answer. (4 marks)

a) Using BADR for Henry
b) Transferring some shares in Henny's Ltd to Henry
c) Utilising Henry's lower tax rate for any gains
d) Henry being employed by Henny's Ltd
e) Using rollover relief

7. What is the current annual exempt amount for tax year 2024/25? (1 mark)

a) 12,790
b) 12,300
c) 3,000
d) 37,700

8. A personal company is one in which the donor holds at least what percentage of the voting rights? (1 mark)

a) 10%
b) 2%
c) 5%
d) 50%

9. A rights issue of shares is not paid for but a bonus issue is. Is this statement true or false? (1 mark)

Task 9 (8 marks)

This task is about trading losses.

Kormoraunt Limited has the following results for the 3 years to 31 March 2024.

- (£15,000) loss 2022
- £7,000 profit 2023
- £10,000 profit 2024
- £5,000 non-trade interest 2023
- £4,000 non-trade interest 2024

Carry forward loss relief is to be relieved as soon as possible and claims to be made.

a) Complete the template below for corporation tax for the 3 years. Use a minus sign for any deductions and a 0 for any boxes not requiring a figure.

Corporation Tax Computations	2022	2023	2024
	£	£	£
Trading profit/(loss)			
Add: Non-trade Interest			
Total profits			
Less: Loss relief			
Less: Qualifying charitable donations			
Taxable total profits (TTP)			

b) Complete the loss memorandum workings.

Loss Memorandum workings	£
Year ending 31 March 2024	

Task 10 (10 marks)

This task is about business disposals.

1. Which of the following are eligible for Business Asset Disposal Relief? (1 mark)

    a) Limited company that has been trading for at least 2 years before sale.
    b) Partner in a business partnership who has owned the business for at least 12 months before sale.
    c) Sole trader who has owned the business for at least 2 years before sale.
    d) Sole trader who has owned the business for at least a year before sale.

2. Tina has run her sole trader business for over 10 years. At the end of December 2024, she decides she wants to retire and gifts her business to her son Turner.

Tina pays income tax at the higher rate and has not made any earlier capital disposals. At 31 December 2024, the business assets were valued as:

	Market Value £	Original cost £	TWDV £
Warehouse	180,000	80,000	
Plant	15,000	25,000	1,500
Goodwill	40,000	0	

Identify any capital gain or loss that may arise on the disposal of each asset assuming no reliefs are claimed. If no gain or loss arises, enter 0. Any loss should be shown as a negative figure using a minus sign. (3 marks)

Asset	Capital gain/(loss) £
Warehouse	
Plant	
Goodwill	

3. On 4 June 2024, Giuseppe gave 80% shareholding in his personal company (market value £1.75 million) to his daughter Aurora.

The resulting gain for the purposes of CGT was £350,000.

Complete the following showing the chargeable gain, if any for Giuseppe and the capital gains base cost for Aurora. (6 marks)

	Giuseppe £		Aurora £
Market value		Market value	
Less: cost			
Less: gift relief		Less: held over gain	
Chargeable gain		CGT base cost	

Taxation references 24/25

Income Tax			
Trading allowance			£1,000
Personal allowance			£12,570
	Basic rate (£0 - £37,700)	Higher rate (£37,701 - £125,140)	Additional rate (Above £125,140)
Salary	20%	40%	45%
Dividends	8.75%	33.75	39.35%
Trading income	20%	40%	45%

National Insurance (NI)	
Class 4 contributions on trading profits between £12,570 and £50,270	6%
Class 4 contributions on trading profits above £50,270	2%

- Dividends are not subject to NI
- Salaries are subject to:
  - Employee NI at 8% between £12,570 and £50,270 and 2% above £50,270.
  - Employer NI at 13.8% above £9,100 (an employment allowance of £5,000 is available).
- Calculations of NI on salaries will not be required in assessment but the rates may be used in tax planning discussions.

Capital gains tax	
Annual exempt amount	£3,000
Basic rate	10%
Higher rate	20%
Business asset disposal relief	10%
Business asset disposal relief lifetime allowance	£1,000,000

Corporation Tax	
Main rate of corporation tax	25%
Small profits rate of Corporation tax	19%
Upper limit	£250,000*
Lower limit	£50,000*
Marginal small company relief	3/200 x (upper limit – TTP)

- Reduced it:
- -accounting period <12 months
- Associated companies

Capital allowances	
Annual investment allowance	£1,000,000
Writing down allowance	18%
Full expensing – expenditure by companies after 1 April 2023	100%
Writing down allowance cars: CO_2 emissions 0g/km CO_2 emissions up to 50 g/km CO_2 emissions over 50 g/km	 100% 18% 6%
Small pools allowance	£1,000
Structures and buildings allowance	3%

Disallowed expenditure		
Types of expense	**Disallowable in calculation of trading profit**	**Notes**
Fines and penalties	Fines on the business, directors/owner.	Employee fines are not disallowed if incurred in the course of their employment.
Donations	Political donations and donations to national charities.	Donations to local charities are allowable (these will only be examined for unincorporated businesses.
Capital expenditure	Depreciation. Gain/loss on disposal. Capital items expensed.*	Capital allowances may be available.
Legal and professional	Capital items including the purchase of leases and renewal of long leases* Breaches of law/regulations. Settling tax disputes.	Legal fees on the renewal of a short lease (50 years or less) are allowable.
Entertaining and gifts	Customer gifts (unless <£50 per annum, not food, drink, tobacco, or cash vouchers and contains business advertising).	Staff gifts and staff entertaining are allowable.

	Customer/supplier entertaining.	
Cars	Depreciation. Private use by owners. 15% of lease cost if leased car >50g/km CO2 emissions.	Capital allowances may be available
Private expenditure of owner	Goods taken for own use. Salary of owners. Private use % by owners. Private expenditure	Reasonable salaries of family members are allowable.

- Capital items and associated legal expenses are not disallowed under the cash basis providing the expense does not relate to the acquisition or disposal or a business, land, cars or an asset not acquired for use in the trade.

Trading losses		
Loss option	**Sole trader/Partner**	**Company**
Carry forward	Against future profits of the same trade only. Applies automatically to first available profits. Applies after any other elections or if no elections are made.	Losses not relieved in the current accounting period or previous 12 months are carried forward and an election cab be made to set against total profits in future periods.
Current year/carry back	Against total income in the current and/or previous tax year in any order. If opted for in either year, the amount of loss used cannot be restricted to preserve the personal allowance. Make claim by 31 January 2027 for 2024/25 tax year.	Can elect to set trading losses against current accounting period 'total profits'. QCDs will remain unrelieved. If the above election is made, can also carry back trading loss to set against 'total profits' within the previous 12 months. Claim within 2 years of the end of the loss-making period.
Opening year loss relief – loss in first four years of trade	Against total income of the previous three tax years on a FIFO basis. If opted for, losses will be used to reduce total income as much as possible in each year and cannot be restricted to preserve the personal allowance. Make claim by 31 January 2027 for 2024/25 tax year.	N/A

Terminal loss relief	Against trading profits of the previous 3 years on a LIFO basis. Claim within 4 years from the end of the last tax year of trade.	Against total profits of the previous 3 years. Claim within 2 years of the end of the loss-making period.

Chargeable gains - reliefs	
Relief	**Conditions**
Rollover relief	Available to individuals and companies. Examinable for companies only. Qualifying assets (original and replacement) - must be used in a trade and be land and buildings or fixed plant and machinery. Qualifying time period – replacement asset must be purchased between one year before and three years after the sale of the original asset. Partial reinvestment – if only some of the sales proceeds reinvested then the gain taxable is the lower of the full gain and the proceeds not reinvested.
Gift relief	Available to individuals only. Qualifying assets – assets used in the trade of the donor or the donor's personal company, shares in any unquoted trading company or shares in the donors personal trading company. A personal trading company is one where the donor has at least 5%.
Business asset disposal relief	Available to individuals only. Gain taxable at 10%. £1m lifetime limit. For 2024/25 a claim must be made by 31 January 2027. Qualifying assets: - The whole or part of a business carried on by the individual (alone or in partnership). The assets must have been owned for 24 months prior to the sale. - Assets of the individual's or partnership's trading business that has now ceased. The assets must have been owned for 24 months prior to cessation and sale must be within 3 years of cessation. - Shares in the individual's personal trading company (own at least 5%). The individual must have owned the shares and been an employee of the company for 24 months prior to sale.

Payment and administration		
	Sole traders/partners	**Company**
Filing date	31 October following the end of the tax year if filing a paper return. 31 January following the end of the tax year if filing online. Amendments can be made within 12 months of filing.	Filed on the later of 12 months after end of AP or 3 months after the notice to deliver a tax return has been issued. Company can amend return within 12 months of the filing date.
Payment date	31 January following the end of the tax year. If payments on accounts are due: • First POA – 31 January during tax year • Second POA – 31 July after tax year • Balancing payment – 31 January after tax year POA's are each 50% of the previous years' income tax and class 4 NICs due by self-assessment. POA's are not required for capital gains or class 2 NICs. POA's are not due if prior year tax payable by self-assessment is less than £1,000 OR if >80% of prior year tax was collected at source.	Small companies (annual profits less than £1.5 million): 9 months + 1 day after end of the accounting period (AP). Large companies (annual profits greater than £1.5 million) must estimate the year's tax liability and pay 25% of the estimate on the 14th day of each of the 7th, 10th, 13th and 16th month from the start of the accounting period.
Interest	Charged daily on late payment.	Interest charged daily on late payment. Overpayment of tax receives interest from HMRC. Interest is taxable/tax allowable as interest income.
Penalties for late filing	£100. After 3 months, £10 per day for up to 90 days. After 6 months, 5% tax due (or £300 if greater). After 12 months, 5% tax due (or £300 if greater) if not deliberate. After 12 months, 70% of tax due (or £300 if greater) if deliberate and not concealed.	£100. After 3months £100. After 6 months 10% of unpaid tax. After 12 months 10% of unpaid tax.

	After 12 months, 100% tax due (or £300 if greater) if deliberate and concealed.	
Late payment	30 days ate – 5% of tax outstanding at that date. 6 months days late – 5% of tax outstanding at that date. 12 months late – 5% of tax outstanding at that date	N/A
Notify of chargeability	5 October following the end of the tax year.	Within 3 months of starting to trade.
Enquiry	Within 12 months of submission of return. Penalty for failure to produce enquiry documents = £300 + £60 per day.	Within 12 months of submission of return. Penalty for failure to produce enquiry documents £300 + £60 per day.
Record retention	Five years from filing date. Penalty for failure to keep records is up to £3,000.	Six years after the end of the relevant accounting period. Penalty for failure to keep proper records is up to £3,000.

Penalties for incorrect returns			
Type of behaviour	**Maximum**	**Unprompted (min)**	**Prompted (min)**
Careless error and inaccuracy are due to failure to take reasonable care	30%	0%	15%
Deliberate error but not concealed	70%	20%	35%
Deliberate error and concealed	100%	30%	50%

Glossary

Accounting period	Period that Corporation tax is payable, cannot be longer than 12 months.
Accounting profit	Profit shown in the accounts before taxation.
AEA	Annual exempt amount.
AIA	Annual investment allowance.
Allowable expenses	Revenue and not capital in nature and wholly and exclusively for the purpose of the trade.
AML	Anti-money-laundering.
BADR	Business asset disposal relief.
Badges of trade	Determines whether a trade is operating.
Balancing allowance	Used where proceeds are less than the written down value.
Balancing charge	Used where the proceeds are more than the written down value.
Basis periods	Profits applied to periods within a tax year.
Bonus shares	Issued free to existing shareholders as per their current holding.
CAP	Chargeable accounting period for corporation tax.
Capital expenditure	The expense of a high value item that brings long-term benefit to the business, like machinery.
CGT	Capital gains tax.
Chargeable asset	Any asset that is not an exempt asset.
Chargeable disposal	Sale or gift of an asset.
Chargeable gains	Gain on the sale or disposal of an asset.
Chargeable person	An individual or company.
Chattel	A tangible moving thing.
CPD	Continuing professional development.
Confidentiality	Keeping client information confidential unless there is a legal obligation to disclose.

Corporation Tax	A tax on limited companies.
Depreciation	A reduction in the value of assets owned by the business.
Disallowed expenses	Expenses that cannot be deducted in computing taxable trading profits.
Dividend income	Income from dividends from shares in companies.
FYA	First year allowance.
IA	Indexation allowance.
Income Tax	A tax on individuals.
Inheritance Tax	A tax levied on the estates of the deceased.
Integrity	Being honest, transparent and fair in all business relationships.
ISA	Individual savings account.
Long life asset	Asset with a lifespan of at least 25 years.
N. I.	National insurance.
Non-savings income	Income from employment, self-employment, pensions, state benefits, etc.
Objectivity	Having an unbiased view and not allowing conflicts of interest or undue influence to affect professional judgement.
Overlap profits	Profits that are taxed more than once when a business starts trading.
PAYE	Pay as you earn.
Period of account	Period that a business prepares its financial statements.
Personal trading allowance	Applies to low level earners currently £1,000.
Private use asset	Only applies to individuals and restricts capital allowances.
Professional behaviour	Being compliant with all rules and regulations and not bringing the profession into disrepute.
Professional competence and due care	Keeping knowledge and skills up to date and being competent and acting diligently at all times.

QCDs	Qualifying charitable donations – gifts that receive tax relief.
Revenue expenditure	Regular everyday expenses which bring benefit in the period it is made.
Rights issue	Shares offered to existing shareholders as per their current holding but paid for.
Savings income	Income from banks and building societies, ISAs and investments.
Short life asset	Sold or disposed of within eight years.
SRA	Special rate allowance.
Taxable profit	Profit determined by the taxation authorities regulations and rules that are relevant for taxation.
Tax avoidance	Using loopholes to reduce or avoid paying tax.
Tax evasion	Always illegal and can incur fines and imprisonment.
Tax planning	Legally being able to reduce tax liability by using available legal exemptions and deductions.
TTP	Taxable total profits – on which tax applies.
Wasting chattel	An asset with a useful life of less than 50 years.
WDA	Writing down allowance.

This page is left intentionally blank.

Answers to Chapter 1 Activities

Answer to Activity 1.1

a) An agent code is only required for authorisation for self-assessment. Is this statement true or false?

False, an agent code is required for every individual service you are required to assist your client with completing.

b) Which of the following statements regarding a tax agent for a business is/are incorrect?

i) **A business must only appoint one tax agent for their tax affairs.** ✓
ii) A business can appoint more than one agent to deal with their tax affairs.
iii) **A tax agent is entirely responsible for the payment of the business tax on time.** ✓
iv) A tax agent can file the business tax returns on behalf of the business.

Both i) and iii). More than one agent can be used for a business and it is the business that is responsible for ensuring the payments of tax are made on time.

c) Match the correct word/s to the relevant description in the table below:

Description	Word/s
Allows the client to give you authorisation to act on their behalf.	**Form 64-8**
Sets out the expectations from HMRC by Agents.	**HMRC standard for Agents**
Required to register as an Agent online.	**Government Gateway User ID and password**

Answer to Activity 1.2

a) Give a brief description with details of any items that may be relevant to the question.

Answer: **It is legal, however, it is an example of tax avoidance and you should not comply with the request but advise your client that most tax avoidance schemes simply do not work and those who engage in it can sometimes be forced to pay more tax than the tax saved if HMRC successfully challenges them.**

b) Which of the fundamental principles could be breached if you agreed to the amendment in question 1 above?

Fundamental principle	Breached Yes/No?
Integrity	YES
Professional competence and due care	NO
Professional behaviour	YES
Confidentiality	NO
Objectivity	YES

Integrity – has been breached as tax practitioners must ensure that all tax returns submitted on behalf of clients are completed fairly and honestly with no attempt to under-declare the amount of taxes owing by the taxpayer.

Professional behaviour – a tax practitioner must comply with relevant laws and regulations and avoid any action that may bring disrepute to the profession.

Objectivity – could be breached as there has been an influence by the Managing Director to use a loophole and this is not really being honest, transparent and fair.

c) A Limited Company would be liable to pay Income Tax on its annual profits.

Is this statement, True or False and why?

False, it would be liable to pay Corporation tax, not income tax.

d) Which of the following types of businesses would not pay corporation tax?

i) Whillans & Son (window cleaners) ✓

ii) Fox Fixtures Ltd (Furniture makers)

iii) Motor Emporium Plc (Nationwide car sales)

iv) CF Counts & Co (partnership of accountants) ✓

The window cleaners are sole traders and the firm of accountants is a partnership, therefore they would not pay corporation tax but the furniture makers and nationwide car sales businesses would as they have Ltd and plc at the end of their business names.

Answer to Activity 1.3

What is the taxable income for Benjamin?

£3,230

£15,800 - £12,570 personal allowance = £3,230

Answer to Activity 1.4

What will Ralph's tax liability be for the year?

£5,026

£37,700 - £12,570 personal allowance = £25,130 taxable income @ 20% liability = £5,026

Answer to Activity 1.5

What would be Sylvester's tax liability for 2024/25?

£37,700 @ 20% = **£7,540**

£87,440 @ 40% = **£34,976**

£46,860 @ 45% = **£21,087**

Total tax liability = **£63,603**

Answer to Activity 1.6

a) Whull Limited was incorporated and started trading on 5 March 2024 and its period of account end date is 31 March 2025.

1) What will be the first accounting period for Corporation Tax?

Answer: First accounting period for CT ends 4 March 2025 (12 months from 5 March 2024).

2) What will be the second accounting period for Corporation Tax?

Answer: Second accounting period for CT ends 31 March 2025 covering the period from 5 March 2025 to 31 March 2025

b) Choose from the following to give the final chargeable accounting period for CT.

a) 1 September 2024 to 31 August 2025
b) 1 February 2025 to 31 August 2025 ✓

1 February 2025 to 31 August 2025. From the date the administrator is appointed to the date of cease of trading.

Answer to Activity 1.7

a) What is the start date of the final chargeable accounting period for corporation tax purposes?

The start date of the final chargeable accounting period is the date they entered into administration being 1 January 2025.

b) What is the end date of the final chargeable accounting period for corporation tax purposes?

The end date is the date they ceased trading being 31 July 2025.

Answers to Chapter 2 Activities

Answer to Activity 2.1

Would Andrew be classed as an art collector or an art dealer? What badge of trade, if any, would determine that trading is happening?

A written summary explaining your answer should be given:

While Andrew displays or keeps the art for himself on a small basis as a hobby over a long period of time, this would not be seen to be trading but would be more of an investment so he could be classified as an art collector at this stage.

However, when he starts to resell the art on a regular basis, the low length of ownership would indicate trading.

The badge of profit seeking motive would apply as he intends to sell these items on at a higher value than purchased on the market stall.

There would also be a change in the frequency and number of transactions as more sales would be achieved on a more regular basis.

Upon retiring from employment and while selling the art on a regular basis he could be classified as an art dealer.

Answer to Activity 2.2

What would be the adjusted trading profit for Kirstie?

£14,900

Steps	Adjustment of Profits	£
1	Net profit before tax as per accounts	15,000
	Add	
2	Disallowable expenses	2,300
3	Income not included in the accounts but taxable as trading income	0
		17,300
	Deduct	
4	Income in the accounts not taxable as trading income,	0
	Adjusted trading profit before deduction of capital expenses	17,300
5	Expenditure deductible from trading profits, e.g. capital allowances	(2,400)
6	**Adjusted trading profit**	14,900

Answer to Activity 2.3

Identify which of the following are revenue or capital by ticking the correct box:

	Revenue ✓	Capital ✓
Buying a vehicle		✓
Repainting an existing office	✓	
Purchasing new premises		✓
Extending existing premises		✓
Paying rent on shop outlet	✓	
Paying for repairs to machinery	✓	

Answer to Activity 2.4

The following expenses have been incurred by a limited company. You are required to determine whether any or all of the expenses are allowable for tax purposes:

Expense	Amount £	Allowable Yes or No?
Staff outing to the races for 30 employees.	3,600.00	Yes
A gift to a customer of a bottle of aged port with the company emblem on the bottle.	49.99	No
A floral gift to an employee who has just given birth.	25.00	Yes
Company embossed diaries of £15 each to customers at Christmas.	450.00	Yes
Donation to the local conservative party.	200.00	No
Speeding fine incurred by a director.	75.00	No
Donation to the local hospice.	100.00	Yes

Answer to Activity 2.5

Show whether the following should be allowed, disallowed and added back disallowed and deducted.

	Allow	Disallow and add back	Disallow and deduct
Owner's parking fine		✓	
Decrease in general bad debt provision			✓
Depreciation charge		✓	
Donation to a local charity	✓		
Patent registration legal fees	✓		
Rental income received			✓
£7 stolen from petty cash by employee	✓		
Employees salaries	✓		
Fee for chasing an irrecoverable debt	✓		
Entertaining suppliers		✓	

Answer to Activity 2.6

How much, if any should be added back in the calculation of adjusting trading profit?

The 40% for business use is allowable but the 60% of personal use must be added back as disallowable.
60% x £3,000 = £1,800

Answer to Activity 2.7

Calculate the taxable profit by making relevant adjustments to the accounting net profit.

Adjustment of Profits	£
Net profit before tax as per accounts	81,950
Add	
Depreciation charges	12,300
Entertainment	3,000
General allowance for doubtful receivables	1,800
Adjusted trading profit before deduction of capital expenses	99,050
Capital allowances	(8,200)
Adjusted trading profit	90,850

The depreciation, entertainment and bad debt provision are all disallowable expenses for tax purposes and therefore added to the net profit, which increases the net profit, the capital allowances are allowable expenses therefore deducted from the net profit which then decrease the net profit and the tax liability.

Answer to Activity 2.8

What would be the total disallowed expenditure for the financial year ending 31 December 2024?

£675

£6,500 for the first car will be allowed. The second car will have a disallowed element as the CO^2 emissions are higher than the 50g/km restriction. Therefore 15% of £4,500 being £675 will be disallowed.

Answer to Activity 2.9

Calculate IKA Ltd.'s tax adjusted trading profit for the year ending 31 March 2025 using the following template.

Add back disallowed items and subtract the items that are not taxable as trading income, placing brackets () around them to show that they are to be subtracted.

Steps	IKA Ltd Adjustment of Profits	£
1	Profit before tax as per accounts	11,436
	Add	
2	Asset repair/improvement Depreciation charge Loss on sale of asset Legal fees for breach of official regulations Director's fine Entertaining customers	1,800 4,200 480 4,500 3,000 3,600
	Less	
3	Bank deposit interest	(1,920)
	Dividends received	(4,800)
	Adjusted trading profit before deduction of capital allowances	22,296

Irrecoverable debts written off recovered are allowable.

Improving an asset is disallowed as this is capital expenditure.

Repairs to the wall are allowable as a revenue expense.

Motor expenses are allowable as every day running expenses.

Depreciation and loss on the sale of an asset are both disallowed.

Accountancy fees are everyday running expenses.

Legal fees for breach of regulations are disallowed as they are an infringement of the law.

Director's fines are never allowable.

Legal fees for debt collection are allowable as a revenue expense along with trade subscriptions.

Entertaining customers is disallowable but the gifts under £50 with the company logo are allowable as an expense.

Bank deposit interest received is non-trading interest received and is required to be deducted from net profit as it will be accounted for in the corporation tax computation for limited companies.

Dividends received should not have been included in the net profit calculation and if they have they need deducting as part of the adjusted trading profit.

This page is left intentionally blank.

Answers to Chapter 3 Activities

Answer to Activity 3.1

Identify which of the following would be defined as plant and machinery for capital allowances calculations:

Description	Plant and Machinery, Yes or No
An item of land purchased for £200,000	**No, plant does not include land**
Printing press for a business selling magazines	**Yes, plant for active function**
Heating and ventilation system in new offices	**Yes, integral feature**
An additional wall to an existing building	**No, treated as building**
Drainage ditch around premises	**No, treated as building**
False ceiling to hide pipework	**No, classed as setting**
Shower unit in bathroom facilities	**Yes, treated as plant**
Advertising hoarding signage on building front	**Yes, treated as plant**

Answer to Activity 3.2

a) What is the total of the eligible assets for AIA for the period?

£180,000 + £30,000 + £50,000 = £260,000
The car is not eligible for AIA.

b) What is the maximum entitlement for AIA for the period?

April 2024 to December 2024 = 9 months.

£1,000,000/12 x 9 = £750,000 (round up)

Or 9/12 x 1,000,000 = 750,000

c) How much can Jeap & Sons claim against AIA for the CAP?

Jeap & Sons can claim the total of the eligible assets for the 9-month period of £260,000 as this is below the maximum entitlement of £750,000.

Answer to Activity 3.3

Calculate the taxable profit for WV Ltd for the year ending 30 November 2024.

Adjusted trading profit before deduction of capital allowances	**257,000**
Less FE claimed FYA claimed	 **(105,000)** **(22,000)**
Taxable profit	**130,000**

WV Ltd can claim full 100% First year allowance against the energy efficient car.
WV Ltd can claim 100% Full Expensing for the other assets.

Answer to Activity 3.4

How much can Beach Ltd claim against capital expenditure and how much if any would be eligible for WDA for the financial year ending 30 November 2024?

	Additions	FE/AIA	General pool	Special rate pool	Total allowances
		£	£	£	£
Additions	**Machinery**	**1,000,000**			
Less allowance		**(1,000,000)**			**1,000,000**
Transfer to general pool			**0**		
Additions for WDA	**Car emissions 100g/km**			**15,000**	
Balance				**15,000**	
WDA 18%					
WDA 6%				**(900)**	**900**
Allowances for period					**1,000,900**
Balance c/f				**14,100**	

£1,000,000 can be claimed under full expensing. The car is not eligible for FE or AIA and would need to be written down under WDA of 6% under the special rate pool.

Answer to Activity 3.5

Complete the following template showing the addition of new assets against the relevant allowances and calculating the total allowances for the period and the total c/f to the following period.

Additions	AIA	FE	FYA	General pool	Special rate pool	Total allowances
	£	£	£	£	£	£
TWDV b/f				37,500	8,000	
FYA zero emissions goods vehicle			31,000			
FYA allowance			(31,000)			31,000
Machinery		497,000				
Plant		650,000				
FE/AIA allowance		(1,147,000)				1,147,000
Transfer to general pool				0		
WDA additions					28,000	
Balance				37,500	36,000	
WDA 18% / 6%				(6,750)	(2,160)	8,910
Allowances for period						1,186,910
c/f total				30,750	33,840	

100% FYA can be claimed against the zero emissions goods vehicle.

Full expensing of 100% can be claimed against the plant and machinery.

18% can be claimed against the balance in the general pool and 6% can be claimed against the balance in the special rate pool.

£31,000 + £1,147,000 + £8,910 = £1,186,910.

Answer to Activity 3.6

All additions and disposals have occurred within the accounting period. From the above information and the layout provided calculate the total capital allowances eligible for Horthorn Limited and the balances to be carried forward to the next accounting period.

Additions	FE/AIA	FYA	General pool	Special rate pool	Total allowances
	£	£	£	£	£
TWDV b/f			158,100	25,050	
FYA electric points		23,750			
FYA allowance		(23,750)			23,750
Machinery	164,000				
Computer	3,000				
Office furniture	37,000				
FE/AIA allowance	(204,000)				204,000
Transfer to general pool			0		
WDA additions				32,250	
Disposal				(17,000)	
Balance			158,100	40,300	
WDA 18%/6%			(28,458)	(2,418)	30,876
Allowances for period					258,626
c/f total			129,642	37,882	

The special rate pool had a TWDV of £25,050 and the high emissions car £32,250 is added to this pool. The disposal of the car for £17,000 which is lower than cost is also put into this pool but is deducted.

Answer to Activity 3.7

Calculate the final period for Pyne Ltd.

	Additions/ Disposals	General pool	Total allowances
		£	£
TWDV b/f		16,000	
Additions	8,750		
Disposals	(23,500)		
Transfer to general pool		(14,750)	
Balancing allowance +		(1,250)	1,250
Balancing charge -			
Balance		0	
Allowances for period			1,250

Answer to Activity 3.8

Calculate the capital allowances for the 8 months ending 31 December 2024 showing the TWDV c/f using the following layout. Use whole figures in your calculations.

Additions	AIA/FE	General pool 18%	Total allowances
		£	£
TWDV b/f		26,400	
Plant	750,000		
Allowance	(750,000)		750,000
Transfer to general pool		0	
Balance		26,400	
WDA 18%		(3,168)	3,168
Allowances for period			753,168
Balance c/f		23,232	

WDA £26,400 x 18% = £4,752 / 12 x 8 = £3,168

Answer to Activity 3.9

1) How much would qualify for the full expensing allowance for the period ending 31/3/2025?

a) £91,700
b) £96,700 ✓
c) £8,500
d) £88,200

£96,700 as the alterations to the floor also qualify for full expensing

2) How much WDA can be claimed for the vehicle for the period ending 31/3/2025?

a) £18,900
b) £3,402
c) £1,985 ✓
d) £1,134

£1,985 as the vehicle falls under purchased after April 21 and is written down in the general pool by 18%. £18,900 x 18% = £3,402 / 12 x 7 = £1,985.

Answer to Activity 3.10

Thompson Limited has a period of account that runs from 1 July to 30 June.

Thompson Limited constructed a qualifying building costing £1,000,000 which was brought into use on 1 October 2023.

What can Thompson Limited claim against Structures and Buildings allowance for the chargeable period during which the building is brought into use?

9-month period 1 Oct 2023 to 30 June 2024. **Total claim for period = £1,000,000 x 3% x 9/12 = £22,500**

Answers to Chapter 4 Activities

Answer to Activity 4.1

As at 1 May 2024, Todd, owner of a sole trader business has the following TWDV:

- Car with CO² emissions 175 g/km (25% private use) £22,000
- Car with CO² emissions 45 g/km (25% employee use) £15,000

Additions	General pool	Private use pool	Total allowances
	£	£	£
TWDV b/f	15,000	22,000	
Balance	**15,000**	**22,000**	
WDA 18%/6%	**(2,700)**	**(1,320)**	**3,690**
Allowances for period			**3,690**
Balance c/f	**12,300**	**20,680**	

The employee car does not have any restrictions for private use and is therefore put in the general pool and written down at 18% as it has emissions below 50 g/km = £2,700.
The owner's car is restricted to 75% business use = £990.
Total allowances £2,700 + £990 = £3,690. The private use pool shows the actual full 100% reduction to ensure the balance c/f is correct.

Answer to Activity 4.2

a) Complete the capital allowances calculations for this first accounting period.

Additions	AIA	General pool	Special rate pool	Total allowances
	£	£	£	£
Furniture	**5,400**			
AIA allowance	**(5,400)**			**5,400**
Transfer to general pool		**0**		
WDA additions			**22,000**	
Balance			**22,000**	
WDA 6%			**(1,760)**	**1,760**
Allowances for period				**7,160**
Balance c/f			**20,240**	

WDA special rate pool as the car is over 110 g/km for purchasing in that period.
WDA is scaled up for a 16 month period. £22,000 x 6% x 16 / 12 = £1,760.

b) What would be the total capital allowances available under AIA for the period?

Total AIA capital allowances would be £1,000,000 + (£1,000,000 x 4 / 12 = £333,333)

Total £1,333,333 for the period.

Answers to Chapter 5 Activities

Answer to Activity 5.1

Calculate the taxable total profits for the year ending 31 December 2024 using the templates below:

Adjusted trading profit before deduction of capital allowances	**250,300**
Less Expenditure deductible from trading profits e.g. capital allowances	**(13,000)**
Adjusted trading profit	**237,300**

Corporation Tax computation for 12 months ended December 2023	
	£
Trading profit (trading income)	**237,300**
Add:	
Non-trade Interest	**8,000**
Property Income	**16,000**
Chargeable gains	**0**
Total profits	**261,300**
Less:	
Qualifying charitable donations	**(7,000)**
Taxable total profits (TTP)	**254,300**

Non-trade interest calculation:
Building society interest received less loan interest payable = £10,000 - £2,000 = £8,000 non-trade interest.

Answer to Activity 5.2

Calculate the Corporation tax liability for the year ending 31 March 2025.

Corporation Tax computation for 12 months ended 31 March 2025	
	£
Trading profit (trading income)	**260,000**
Add:	
Non-trade Interest	**3,750**
Property Income	**0**
Chargeable gains	**8,000**
Total profits	**271,750**
Less:	
Qualifying charitable donations	**0**
Taxable total profits (TTP)	**271,750**
Tax rate	**25%**
Tax liability	**67,937.50**

£271,750 x 25% main rate = £67,937.50 tax liability
Dividends paid are not part of the CT computation

Answer to Activity 5.3

Calculate the corporation tax liability for Slater Limited for the two accounting periods.

First 12 months:

£447,600 / 16 months = £27,975 per month

1 March 2023 to 31 March 2023

1 month £27,975 x 19% = £5,315.25

1 April 2023 – 28 February 2024

11 months £307,725 x 25% = £76,931.25

£5,315.25 + £76,931.25 = £82,246.50

Following 4 months:

1 March 2024 to 30 June 2024
£27,975 x 4 = £111,900 x 25% = £27,975

Answer to Activity 5.4

Calculate the two CAPs for the 15-month period based on the relevant apportionment rules.

Corporation Tax computation		
	£	**£**
	01/04/23 to 31/03/24	01/04/24 to 30/06/24
Trading income	**359,000**	**88,500**
Add:		
Non-trade Interest	**3,840**	**960**
Property Income	**15,040**	**3,760**
Chargeable gains	**35,500**	
Total profits	**413,380**	**93,220**
Less:		
Qualifying charitable donations	**(6,000)**	**(2,000)**
Taxable total profits (TTP)	**407,380**	**91,220**

2023									**2024**						
1	2	3	4	5	6	7	8	9	10	11	12	13	14	15	
A	M	J	J	A	S	O	N	D	J	F	M	A	M	J	
12 months April to March 2024												3-month Apr-Jun			

Workings:

£480,000 / 15 = £32,000 x 12 = £384,000 - £25,000 capital allowance = £359,000.
£32,000 x 3 = £96,000 - £7,500 capital allowance = £88,500.

Non-trade interest £3,000 - £1500 = £1,500 + £2,800 + £500 = £4,800/15 = £320
£320 x 12 = £3,840. £320 x 3 = £960

Property Income £18,800 / 15 = £1,253.33 x 12 = £15,040. £1,253 x 3 = £3,760

Chargeable gains 31/05/23 = first 12 months £16,500

31/03/24 = first 12 months £19,000. Total £35,500

QCDs paid 31/12/23 first 12 months £3,000
paid 31/03/24 first 12 months £3,000. £6,000 total first CAP.
paid 30/06/24 second 3 months £2,000

Answers to Chapter 6 Activities

Answer to Activity 6.1

Jake is self-employed and has a 31 December accounting date. Which of the following will he be required to make his accounts up to to be able to complete his 2024/25 tax return?

a) 1 January 2024 to 31 December 2024 and 1 January 2025 to 31 December 2025.

b) 6 April 2024 to 5 April 2025 and 6 April 2025 to 5 April 2026.

c) 1 January 2023 to 31 December 2023 and 1 January 2024 to 31 December 2024.

d) 6 April 2023 to 5 April 2024 and 6 April 2024 to 5 April 2025.

The self-employed profits for his 2024/25 return would be made up of 9 months profit from the year ended 31 December 2024 and 3 months profit from the year ended 31 December 2025.

This would be only 1 month before the online filing deadline of 31 January 2026.

Answer to Activity 6.2

Using the templates provided, calculate the trading income assessments for each of the partners that will be based on the adjusted profits for this period.

Appropriation Account	Total £	Morris £	Valerie £
Profit/ (loss) for the year	118,500		
Add			
Interest on drawings	1,625	875	750
Less appropriation of profits			
Partner's salaries	20,000	0	20,000
Interest on capital	4,200	2,450	1,750
Profit available for distribution	95,925		
Profit Share			
Morris	57,555		
Valerie	38,370		
Total profit distributed	95,925		

Profit for tax purposes	Morris £	Valerie £
Salary		20,000
Capital interest	2,450	1,750
Profit share	57,555	38,370
Less drawings interest	(875)	(750)
Totals	59,130	59,370

Answer to Activity 6.3

Adjust the net profit for tax purposes and complete a profit appropriation showing each partner's share of profits for tax purposes.

Adjustment of Profits	£
Net Profit before tax as per accounts	52,814
Add	
Depreciation	5,130
Doubtful receivables provision	591
Entertaining customer	150
Private fuel	500
	6,371
Deduct	
	0
Adjusted trading profit before deduction of capital expenses	59,185
Capital allowances	(35,000)
Adjusted trading profit (trading income)	24,185

State the adjusted trading profit £24,185

State the share of profit after appropriation £24,185

State the value of profit for tax purposes for James £12,092.50

State the value of profit for tax purposes for Jonathan £12,092.50

As there is no partnership agreement, the profit is shared equally £24,185 / 2 = £12,092.50.

Again, as there is no partnership agreement, interest on capital balances and interest charged on drawings is not allowed, therefore no further adjustment is required for tax purposes.

Answer to Activity 6.4

Calculate the trading profits for each partner by completing the missing entries in the appropriation of profits below. All entries should be stated to the nearest £.

	Priyanka £	Jen £	Grace £	Total £
Period to 30/11/24				
Salary	15,000	16,000	0	31,000
Profit share	86,535	86,535	0	173,070
Total	101,535	102,535	0	204,070
Period to 31/01/25				
Salary	3,200	3,500	2,500	9,200
Profit share	12,646	9,484	9,484	31,614
Total	15,846	12,984	11,984	40,814
Total for year	117,381	115,519	11,984	244,884

Period 1/2/2024 to 31/1/2025 – This covers two tax periods of FY23 and FY24.

First period before Grace joins = 1/2/24 to 30/11/24 = 10 months

Second period 1/12/24 to 31/1/25 = 2 months

Priyanka salary £1,500 x 10 months = 15,000. Jen salary £1,600 x 10 months = 16,000

£244,884 taxable profits / 12 x 10 = 204,070. x 2 = 40,814.

Profit share first period = 204,070 – 31,000 = 173,070 / 2 = 86,535

Priyanka salary £1,600 x 2 months = £3,200. Jen salary £1,750 x 2 = £3,500. Grace £1,250 x 2 = £2,500.

Profit share second period = £40,814 - £9,200 = 31,614 / 100 x 40 = £12,646. 31,614 – 12,646 = 18,968 / 2 = 9,484

Answer to Activity 6.5

Calculate Joshua's total NIC liability for 2024-25.

Joshua will pay class 4 NIC at the following rates:

(£50,270 - £12,570) £37,700 x 6% = £2,262.00

(£60,000 - £50,270) £9,730 x 2% = £194.60

Class 4 NIC liability would be: £2,262.00 + £194.60 = £2,456.60

Answer to Activity 6.6

Calculate the class 4 NIC each partner will be charged in respect of their taxable profits.

Dom = £2,583.08

£50,270 – £12,570 = £37,700 x 6% = £2,262

£66,324 – £50,270 = £16,054 x 2% = £321.08 + £2,262 = £2,583.08

Dick = £1,898.88

£44,218 – £12,570 = £31,648 x 6% = £1,898.88

Dell = £2,453.94

£50,270 – £12,570 = £37,700 x 6% = £2,262

£59,867 – £50,270 = £9,597 x 2% = £191.94 + £2,262 = £2,453.94

Answers to Chapter 7 Activities

Answer to Activity 7.1

Identify whether the following disposals give rise to a chargeable gain or are exempt.

Disposal	Chargeable or Exempt?
A painting which cost £750 and sold for £9,000	Chargeable
An antique ornament costing £3,000 which sold for £5,500	Exempt
A classic car sold for £40,000	Exempt
Inventory that has become obsolete sold for £6,000	Exempt
Land sold for £5,900 purchased for £2,900	Chargeable

The painting is a non-wasting chattel which sold for more than £6,000.
The antique ornament is a non-wasting chattel but sold for less than £6,000 so is exempt.
Classic cars are exempt irrespective of the gain.
Inventory is part of trading so is therefore exempt.
Land is chargeable as it is not a moveable property so not classified as a chattel even though it was sold for less than £6,000.

Answer to Activity 7.2

Calculate the chargeable gain arising on the sale of the asset and complete the computation table. Indexation factors: August 2010 to December 2017 = **0.239**.

Chargeable gains computation		£
Disposal proceeds		53,000
Less: incidental cost of disposal		0
Net sale proceeds		53,000
Less original costs for acquisition		(35,000)
Less cost of enhancements		0
Less incidental cost of acquisition		0
Unindexed gain/loss		18,000
Indexation allowance on original costs	0.239	(8,365)
Indexation allowance on enhancement		0
Indexed chargeable gain		9,635

Indexation is applied to the original cost of £35,000 and not to the unindexed gain of £18,000. £35,000 x 0.239 = £8,365.

Answer to Activity 7.3

Complete the chargeable gains table showing the gain on disposal:

Indexation allowance on original costs = 22,000+550 = £22,550 x 0.680 = 15,334
Indexation allowance on enhancement = £4,000 x 0.372 = £1,488

Chargeable gains computation		£
Disposal proceeds		**52,000**
Less: incidental cost of disposal		**(1,600)**
Net sale proceeds		**50,400**
Less original costs for acquisition		**(22,000)**
Less cost of enhancements		**(4,000)**
Less incidental cost of acquisition		**(550)**
Unindexed gain/loss		**23,850**
Indexation allowance on original costs	0.680	**(15,334)**
Indexation allowance on enhancement	0.372	**(1,488)**
Indexed chargeable gain		**7,028**

Answer to Activity 7.4

a) How much net chargeable gain/(loss) will be included in the CT calculation for the year ending 31 March 2025?

Chargeable accounting period ending 31 March 2025	£
1) Chargeable gain	**15,000**
2) Chargeable gain	**11,600**
Gross chargeable gains current CAP period	**26,600**
3) Allowable loss	**(3,000)**
Net chargeable gains/(losses) current CAP period	**23,600**
Less: Capital losses b/f previous period	**(2,300)**
Net chargeable gains	**21,300**

b) Complete the relevant boxes in the CT600 return.

Chargeable gains

Box	Description	£
210	Gross chargeable gains	26600·00
215	Allowable losses including losses brought forward	5300·00
220	Net chargeable gains - box 210 minus box 215	21300·00

Answer to Activity 7.5

Calculate the value of the rollover relief available (if applicable) and complete the base cost of the new asset and any chargeable gains on the old asset.

Disposal proceeds from old asset = £449,850 less new asset cost £415,000 = £34,850 proceeds not re-invested.

Revision of base cost of new production machine	£
Original cost	**415,000**
Less partial rollover relief **£140,345 - £34,850**	**(105,495)**
Revised base cost	**309,505**

Chargeable gains computation	£
Indexed chargeable gain before reliefs	**140,345**
Less: Partial Rollover Relief **£140,345 - £34,850**	**(105,495)**
Chargeable gain	**34,850**

Answer to Activity 7.6

a) Complete the chargeable gain for any first matching rules:

Chargeable gains computation	£
Total disposal proceeds £30,000 **Sale proceeds for 2,000/5,000 x £30,000**	**12,000**
Less original costs for acquisition	**(6,000)**
Chargeable gain	**6,000**

b) Complete the chargeable gain for any second matching rules:

Chargeable gains computation	£
Total disposal proceeds £30,000 **Sale proceeds for 1,500/5,000 x £30,000**	9,000
Less original costs for acquisition	(5,000)
Chargeable gain	4,000

c) Complete the share pool calculations showing the purchases and sales including re-indexing.

Index rate from July 2000 – December 2015 **0.528**
Index rate from December 2015 – December 2017 **0.067**
1,500/6,000 x cost £13,000 = £3,250 cost
1,500/6,000 x indexed cost £17,251 = £4,313

Events	Number	Cost £	Indexed cost £
Purchase July 2000	3,000	6,000	6,000
Index to next event 0.528			3,168
Purchase December 2015	3,000	7,000	7,000
	6,000	13,000	16,168
Index to next event 0.067			1,083
	6,000	13,000	17,251
Sale 15/2/25	(1,500)	(3,250)	(4,313)
Pool c/f	4,500	9,750	12,938

d) Complete the chargeable gains computation for the shares from the share pool.

Chargeable gains computation	£
Total disposal proceeds £30,000 **Sale proceeds for 1,500/5,000 x 30,000**	9,000
Less original costs for acquisition	(3,250)
Chargeable gain	5,750
Indexation allowance 4,313 – 3,250	(1,063)
Chargeable gain	4,687

e) What are the total chargeable gains on the complete 5,000 shares disposal?

£6,000 + £4,000 + £4,687 = £14,687

Answer to Activity 7.7

The indexed rise from June 2004 to Feb 2006 is 0.038, and from February 2006 to December 2017 is 0.432. What is the chargeable gain on the disposal of the 2,000 shares sold on 21 September 2024?

Events	Number	Cost £	Indexed cost £
Pool b/f June 2004	2,000	4,000	5,250
May 2005 bonus issue 1 / 2 x 2,000	1,000	NIL	NIL
	3,000	4,000	5,250
Indexed rise to Feb 2006 £5,250 x 0.038			200
	3,000	4,000	5,450
Rights issue 1 for 5 @ £2.50 share	600	1,500	1,500
	3,600	5,500	6,950
Indexed rise to Dec 2017 £6,950 x 0.432			3,002
	3,600	5,500	9,952
Sale September 2024	(2,000)	(3,056)	(5,529)
Pool c/f	1,600	2,444	4,423

Chargeable gains computation	£
Total disposal proceeds	6,000
Less allowable costs	(3,056)
Unindexed gain	2,944
Less Indexation allowance £5,529 – £3,056 =	2,473
Chargeable gain	471

This page is left intentionally blank.

Answers to Chapter 8 Activities

Answer to Activity 8.1

Using the template provided, show Lawrence's CGT computation for 2024-25 and calculate any loss carried forward to 2025-26.

Summary of net chargeable gains	£
Current year chargeable gains	18,970
Less current year allowable losses	(14,180)
Net chargeable gains/(losses)	4,790
Less AEA	**(3,000)**
	1,790
Capital losses b/f	(1,790)
Taxable gains	**0**
Capital losses c/f to 2025/26	**12,110**

£1,790 of the loss b/f is utilised and the balance of £12,110 is c/f to 25/26

Answer to Activity 8.2

How much of the gain on the sale of the business is taxed at 10%? Complete the workings template given below.

a) £500,000

b) £481,000

c) £478,000 ✓

d) £497,000

Summary of net chargeable gains	£
Chargeable gains	**500,000**
Less: Annual exempt amount	(3,000)
Chargeable gain after the AEA deduction	**497,000**
Less capital losses b/f	**(19,000)**
Taxable gains	**478,000**

The taxation for the business under BADR will be at 10%.

Answer to Activity 8.3

Complete the template showing the total CGT payable by Carloz.

	Qualifying for BADR £	Not qualifying for BADR £	CGT due
Eligible gains	10,000		
Ineligible gains		42,750	
AEA		(3,000)	
Gains to be taxed	10,000	39,750	
BADR relief 10%	1,000		1,000
Basic rate band 10%		225	225
Higher rate band tax 20%		7,500	7,500
Total CGT due			8,725

Basic rate band £37,700 – taxable income £25,450 - £10,000 BADR = £2,250 basic band rate remaining.

£2,250 x 10% = £225

£39,750 - £2,250 = £37,500 x 20% = £7,500

Answer to Activity 8.4

1) Who must the gift relief claim be claimed by?

a) Frances only

b) Assisi only

c) Both Frances and Assisi ✓

2) What is the chargeable gain on disposal for Frances? NIL

3) What is the base cost for Assisi? £122,000

	Frances £		Assisi £
Market value	215,000	Market value	215,000
Less: cost	(122,000)		
	93,000		
Less: gift relief	(93,000)	Less: held over gain	(93,000)
Chargeable gain	NIL	CGT base cost	122,000

Answer to Activity 8.5

Calculate the following CGTs where a) a claim for gift relief has been made and b) where a claim for gift relief has not been made.

a) If gift relief is not claimed Valerie's chargeable gain would be £35,000.

Chargeable gains computation	£
Deemed sale proceeds at market value	75,000
Less original costs for acquisition	(40,000)
Gain/loss	35,000

Alison's chargeable gain would be £13,000.

Chargeable gains computation	£
Net sale proceeds	88,000
Less original costs for acquisition (Market value)	(75,000)
Gain/loss	13,000

b) If gift relief is claimed Valerie's chargeable gain would be £ 0.

Alison's chargeable gain would be £48,000.

	Valerie £		Alison £
Market value	75,000	Market value	75,000
Less: cost	(40,000)		
	35,000		
Less: gift relief	(35,000)	Less: held over gain	(35,000)
Chargeable gain	NIL	CGT base cost	40,000

Chargeable gains computation	£
Net sale proceeds	88,000
Less original costs for acquisition (Market value)	(75,000)
Held over gift relief	35,000
Gain/loss	48,000

Answers to Chapter 9 Activities

Answer to Activity 9.1

Use the loss as soon as possible to relieve trading profits and complete the Corporation Tax computations and Loss Memorandum working sheet.

Corporation Tax Computations	2023	2024	2025
	£	£	£
Trading profit/(loss)	15,000	11,000	NIL
Add: Non-trade Interest	400	500	600
Chargeable Gains			3,500
Total profits	15,400	11,500	4,100
Less: Loss relief – current year			(4,100)
Loss relief – carry back		(11,500)	
	15,400	NIL	NIL
Less: Qualifying charitable donations	(300)	Wasted	Wasted
Taxable total profits (TTP)	15,100	0	0

Loss Memorandum workings	£
Year ending 31 March 2025	
Current period loss 31 March 2025	38,000
Loss relieved in current period 31 March 2025	(4,100)
Loss relieved in previous period 31 March 2024	(11,500)
Loss c/f	22,400

The loss cannot be carried back as far as 2023 therefore the computation for 2023 is not affected.

QCDs for 2025 and 2024 would be wasted as profits have already been reduced to zero by the loss relief.

Answer to Activity 9.2

a) How much loss can Jooser Limited relieve in the first year ending 31/3/24?

1) nil
2) £12,000
3) **£32,000 ✓**
4) £31,000

b) How much loss should Jooser Limited relieve in the year ending 31/3/2025?

1) £117,000
2) £102,000
3) £148,000
4) **£116,000 ✓**

The amount carried forward can be offset against total profits. They can specify the amount to be claimed and avoid wasting the QCDs.

Corporation Tax Computation	2024	2025
	£	£
Trading profit/(loss)	NIL	90000
Add: Property Income	12000	12000
Chargeable Gains	20000	15000
Total profits	32000	117000
Less: Loss relief – current year	-32000	
Loss relief – carry forward		-116000
		1000
Less: Qualifying charitable donations	Wasted	-1000
Taxable total profits (TTP)	0	0

Answer to Activity 9.3

Panza Limited expect to incur a non-trading loan relationship deficit in the year ending 31 March 2025 and needs to make a decision on its options for claiming any available relief. Which of the following is **not** an acceptable way of claiming relief for the non-trading loan deficit?

a) The deficit can be relieved against non-trading loan relationship credits within the previous 12 months.

b) The deficit can be relieved against total profits in the future.

c) **The deficit can be relieved against the previous 12 months' total profits.** ✓

d) The deficit can be relieved against total profits from the same accounting period.

Non-trading Loan relationship Deficits

Non-trading loan relationship deficits can be carried back 12 months, but can only be relieved against non-trading loan relationship credits of the previous 12 months and not against total profits of the previous 12 months.

This page is left intentionally blank.

Answers to Chapter 10 Activities

Answer to Activity 10.1

The filing due date of a CT Return is the later of:

a) 6 months from notice to deliver and 12 months from the end of the period of account.

b) 12 months from notice to deliver and 6 months from the end of the period of account.

c) **12 months from the end of the period of account and 3 months from notice to deliver. ✓**

Answer to Activity 10.2

Wiske Limited has prepared accounts for the 18 month period to the end of December 2023.

What is the filing date of the first CT return covering the first 12-month period?

a) 30 June 2024

b) **31 December 2024 ✓**

c) 31 March 2024

d) 30 June 2023

Answer to Activity 10.3

Read the following and decide whether the statements are true or false.

Statement	True or False?
A CT return that is filed 7 months late with a liability of £27,000 would incur a penalty of £200 and £5,400 ***False, £200 and £2,700 (10%).***	**False**
A company whose period of account ends on 30 June 2024 should file their return by 30 June 2025. ***True, as this is 12 months from 30 June 2024.***	**True**
The maximum HMRC can charge as a penalty for a late filing of a CT return is £200. ***False, a percentage can also be applied depending on how late the return is.***	**False**
If a tax return is filed on 15 July 2025 for the year ending 30 July 2024 a penalty of £100 will be incurred. ***False within the deadline for filing – no penalty.***	**False**

Answer to Activity 10.4

Decide whether the following companies would incur penalties from HMRC and what type of penalty and % would be applied where applicable.

a) Skales Limited, a micro entity has unknowingly entered an incorrect figure in their CT return ending 31 March 2025 even though the return was thoroughly checked. After realising their mistake, they inform HMRC on 5 April 2025.

As this is a genuine mistake and the disclosure was unprompted this would not incur a penalty.

b) Jugg Limited, a small entity struggled to meet the deadline for filing and therefore sent in the CT return without it being checked carefully. Within the month following filing, a number of substantial errors were identified at which time the details were sent to HMRC.

Jugg Limited has shown a lack of reasonable care in not checking the return before submitting and the maximum percentage is 14%. As this was an unprompted disclosure the minimum percentage is 0%.

c) Boule Limited, a small entity had deliberately concealed information which resulted in an understatement of tax. HMRC have realised and has requested disclosure and Boule Limited has assisted them with the request.

Boule Limited have deliberately understated and concealed the information which can incur the maximum 100% penalty. As they are assisting HMRC with a prompted disclosure of information the minimum penalty % would be 50%.

Answers to Mock Exam

Task 1 (8 marks)

Calculate the taxable trading profit for Herron Ltd by entering adjustments to the accounting profit below. If no adjustment is required, you should enter a zero. If any adjustments are deducted from accounting profits, these should be shown as a negative figure using minus signs (for example, a deduction of 1,000 should be shown as -1000 or -1,000.

	£	Marks
Accounting profit	**45,225**	*1*
Depreciation	**12,444**	½
Property rental income	**-9,000**	½
Interest received non-trading	**-690**	½
Repair to factory floor	**0**	½
Entertaining customers	**675**	½
Donation to local charity	**0**	½
Political donation	**400**	½
Patent registration	**0**	½
Dividend received	**-2,000**	½
Decrease in general bad debt provision	**-1,300**	½
Profit on sale of machine	**-2,800**	½
Interest payable	**0**	½
Taxable profit	**42,954**	*1*

The repair to the factory floor is allowable.

The donation to a local charity is allowable but the political donation is not.

Patent registration is allowable.

Interest payable for the trading loan is allowable as it refers to trading. However, the interest received for non-trading is not.

Task 2 (12 marks)

This task is about capital allowances.

1. Complete the capital allowance computation for the period ending 31 December 2024. The brought forward figures have already been entered. (9 marks)

Additions	AIA	General pool	Private use asset	Total allowances	Marks
£	£	£	£	£	
TWDV b/f		55,950	0		
Plant & Machinery	31,554				1
AIA allowance	-31,554			31,554	1
Transfer to general pool		0			
Other additions		0	32,975		½
Disposals		-250	0		½
Balance		55,700	32,975		1
WDA 18%		-10,026	0	10,026	1 ½
WDA 6%		0	-1,979	1,385	1 ½
Allowances for period				42,965	1
c/f total		45,674	30,996		1

2. Complete the capital allowances template showing either a negative or positive balancing charge. Enter a 0 in any boxes not requiring a figure and use a minus sign for any deductions. (3 marks)

	Additions/ Disposals	General pool	Total allowances	Marks
		£	£	
TWDV b/f		18,460		
Additions	6,000			½
Disposals	-33,500			½
Transfer to general pool		-27,500		½
Balancing allowance		0	0	½
Balancing charge		9,040	-9,040	½
Balance		0		
Allowances for period			-9,040	½

Task 3 (8 marks)

a) Calculate the trading profits for each partner by completing the missing entries in the appropriation of profits below. All entries should be stated to the nearest pound. Complete all boxes and any values that are nil, enter a 0. (6 marks)

	Dave £	Sue £	Tim £	Total £	Marks
Period to 30 April 2024					
Profit share	60,750	20,250	0	81,000	*2*
Period to 31 July 2024					
Salary	0	0	3,000	3,000	*1*
Profit share	9,600	9,600	4,800	24,000	*2*
Total profit for the year	70,350	29,850	7,800	108,000	*1*

108,000 / 12 = 9,000 per month. 9,000 x 9 months = 81,000. 81,000 / 4 = 20,250
20,250 for Sue. 20,250 x 3 = 60,750 for Dave
9,000 x 3 (remaining 3 months of the year) 27,000
Tim's salary 12,000 / 12 x 3 months = 3,000
27,000 – 3,000 salary = 24,000 remaining profit
24,000 / 5 = 4,800. 4,800 for Tim. 4,800 x 2 = 9,600 for Dave. 4800 x 2 = 9,600 for Sue

b) Calculate Sarah's Class 4 national insurance contributions for 2024/2025. Your answer should be to the nearest penny and if your answer is zero or nil, enter 0. (1 mark)

NIC	Amount payable (£)
Class 4 at 6%	0

No class 4 as below the threshold of £12,570

c) Calculate the amount of class 2 and class 4 NICs that would be payable. Your answer should be to the nearest pound and if your answer is zero or nil, enter 0. (2 marks)

NIC	Amount payable (£)
Class 4 at 6%	1,046

£30,000 - £12,570 = £17,430 x 6% = £1,046

Task 4 (8 marks)

a) Calculate the chargeable gain to be included in the corporation tax computation of Greab Ltd for the year ended 31 December 2024.

Any amounts to be deducted in calculating the gain should be shown as a negative figure using minus signs. All entries should be stated to the nearest £. (6 marks)

Chargeable gains computation	£
Proceeds	**550,000**
Cost including acquisition expenses	**-245,000**
Unindexed gain/loss	**305,000**
Indexation allowance	**-109,515**
Indexed chargeable gain before reliefs	**195,485**
Less relief	**-165,485**
Chargeable gain	**30,000**

Disposal proceeds are £550,000 and the new asset is £520,000 therefore £30,000 will be the chargeable gain on the sale of the old asset and the rollover relief will be £195,485-£30,000 = £165,485.

b) Identify whether the following statements are true or false. (2 marks)

Statement	True or False?
The new assets must be bought within 3 years of selling or disposing of the old ones, or up to one year before.	**True**
As the Indexation Allowance was frozen in December 2018, indexation can only be applied for ownership of the asset up to December 2018	**False, should be Dec 2017**

Task 5 (9 marks)

a) Complete the share pool for Dimecross Ltd. The purchase in March 2010 has already been included. Show the balance of shares carried forward and give your answers to the nearest £. You may have been given more spaces than you will need. (5 marks)

Events Description	Number of shares	Cost £	Indexed cost £	Marks
Purchase March 2010	**2,800**	**56,000**	**56,000**	
April 2011 bonus issue 1 / 4 x 2,800	700	NIL	NIL	*1*
	3,500	56,000	56,000	
Indexed rise to Nov 2012 £56,000 x 0.126			7,056	*1*
	3,500	56,000	63,056	
Rights issue 1 for 2 @ £22 share	1,750	38,500	38,500	*1*
	5,250	94,500	101,556	
Indexed rise to Dec 2017 £101,556 x 0.135			13,710	*1*
	5,250	94,500	115,266	
Sale October 2024	-1,000	-18,000	-21,955	*1*
Pool c/f	4,250	76,500	93,311	

b) Calculate the chargeable gain or allowable loss on the disposal of the shares in Creative Products Ltd by Domecross Ltd in the year ended 31 October 2024. You may have been given more spaces than you will need. (4 marks)

Chargeable gains computation	£
Proceeds 3,000 x £42	126,000
Shares not pooled 2,000 x £40	-80,000
From share pool	-21,955
Chargeable gain/loss	24,045

Task 6 (10 marks)

a) Calculate the total corporation tax liability of D&C Engineers Ltd for the 16-month trading period using the table below. Any items that should be deducted should be indicated with a minus sign (-). Any boxes that are nil enter a '0'. (6 marks)

	Year ended 30 November 2024	Four Months ended 31 March 2025	Marks
	£	£	
Trading profit	**120,000**	**40,000**	*1*
Rental income	**33,000**	**11,000**	*1*
Chargeable gain	**122,000**	**0**	*½*
Charitable donation	**-6,000**	**0**	*½*
Total taxable profits	**269,000**	**51,000**	*1*
Corporation tax liability	**67,250**	**12,265**	*1*
Total corporation tax liability	**79,515**		*1*

Trading profit = 160,000 / 16 months = £10,000 x 12 months = £120,000. 10,000 x 4 months = 40,000. Rental income = 44,000 / 16 x 12 = 33,000. 44,000 / 16 x 4 = 11,000. Chargeable gain = add on 122,000, 11 Nov 2024, during the period ended 30 November 2024, no apportionment needed. Charitable donation = Deduct 6,000, 1 July 2024, during the period ended 30 November 2024, no apportionment needed. Total taxable profits = add them all up. Corp tax = (£269,000 x 25% = £67,250) (£51,000 x 25% = £12,750 less marginal relief of £485 = £12,265). Marginal relief 4-month period = reduced limits of 16,667 and 83,333.
3/200 x (upper limit – TTP)
3/200 x (83,333 – 51,000) = 3/200 x 32,333 = 485.
£67,250 + £12,265 = £79,515.

b) Calculate the corporation tax payable for the period ending 31 December 2024. State your answer to the nearest pound (£). (2 marks)

£33,750

As it is a 6 month period the upper limit of marginal relief is £125,000, therefore the main rate is still 25%.
£135,000 x 25% = £33,750

c) Calculate the corporation tax payable for the period ending 31 March 2025. State your answer to the nearest pound (£). (2 marks)

£35,000

As there is an associated company, the marginal relief is divided by 2 making the upper limit £125,000. Therefore, the main rate is still 25%.
£140,000 x 25% = £35,000

Task 7 (15 marks)

This task is about the administrative requirements for UK tax law.

1. Identify the correct deadline for the actions below from the following options. (4 marks)

The filing date of the company's corporation tax return for the year ended 30 June 2024 is:	**30 June 2025**
The payment date of the corporation tax for the year ended 30 June 2024 is:	**1 April 2025**

2. Complete the following table to show when the instalments are due. Enter your dates in the format of XX/XX/20XX. (4 marks)

Instalment	Payment Date
First	**14/10/2024**
Final	**14/07/2025**

3. Identify whether the following statements are true or false. (6 marks)

	True or false
a) The maximum penalty for late filing of an income tax return if it is less than 3 months late is £100.	**True**
b) The maximum penalty for submitting a corporation tax return more than 6 months but less than 12 months late is £200 + 10% of the tax due.	**True**
c) The penalty for failure to keep records for 6 years is up to £3,000 in total.	**False**
d) The maximum penalties for errors made by individuals in their tax returns can vary from 20% to 100%.	**False**
e) An individual has up to one year from the date of the filing deadline to amend a return, not the date of submission.	**True**
f) Late payment penalties are only payable for late payment of balancing payments, not payments on account.	**True**

4. Jai made a sudden voluntary disclosure to HMRC, who then considered it to be a deliberate error was concealed by Jai. HMRC has decided that a further £6,000 is payable. (1 mark)

	£
What is the minimum penalty he may incur?	**1,800**
What is the maximum penalty he may incur?	**6,000**

Task 8 (12 marks)

This task is about tax planning and the responsibilities of the business and agent.

1. HMRC has an area which has a source of tax guidance. Does this guidance have force of law? (1 mark)

No, HMRC reference material does not have force of law.

2. Parhut Limited has decided not to include some income from renting out part of their business premises on their Corporation Tax return. Does this omission constitute? (1 mark)

   a) **Tax evasion** ✓

   b) Tax avoidance

   c) Tax planning

Tax evasion, as it is a deliberate omission of income applicable to tax.

3. What would be the maximum dividends that Annie will be able to take each year? (1 mark)

£28,350

£35,000 x 19% small profits rate = £6,650. £35,000 - £6,650 = £28,350

4. From 1 January 2025 the Annual investment allowance is £1,000,000. Is this true or false? (1 mark)

True, remains at this amount until 31 March 2026.

5. To operate as a tax practitioner, you must have an agent code before you can set up agent authorisation for tax, to be able to deal with your client's tax details. Is this true or false? (1 mark)

True, required for both online and paper filing and obtained in writing from HMRC.

6. Which of the following would be advantageous to Henrietta and Henry for keeping their taxes low? There may be more than one answer. (4 marks)

   a) Using BADR for Henry
   b) **Transferring some shares in Henny's Ltd to Henry** ✓
   c) **Utilising Henry's lower tax rate for any gains** ✓
   d) Henry being employed by Henny's Ltd
   e) Using rollover relief

Henry does not work for Henny's Ltd therefore BADR would not be appropriate.

If Henry was employed by Henny's there would not be full time care for the children and he would start paying tax at the basic rate.

Rollover relief does not apply in these circumstances.

7. What is the current annual exempt amount for tax year 2024/25? (1 mark)

    a) 12,790
    b) **3,000** ✓
    c) 12,700
    d) 37,700

8. A personal company is one in which the donor holds at least what percentage of the voting rights? (1 mark)

    a) 10%
    b) 2%
    c) **5%** ✓
    d) 50%

9. A rights issue of shares is not paid for but a bonus issue is. Is this statement true or false? (1 mark)

    False, the rights issue is paid for but the bonus issue is not.

Task 9 (8 marks)

This task is about trading losses.

a) Complete the template below for corporation tax for the 3 years. Use a minus sign for any deductions and a 0 for any boxes not requiring a figure.

Corporation Tax Computations	2022	2023	2024	Marks
	£	£	£	
Trading profit/(loss)	NIL	7,000	10,000	*1*
Add: Non-trade Interest	0	5,000	4,000	*1*
Total profits	NIL	12,000	14,000	
Less: Loss relief	0	-12,000	-3,000	*1*
Less: Qualifying charitable donations	0	0	0	
Taxable total profits (TTP)	0	0	11,000	*1*

b) Complete the loss memorandum workings.

Loss Memorandum workings	£	Marks
Year ending 31 March 2024		
Loss year ended 31 March 2022	**15,000**	*1*
Less: used in year ended 31 March 2023	**(12,000)**	*1*
Less: used in year ended 31 March 2024	**(3,000)**	*1*
Loss c/f	**0**	*1*

In 2022 the loss of £15,000 is c/f.
In 2023 the profits of 12,000 are relieved by using £12,000 of the £15,000 loss c/f.
In 2024 the profits of 14,000 are partially relieved by using the remaining £3,000 loss c/f and the remaining £11,000 would be taxable.

Task 10 (10 marks)

This task is about business disposals.

1. Which of the following are eligible for Business Asset Disposal Relief? (1 mark)
   a) Limited company that has been trading for at least 2 years before sale.
   b) Partner in a business partnership who has owned the business for at least 12 months before sale.
   c) **Sole trader who has owned the business for at least 2 years before sale.**
   d) Sole trader who has owned the business for at least a year before sale.

2. Identify any capital gain or loss that may arise on the disposal of each asset assuming no reliefs are claimed. If no gain or loss arises, enter 0. Any loss should be shown as a negative figure using a minus sign. (3 marks)

Asset	Capital gain/(loss) £
Warehouse	**100,000**
Plant	**0**
Goodwill	**40,000**

Warehouse MV £180,000 – cost £80,000 = £100,000
Plant Usually, these assets don't trigger CGT, as they are subject to capital allowances. However, if sold for more than their tax written down value, a balancing charge may arise, which is treated as income and will affect trading profit.
Gain of £40,000 on goodwill

3. Complete the following showing the chargeable gain, if any for Giuseppe and the capital gains base cost for Aurora. (6 marks)

	Giuseppe £		Aurora £
Market value	1,750,000	Market value	1,750,000
Less: cost	(1,400,000)		
Less: gift relief	(350,000)	Less: held over gain	(350,000)
Chargeable gain	NIL	CGT base cost	1,400,000

£1,750,000 - £350,000 = £1,400,000

BVPRI - #0012 - 270525 - C0 - 297/210/19 - PB - 9781836902447 - Gloss Lamination